Table of Contents

C000082583

Corporate Watch

THE UK BORDER REGIME

a critical guide

Introduction

Throughout history, human beings have migrated. People move for many reasons: to escape war, oppression and poverty, to make a better life, to follow their own dreams. But since the start of the 20th century, modern governments have found ever more vicious ways to stop people moving freely.

The *border regime* is a name for the overall system that tries to control people's ability to move and live, depending on our immigration status. That fixes our chances in life depending on what "papers" we have, on where we had the luck to be born, on our wealth or education, on the colour of our skin.

The UK border regime includes the state's external borders, where people are checked coming through passport control, and patrol boats and sniffer dogs search for those trying to enter unseen. It also works inside the country, through the bureaucratic nightmare of visa and asylum applications, or the open violence of workplace raids, detention and deportation flights.

In recent years it has been creeping into ever more areas of everyday life: for example, "right to work" and "right to rent" rules, immigration checks in NHS hospitals, or the Schools Census collecting immigration data from children. This move has escalated with Theresa May's "hostile environment" policy, but was already well under way with the previous Labour governments.

The Home Office is the main government department responsible for immigration control. But there are many other players involved too. For example, private security companies running detention centres, or IT firms developing new surveillance tools. Or the media pumping out anti-migrant propaganda, and ambitious politicians posturing to look "tough on immigration".

And the border regime also relies on millions of other people collaborating in small ways, sometimes without even knowing. For example, healthcare or council workers, "just doing their jobs", pass on personal information that may lead to someone being detained and deported. Or any of us who just walk on by when we see someone being stopped or raided. The border regime cannot exist without our consent.

What, and who, is this book for?

The aim of this book is to provide information and ideas to help understand how the border regime works, and to think about how we can fight it effectively.

Our research group, Corporate Watch, has been studying the UK border regime for ten years now. We have produced many articles and reports investigating parts of it, and in particular the private companies that make money from it. We work closely with people fighting the system, and are active in these struggles ourselves. In this book, for the first time, we bring this research together in one place.

The book isn't about *why* the border regime is a problem. It says little about the human cost of borders – the deaths in the seas and deserts, the torture camps our government helps fund in Libya, the routine abuse and destitution faced by refugees who make it to the UK.

It is written for people who are angry about these things and want to stop them happening. For people directly affected by immigration controls, or those involved in groups fighting for free movement, or other people who support these struggles.

The book talks a little bit about how border controls are connected to other forms of oppression and exploitation – about the roles they play in capitalism, colonialism, nationalism and racism. We believe that the fight against borders is tied to struggles against all these structures, and more. But there is a lot more to say on this than can fit in this book.

One crucial point. Migrants, and above all people "without papers", are on the cutting edge of this struggle. But the border regime affects all of us. The rich and powerful use it to spread fear and division, to stop people working together to make a world where everyone can live a decent life. As such, it can only be defeated with solidarity, by people both with and without papers fighting side by side.

What's in this book (and what isn't)?

This book contains:

- detailed profiles of different parts of the border regime and how they function, from databases and detention to media propaganda;

- information on border profiteers and their contracts, from security giants like G4S to data gatherers like Experian;

- some thoughts on how the system works together as a whole;

- examples of resistance over the last 20 years, looking at why actions have been effective, with a few thoughts on strategy.

We certainly don't cover everything. Except for Calais, we don't look much at the UK's frontier controls. We don't say much about how the UK works with the European Union to help build a "Fortress Europe" against Africa and Asia. There is lots more to investigate about how the UK, like other European states, tries to "externalise" its borders by making deals with ex-colonial countries. We barely scratch the surface of the connections between the border regime and the global economy. Also, at this point any comment on how Brexit will affect all this would just be speculation, so we say little about that.

All of these are crucial topics, but this book is pretty big and heavy as it is.

Acknowledgements

Like all human productions, this book is a collective effort, and there is no way to count all the people who have played a part in its making.

This is one reason why we have decided not to name individual authors or contributors. Another is that, particularly given the nature of the struggle we are writing about, we don't want to recognise only those people who are able to give their names, or who feel more comfortable in doing so.

Chapter 9, "Calais", was written jointly by the Calais Research Network. This is a joint project involving some people from Corporate Watch, Calais Migrant Solidarity, and other friends. For the rest of the book, Corporate Watch take overall responsibility for the writing and editing, and any mistakes are ours alone.

In Chapter 10, "Hostile Environment", the research on housing and rough sleeper raids was carried out in collaboration with friends involved with North East London Migrant Action (NELMA) and Housing Action Southwark and Lambeth (HASL).

We have received big help from people involved with the Anti Raids Network, End Deportations, and the Unity Centre. We also need to thank people involved with the Campaign to Close Campsfield, Coventry Asylum and Refugee Action Group (CARAG), Institute of Race Relations (IRR), International Federation of Iraqi Refugees (IFIR), Migrants' Rights Network, Migreurop, Right to Remain, Spinwatch, South Yorkshire Migrant and Asylum Action Group (SYMAAG).

But most of all, all the unnamed individuals who have lived at the cutting edge of this struggle, and have shared their knowledge, experience and ideas.

Summary

We have tried to divide the book up into self-contained sections so that you can skip to the parts you need. Here we'll give a quick run-through of the main points of the book.

In addition, the final Annex to the book contains further information on border profiteers: a list of major Home Office contracts, and then mini-profiles of six companies. These are detention managers G4S, Mitie, Serco and GEO Group; plus deportation contractors Carlson Wagonlit Travel and Titan Airways. You can also find more detailed company profiles, and updates, on the Corporate Watch website.

Part One: Background

We start by looking at the history of the UK border regime. Attacks on migrants go back at least to the Middle Ages, but the idea of systematic border controls really kicked off with newspaper campaigns against Jewish refugees from Eastern Europe, which led to a 1905 law called the Aliens Act. More recently, the border regime has grown in three main phases, each involving both new laws and increased resources such as guards and detention centres. In each case we see a common pattern: media push scare stories targeting new scapegoat groups, politicians respond with clampdowns. In the 1970s, the targets were Black and Asian workers from Britain's old empire; in the 2000s, asylum seekers from the wars in the Balkans and the Middle East; most recently, so-called "illegals".

Chapter 2 takes a quick glimpse at the Home Office, its structures and resources. In Chapter 3, we look at how the border regime relies on identifying people and sorting us into categories: citizens vs. migrants, refugees vs. "economic migrants", "genuine" vs. "bogus" asylum-seekers, "legal" vs. "illegal". Some of these labels come from official definitions, such as the various "tiers" of the visa system, or the asylum process. Others are more informal. For example, there is actually no legal definition of an "illegal immigrant" – this label is the creation of newspapers and political speeches.

Chapter 4 looks a bit deeper at "what is the border regime". This is the most theoretical bit of the book, introducing the idea of a *system of control*. To make the theory more real, we illustrate it with a diagram: a picture of a kind of Frankenstein's Monster. The border regime is a monster, it has teeth and does real harm to people's lives. But it is not unstoppable. It is made up of many parts, many of which are weak or rusty, many of which don't work well together. When we can identify its joints and weak points, we can see where it is vulnerable and can be beaten.

Part Two: Control

This is the biggest part of the book, with nine chapters. The first seven look in detail at different parts of the border regime. These are:

- **In limbo:** the reporting and asylum dispersal systems.
- **Raids:** the work of the 19 Immigration Enforcement raid squads, looking particularly at workplace raids.
- **Detention:** an overview of the immigration detention system and the private companies that run most of them.
- **Deportations:** the "removal" system, with a particular focus on mass deportations using charter flights.
- **Calais:** the ultimate hostile environment on the UK-France border.
- **Hostile Environment:** a run-through of 12 main anti-migrant measures introduced under Theresa May's recent hostile environment approach.
- **Hostile data:** how the Home Office tracks people with its current databases – and how it wants to expand them into One Big Datasphere.

In each chapter, we also look at how people are fighting back – and at the impacts of this resistance. From the revolts that forced the government to scale down its detention plans, and the countless cases of people beating deportations, to the legal and political battles that have ended charter flight routes and blocked or delayed recent hostile environment policies.

Chapter 12 looks deeper at how the border regime relies on the collaboration of many people outside the Home Office, from landlords and banks to nurses and teachers. It investigates the different ways the government tries to persuade people to collaborate. For example, not just threatening fines and prison sentences, but also seeking to shift the culture inside institutions like the NHS.

In Chapter 13 we ask: so what do all these attacks on migrants actually achieve? The border regime certainly makes many people's lives a misery. But it doesn't come close to achieving the official goal of "controlling immigration". Since the 2000s, many policies have been based on the *deterrent dogma*: the idea that tough measures will persuade people to leave the UK, or not come in the first place. But the evidence suggests this doesn't work. Indeed, the government's own figures show "voluntary returns" have been going down since the start of the new hostile environment approach. The one factor that has actually affected immigration numbers is not a Home Office policy, but the Brexit vote scaring off investment and European workers.

In fact, we argue, the border regime will never succeed in effectively controlling immigration. At least, not so long as the UK remains a democratic state with limits on the use of visible violence, and a capitalist economy that demands migrant labour. This leads us to the question: so what are tough immigration policies really for?

Part Three: Consent

This part of the book digs a level deeper, to look at the forces that drive the border regime.

We suggest that hostile policies aren't really about controlling immigration. They are shows, spectacles that "strike a pose" of control. Whipped up by media campaigns, politicians use new laws and clampdowns to pose at being tough.

Who is the show for? Politicians, from both left and right, often say they have to be tough on immigration to satisfy "public opinion". But what does that actually mean? There is no one public opinion about migration: there are millions of different people, with very different views.

In Chapter 14, we look at the evidence from polling surveys on British people's attitudes. In particular, an anxious minority of about 20% of the population say immigration is an important political issue. These are largely older, white people. Some are well-off pensioners living far from any actual immigrants. Others are working class people living in deprived areas, including the dispersal zones where asylum seekers are dumped. Crucially, both these demographic groupings are often key voters chased by politicians in election battles. They are the main target audiences for anti-immigration policies.

These *target publics* have quite different economic situations and experiences, but they share a sense of alienation and anxiety that is pumped up by media propaganda. Chapter 15 looks at how that works. Summarising several valuable studies, we see how media spread the story of migration as a threat – although specific scapegoats shift over the years. And we ask what motivates journalists and media bosses to do this dirty work.

Chapter 16 turns to politicians. We start with election strategy, seeing how politicians court target voter groups. Next we see how a run of Home Office ministers have built their careers posturing as tough on migrants. Finally, we look at how politicians exist in a closed bubble or "ecology of ideas" with the media – the two feed off each other in a vicious spiralling of bad ideas.

Chapter 17 gets to business. Some capitalists directly profit from the border regime. But most, from farmers to the City banks, rely on a constant supply of migrant labour. All major business lobby groups are pro-migration (in this narrow sense). This is why immigration policies never really try to close the borders to all migrants. Instead, policies target smaller scapegoat groups such as asylum seekers or "illegals", who are seen as economically "low value".

Chapter 18 looks at right-wing agitators. Far right parties, more respectable think-tanks like Migration Watch, and the new "alt-right" or "alt-light" internet propagandists, all work to push mainstream politics further against migrants. (Shifting the "Overton window" of what is politically acceptable.) Currently only about 20% of the UK population is strongly anti-migrant. But if these people have their way, the hatred will grow.

Finally, Chapter 19 digs deeper into the nature of anti-migrant propaganda. It is rooted in fear, part of the politics of anxiety that shapes many aspects of our culture today. What does this mean for those who want to fight these ideas?

Part Four: Fighting Back

People are fighting the border regime every day – and winning. Yet there's no denying we're swimming against a strong tide. It's more urgent than ever not just to fight the border regime, but to work out how to fight it *effectively*.

In Chapter 20 we look back over examples of successful resistance, and think about what makes them successful. Actions and campaigns win when they hit the border regime at its limits: from tight budgets and institutional failings, through legal and political constraints, to the ultimate limits of people's consent.

We note that political action – that is, campaigning to get politicians to change policies – is rarely successful in UK migration struggles. To shift the politics of the border regime we need to shift the wider culture in which millions of people give it their consent. This requires building active movements from the grassroots up: taking effective action, spreading victories, inspiring each other.

But while migrants are on the front line of this struggle, they cannot win it alone. We really start to threaten the border regime when people with and without papers come together in common struggles.

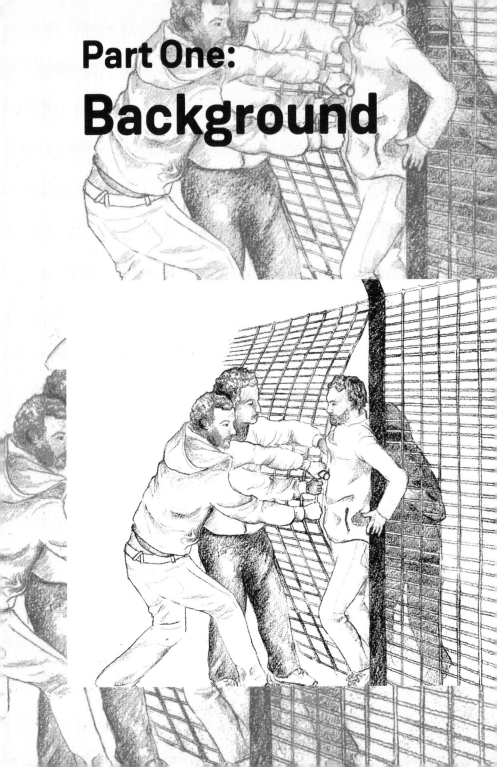

Part One:
Background

1. A brief history of the UK border regime

Immigration control is really a 20th century invention. In the UK, the first systematic immigration law was the 1905 Aliens Act. Since then, the border regime has grown through many gradual steps, becoming an ever greater presence in many people's lives. We can identify three main waves:

- **1970s: Commonwealth immigration panic.** The government stripped rights from citizens of Britain's former colonies, massively expanded the Immigration Service and opened the first detention centre at Harmondsworth. For the first time, the state sought to systematically control migrants not just at the frontiers but also inside the country.

- **1998-2003: Labour's war on asylum seekers.** Immigration enforcement was dramatically escalated. The government criminalised refugees, set targets to deport over 30,000 people a year and built a wave of new PFI-funded detention centres.

- **2012-on: the "hostile environment".** Theresa May's new approach expands the border regime with controls on working, education, housing, healthcare, and other areas of everyday life.

A common pattern emerges from all of these periods: the media stir up anti-migrant scares, then the government responds with "tough" new laws or other measures.

Early days

In English history, the best known early case of a government turning on "foreigners" is the 13th century attack on Jews. Under the reign of Henry III in particular (1216-72), the state imposed an increasingly hostile environment on Jews. A run of laws restricted their freedom to stay in many towns, to work in certain trades, to bury their dead, and more. Under Edward I's statute of 1275, Jews were forced to wear yellow identification badges. Finally, in 1290 the whole Jewish population was expelled.

In medieval times, as today, laws were just one part of the story. Antisemitic propaganda whipped up hatred before the state responded with legal controls. The first recorded "blood libel" in England, accusing Jews of killing Christian children, followed the death of a 12-year old boy called William of Norwich in 1144. Persecutions and pogroms spread across English towns, including massacres in York in 1190 and London in 1264.

Later, other migrant communities became targets. Flemish and Huguenot protestants fleeing religious persecution, Lascar sailors from India, and the large-scale immigration from Ireland were all targeted.

Again, we can see both official and unofficial measures at work. On the one hand, propaganda panics against "strangers" spread from pulpits or pamphlets, leading to anti-foreigner riots by "church and king" mobs (which were often paid by local officials).

On the other hand, governments responded to what nowadays would be called "public opinion" with laws targeting scapegoat groups. These could involve restrictions on residence areas, or on trading or working, registration or reporting requirements, and occasional mass expulsions. Probably the first official reference to "genuine" as opposed to "bogus" refugees appears in a document from 1573, which distinguishes protestant migrants who arrive "for conscience's sake" from those who come "onlie to seeke worke".[1]

These early laws singled out specific ethnic groups, or applied in emergency situations such as wartime. As Steve Cohen puts it in his book *Deportation is Freedom*:[2]

> Prior to the twentieth century, prior to imperialism, there were ad hoc, occasional, unsystematic examples of controls that were directed for particular purposes against particular individuals or groups rather than everyone at large. Controls became generalised, and the construct of 'foreigner' (and therefore of 'immigrant', 'migrant' and 'refugee') fully developed, as the definition of the state became clearer and the norms of civil society themselves became generalised.

1905: The Aliens Act

The Aliens Act of 1905 was the first general attempt to determine who could or couldn't enter the country. People arriving at the frontiers of UK territory were classed as either citizens or "aliens". Aliens were further sorted into those who could legally enter and those who failed on one of four grounds: lacking economic means of support, being insane, being a criminal, or having been refused in the past.

The Aliens Act shows the power of a modern state to make much more systematic efforts at control. It also shows the power of modern mass media. The law came after continual campaigning by the mass circulation newspapers of the "popular press". These called for government intervention to stop arrivals of Jewish refugees fleeing massacres in what was then the Russian empire. The Daily Mail, then as now, was a leading voice but it was not alone.[3] Newspapers also gave a platform to racist pressure groups ("anti-alien societies") such as the Society for the Suppression of the Immigration of Destitute Aliens or the "British Brothers League", and to politicians campaigning in the name of white working class constituents.[4]

The most notorious was the Conservative MP for Stepney, Major William Evans-Gordon. As Teresa Hayter writes in her book Open Borders, his 1902 House of Commons speech calling for an immigration ban:

> sounded much like the speeches vilifying blacks and demanding immigration controls 50 years later. He accused immigrants of living four or five families to a house once they had turned out its proper occupants, threatening to turn the population 'entirely foreign', engaging in criminal activities and prostitution, carrying knives, causing overcrowding in schools and undermining Sundays. 'A storm is brewing', he said, sounding like a less eloquent version of Enoch Powell, 'which if it be allowed to burst, will have deplorable results'. He proceeded, like Powell, to do his best to stoke up that storm. He compared Jewish immigration to the entry of diseased store cattle from Canada.[5]

Such images remain commonplaces in anti-migrant propaganda and policy today. For example, in Chapter 10 we will see how local councils today launch joint operations with Immigration Enforcement against "unsanitary" and "overcrowded" "houses of multiple occupation", "criminality" and "prostitution".

Through the next decades, the Jews and the Irish remained regular targets of newspaper hate campaigns and new laws. The 1914 Aliens Registration Act and 1919 Aliens Restriction Acts introduced powers we now take for granted: the need to show ID documents at the border, the Home Secretary's power of "deportation for the public good", passport stamps and the granting of conditional "leave to remain".

But by today's standards these early controls were minimal. Governments then had far less power to police border crossings, and could do little to register or raid migrants inside the territory.

1970s: "rivers of blood" and the Immigration Act

In the 1960s and 1970s, political and media agitation turned to a new threat: migrants from South Asia and the Caribbean. From 1948, thousands were invited to Britain by the government and by employers keen to recruit workers to fill labour shortages. They became known as the "Windrush generation", named after the ship Empire Windrush which carried 802 immigrants from Jamaica in June 1948. Until 1962, people from ex-colonial countries in the Commonwealth group of nations had the right to British citizenship, and were exempt from controls on "aliens".

It is worth noting that, in fact, during this period more people were leaving the UK than arriving. According to Office of National Statistics figures, in every year through the 1960s and 1970s there were more emigrants than immigrants. This included white British people moving to other Commonwealth countries such as Australia and Canada. Only in 1983 did net migration – the difference between people coming in and out – become positive. 1994 was the first year when there were over 50,000 more people arriving than leaving.[6]

The truth is the immigration panics that began in the 1960s, again stirred by the popular press, had little to do with numbers, and everything to do with race. What scared anxious anti-migrant voters, and fed the rise of far-right politics, was the arrival of Black and brown people from the empire's former colonies.

As one vocal Conservative MP, Sir Cyril Osborne, told the Daily Mail in 1961: "This is a white man's country, and I want it to remain so." Meanwhile Irish immigrants, in Osborne's view, now became acceptably white: "I do not like to regard the Irish as immigrants. I regard the Irish as British as I am."[7]

A range of new players became involved in anti-migrant campaigning. These included resurgent far-right parties such as the original British National Party (founded in 1960) and then the National Front (1966); supposedly non-political pressure groups, often identifying as local residents' associations; through to right-wing Conservative MPs grouped in the "Monday Club". Once again, mass circulation newspapers provided the megaphone.

Enoch Powell became the figurehead of the movement after he gave his notorious 1968 "rivers of blood speech" which warned of race war if "coloured" migration wasn't controlled.[8] Powell was the first ministerial level politician to openly invoke race hatred in a public speech. He was sacked from the Conservatives' shadow cabinet the next day, becoming a martyr for the far right. Teresa Hayter quotes from a National Front organiser at the time:

> We held a march in Huddersfield in support of what Powell had said, and we signed eight people up as members that afternoon. Powell's speech gave our membership and morale a tremendous boost. Before Powell spoke, we were getting only cranks and perverts. After his speeches we began to attract, in a secret sort of way, the right-wing members of the Conservative organisations.[9]

From 1962, governments rolled out a succession of laws restricting Commonwealth citizens' rights. These led eventually to the Immigration Act 1971, which basically downgraded Commonwealth migrants to the same status as other "foreigners". Today's immigration system is still largely based on this Act. Although numerous amendments have been added since, the law remains in force and its principles and terminology still apply. They include Britain's infamous system of indefinite detention, with the Act giving immigration officers powers to lock up migrants without charge or trial.

As well as a new legal framework, governments began to build the physical infrastructure of Immigration Enforcement. The first detention centre, Harmondsworth, was opened near Heathrow Airport in 1970. Its original site only had space for 44 people. From the start, in a pioneering example of prison privatisation, it was run by a private contractor – Securicor, now part of G4S.[10] Although small numbers of migrants had been held in prisons and police stations before, this was the beginning of the detention and deportation system in its own right.

To operate this system, an expanded Home Office "Immigration and Nationality Directorate" was set up in 1972, and given a base at Lunar House in Croydon. The name and structure has changed over the years, but today's Immigration Enforcement and Border Force is still run out of Lunar House.

None of this appeased the racist right. The National Front grew both in votes and as a presence on the streets. Anti-migrant opinion crescendoed: by 1978-9 over a quarter of people in Ipsos Mori's monthly opinion surveys were naming immigration as an important concern (see Chapter 14 on immigration polling).

In 1978, Conservative opposition leader Margaret Thatcher took race politics mainstream. In a famous ITV interview she opined: "people are really rather afraid that this country might be swamped by people with a different culture."[11] Powell had been expelled from the shadow cabinet for saying the same thing just ten years before. But now, as Daniel Trilling tells in the book *Bloody Nasty People*:

> Thatcher brought Powell's ideas back into the heart of Conservative politics, as part of a wider nationalist project that grasped the narrative of imperial decline [...] and turned it around, promising voters that she would make Britain 'great' again.[12]

The Conservatives' embrace of race politics meant that the NF became an irrelevance: its vote share at the 1979 election collapsed to 1.3% (from 3.4% in 1974).[13] The Conservatives won with a landslide.

But although Thatcher adopted anti-migrant posturing, immigration control was never that high up her agenda. Conservative governments of the 1980s and 1990s introduced only relatively small pieces of legislation tightening some aspects of the 1971 Act. The 1981 British Nationality Act, which abolished the right to citizenship of people born on British soil without British parents, was largely based on a previous Labour party plan. The 1996 Asylum and Immigration Act introduced the criminal offence of employing someone without permission to work. But in 1993 there were still only 250 detention places.[14]

2000: Labour's war on asylum seekers

When Tony Blair brought Labour to power in 1997, the party's manifesto was based on five pledges concerning education, the NHS, crime and punishment, youth employment, and frozen tax rates. Migration was not seen as a major election issue. In so far as Labour had an immigration narrative, it was to mirror Tory rhetoric. In 1996, shadow home secretary Jack Straw famously said that "not a cigarette paper" should separate the two parties on immigration.

This began to change around 1998, as the populist press seized on a new campaigning issue: the "asylum crisis". The numbers of refugees arriving in Britain had started to rise after the fall of the Soviet Bloc and the wars in the Balkans. Now media attention focused across the channel on Calais, and particularly the Red Cross refugee centre in Sangatte.[15]

Week after week of headlines and front page splashes in the Daily Mail, Express, Sun, and other papers featured shadowy groups of dark-skinned young men, all apparently plotting to storm the Channel Tunnel and embark on a spree of criminality and "benefit scrounging" at the expense of UK tax payers, spreading diseases and barbecueing the queen's swans.

This media campaigning had an impact. Through the 1980s and much of the 1990s, with the exception of a brief spike in 1985, Ipsos MORI surveys showed less than 10% of people considered immigration an important issue. Then immigration jumped up the rankings in 1999, and since 2001 at least 20% of respondents have named immigration as an important issue in almost every monthly survey.

The new Labour government was particularly obsessed with the media, and their power to sway key voters. Labour politicians also had a worried eye on a return of the far right, this time in the shape of the British National Party (BNP). (We will look at these points closely in Part 3 of this book.)

In fact, in many respects Labour pursued liberal immigration policies, most famously enacting free movement for European Union workers. Immigrant numbers did climb rapidly under Labour. Net migration was over 200,000 for the first time in 1998, and has stayed at that level since. Over half a million people have arrived each year since 2002 (though numbers leaving have also gone up).

Asylum seekers made only a small contribution to these headline figures, and the large majority of new arrivals were EU workers. However, refugees provided an ideal target: they were not important to the economy, but could be used as a convenient scapegoat to try and appease anti-migrant voters.

The new approach was heralded in a 1998 White Paper called "Fairer, Faster, Firmer: A Modern Approach to Immigration and Asylum". This called previous asylum measures "a shambles" and flagged two themes: the need to distinguish between "genuine" asylum seekers and "bogus" ones who are actually "economic migrants"; and minimising "the attractions of the UK" in order to put off potential arrivals.

These ideas would play out over an unprecedented wave of new Immigration Acts, five in under ten years. They were: the 1999 Immigration and Asylum Act; the 2002 Nationality, Immigration and Asylum Act; the 2004 Asylum and Immigration (treatment of claimants) Act; the 2006 Immigration, Asylum and Nationality Act; and the 2009 Borders, Citizenship and Immigration Act. Each successive Labour home secretary had to have one to establish their tough credentials.

Alongside new laws came the new infrastructure to work them – including a rapid expansion of the detention system. Key to this architecture was the introduction of deportation targets, which were set by the Home Office in funding negotiations with the Treasury. We know how these came about thanks to an inquiry published by the prisons and probation ombudsman Stephen Shaw after prisoners in the new Yarl's Wood detention centre revolted in 2002.[16]

The Shaw report revealed how the Home Office set a programme of rising deportation targets in April 2000. They aimed to deport 12,000 people in 2000-1; 30,000 people in 2001-2; 35,000 people in 2002-3; rising to 57,000 in 2003-4. As the Home Secretary Jack Straw wrote in a letter to the Chief Secretary of the Treasury:

> This is a massive increase in anything any Government has previously delivered – compared for example with 8,000 in the current year.

The rationale behind these targets came from asylum predictions. One letter from Home Office manager Peter Wales, dated 22 December 1999, gives a rough working out:

> Based on a current projection of 80,000 asylum applications of whom 66 per cent are unsuccessful, this will be in the order of 50,000 to be removed. Currently, some 30 per cent depart voluntarily. If this remains constant there will still be some 30–35,000 who will require some period in detention prior to removal.

Deportation targets then led plans to expand the detention estate. The same letter explains that if these 30-35,000 people spend an average of a month in detention, 2,750 places would be needed. Another source mentions a Home Office "rule of thumb of 8.75 removals per detention space per year" – which would mean 3,420 spaces for 30,000 deportations. But by 9 March 2000 Jack Straw was thinking even bigger, asking civil servants to advise on "how we would urgently expand detention accommodation to 4,000 places".

Why the jump? The Shaw report concludes that it "was as much to do with deterring potential asylum seekers as removing those that were not so deterred." It quotes the Home Office permanent secretary Sir David Omand, who wrote on 10 March 2000:

> Detention is a key element in effective enforcement and it contributes to the impression potential asylum seekers have of the UK ... We also believe that up to a further 1500 places would significantly enhance the deterrent effect for new asylum seekers.

To build the new detention centres, the government turned to its favourite new funding tool – the Private Finance Initiative (PFI). Under this scheme, similar to a "hire purchase" agreement, a private contractor paid for the building work up front, then was paid back by the government with high management fees over many years.

In 2001, Harmondsworth was substantially rebuilt and expanded, while Yarl's Wood was built from scratch under a PFI deal with Group 4 (now part of G4S) and building contractor Amey. Dungavel opened the same year. But the Home Office never quite met its targets. In particular, the Yarl's Wood rebellion and fire in 2002 was a major set-back to the detention expansion programme, permanently destroying over 400 places (see Chapter 7).

Towards the hostile environment

In any case, the media asylum scare was starting to fade. After peaking at over 84,000 in 2002, refugee numbers began to fall again. Asylum claims dropped below 30,000 in 2005, and bottomed at 17,916 in 2010.

This had little to do with Labour's hard line asylum policies. Refugee movements are overwhelmingly caused by conflicts that drive people from their home countries. In fact numbers of refugees effectively halved across Europe in this period. In particular, the number of Afghan asylum applicants in Europe, who mostly headed for the UK, dropped from over 50,000 in 2001 to under 10,000 per year from 2003 to 2007.[17] Then came the Arab Spring and the collapse of the Syrian revolution, and refugee numbers started to rise again.

Meanwhile, the UK's immigration "debate" also moved on. Although the media's obsession with asylum faded, the fixation on immigration did not. Instead, the xenophobia stirred up against refugees was redirected to new scapegoats such as East European low wage workers, and the new spectre of "illegal immigrants".

Immigration policy moved in line. The last of Labour's big immigration laws, the 2009 Borders, Citizenship and Immigration Act, was the first that didn't mention asylum in the title.[18] Then in 2010 the Conservative Party made the bold step, much criticised by its friends in the business world, of introducing the "net migration target" in the 2010 election manifesto. The party pledged to get net migration below 100,000 per year.[19] Although the target has never been met, it was reaffirmed by the Conservatives again in their 2015 and 2017 election campaigns.

Ed Miliband's Labour leadership got on board too. As the National Front had helped push immigration policy in the 1970s, and the BNP in the 1990s, now both parties were running scared of losing voters to a new right wing force, the United Kingdom Independence Party (UKIP). Labour, in its internal strategy document on targeting potential UKIP in the 2015 election, told activists to admit that "the last Labour government got some things wrong on immigration", and now the country needed "stronger border controls" "to tackle illegal immigration".[20]

This is where Theresa May's "hostile environment" approach comes in. It kicked off in 2012, when May was home secretary under prime minister David Cameron. They set up an "Inter-Ministerial Group on Migrants' Access to Benefits and Public Services", which brought together the Home Office with ten other ministries, discussing ways government departments could work together to attack migrants. Proposals led to two new sets of laws, the 2014 and 2016 Immigration Acts. And alongside these, a host of new rules, protocols, "memoranda of understanding" between government departments, and more. (See Chapter 10).

As Theresa May explained in 2013, the aim was to "create a really hostile environment for illegal migrants". "What we don't want is a situation where people think that they can come here and overstay because they're able to access everything they need."[21]

Like Blairite immigration policy, we could look at the current approach in two ways. On the one hand, the question of overall immigration; on the other, the scapegoating of a particular group for enforcement. In both respects, the Conservatives have set themselves a much harder job. While Labour was relaxed about overall numbers, the Tories are caught in the trap of an impossible net migration target. And rather than the small and relatively easy target of asylum seekers, Immigration Enforcement now has the much bigger and vaguer enemy, "illegals", in its sights.

In Chapter 13, we will pick up the story again to look at a crucial issue: the clampdowns never work. For all the posturing and promises of "tough" immigration policies, they in fact do little to "control" or "deter" immigration. Which will lead us to the question: so what are anti-migrant policies really for?

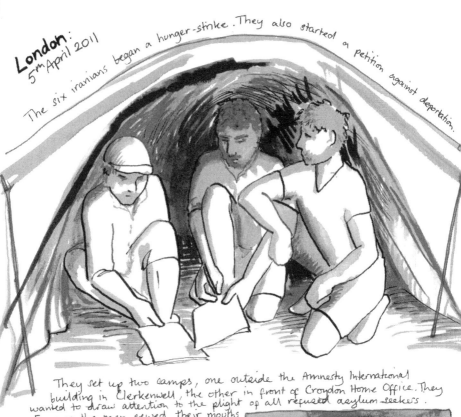

London:
5ᵗʰ April 2011

The six iranians began a hunger-strike. They also started a petition against deportation.

They set up two camps, one outside the Amnesty International building in Clerkenwell, the other in front of Croydon Home Office. They wanted to draw attention to the plight of all refused asylum-seekers.

Four of the men sewed their mouths shut with fishing-line while the other two acted as spokespersons. Journalists and photographers came and went and articles appeared in the mainstream press but the Home Office stayed silent while the men starved.

But they weren't alone. Mehran, Mahyar, Ahmad and Keyvan, Morteza & Kiarash had many friends from the No Borders and refugee support groups who helped support the six by bringing water and newspapers and also to protect them from assaults by passing gangs. In an increasingly weakened state, they became more vulnerable to attacks from racists. One night, a sleeping-bag of one of the men was set on fire.

"I think they would have killed me by now, if I was in Iran"

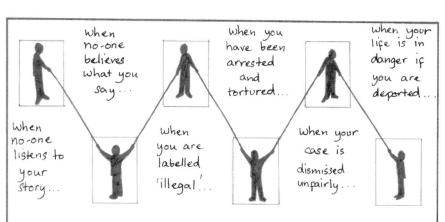

When no-one believes what you say...

When you have been arrested and tortured...

When your life is in danger if you are deported...

When no-one listens to your story...

When you are labelled 'illegal'...

When your case is dismissed unfairly...

...when you have nothing left but your body and the will to resist,

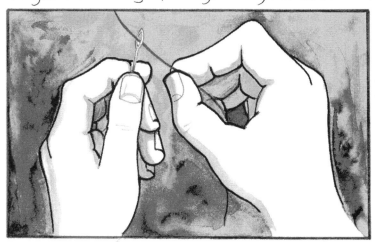

... hunger-strike is the last resort.

"Our closed lips are a response to your closed eyes." Six Iranian hunger-strikers

2. The Home Office: an overview

One government institution has primary responsibility for the UK border regime: the Home Office. This is what most other countries call the "interior ministry". It is in charge of policing and control of the UK territory, including its borders. This chapter gives a quick overview of the Home Office and its jumble of departments and units.

The big boss is the Home Secretary. This is one of the top ministerial jobs, taken by a high-profile politician in the governing party. As we write, this is Sayid Javid MP, who took over from Amber Rudd in April 2018 following the Windrush scandal (where the media exposed the abuse, including deportation, of elderly people who had arrived from the Caribbean in the 1960s and been living in the UK for many decades – it is the only example of a politician resigning for being too tough on migrants, rather than too soft.)

There is also a chief bureaucrat called the Permanent Secretary. This is a career official rather than a politician, who may stay in post guiding decisions behind the scenes as ministers come and go.

In its current set-up, the Home Office has three divisions or "systems":

- **Homeland Security.** Responsible for terrorism and organised crime, includes the security and intelligence services.

- **Public Safety.** Oversees the 43 police forces of England and Wales (Scotland and Northern Ireland have separate ministries), as well as the fire service, and some licensing and other authorities.

- **Borders, Immigration and Citizenship.**

The third "system" is what we're directly concerned with here, the official power of the border regime. Each of these three also has its own subordinate minister and civil service boss. The Immigration Minister, currently Caroline Nokes, is often the public face of immigration policy alongside the Home Secretary.

Immigration Directorates

A first thing to note about the Home Office's immigration division is that it is in a state of perpetual chaos. Perhaps more than any other government department, it is regularly in the firing line of media attention. One common way it responds to criticism is by restructuring – three times in the last two decades.

The main immigration division was called the Immigration and Nationality Directorate until 2007; then restructured as the Border and Immigration Agency (2007-8); and soon after the UK Border Agency (2008-13); before being split up in its current arrangement in 2012 and 2013. These shake-ups confuse and demoralise officials, but don't change the organisation's basic strategies and culture.

In the current arrangement, there are three main "directorates" dealing with immigration control:

- **UK Visas and Immigration.** Responsible for granting or refusing the right to stay by issuing visas, deciding asylum claims, etc.

- **Border Force.** Responsible for control at the frontiers, e.g. passport checks and vehicle searches.

- **Immigration Enforcement.** Responsible for immigration control within the territory, including raids, detention and deportation.

Each directorate is headed by a senior civil servant with the title of Director General (DG). The three directorates between them employ just over 19,000 staff. There are approximately 8,000 Border Force officers, about 6,000 employees handling visa applications, and 5,000 people working in different roles for Immigration Enforcement.[22] But many more people work indirectly through outsourcing to private contractors.

Each of the three directorates in turn has numerous sub-divisions, teams, and units, known by a host of initials. Immigration Officers themselves are known to be frustrated and confused by all this. Here are just a few of the main ones that will crop up in the book.

Border Force is divided into five operational regions, each with a regional command centre: North; Central; Heathrow; South; South East & Europe. The last includes officers working in Calais and the other "juxtaposed controls" posts in France and Belgium (see Chapter 9). There are also national teams including a National Command Centre (NCC) and a "National Intelligence Hub" (BFNIH).

Immigration Enforcement (IE) has a range of divisions. In Chapter 6, we will look at the Immigration, Compliance and Enforcement (ICE) units who carry out raids. There are 19 of these across the country, including five in London (Central, North, South, East and West; both Central and North teams are based in Becket House near London Bridge).[23] Alongside these, Criminal and Financial Investigations (CFI) teams deal with more serious criminal investigations such as smuggling and trafficking, forged documents, and "organised crime".[24]

The Interventions and Sanctions Directorate (ISD) is involved in pushing the newer hostile environment policies, working with the NHS, Department of Education, banks, and other "partners".

The National Removals Command (NRC) organises deportation flights, allocates detention "beds" and authorised detention of people arrested by ICE, and sets targets for rounding up particular nationalities. The Civil Penalties Compliance Team (CPCT) collects fines from, e.g. companies caught employing illegal workers.

There are also various Immigration Intelligence (II) structures supporting enforcement operations with information. These include Operational Intelligence Teams working alongside local ICE teams; four regional Receipt, Evaluation, and Development (RED) units based in Croydon, Solihull, Sheffield and Glasgow; and officers working with foreign agencies as part of the Risk and Liaison Overseas Network (RALON).

The array of officials' ranks and titles can also be confusing. The basic grades are Officer – e.g. Border Force Officer, or Immigration Officer (IO) – and Assistant Officer. For example, as of 2016 a standard Border Force Officer was paid £23,330-£26,831; but could make up to £30,896 if working at Heathrow.[25]

Below these, there are lowly Administrative Assistants. Above come Chief Immigration Officers (CIOs), Inspectors, and Assistant Directors.

Tight budgets

The Home Office spent nearly £16 billion overall in 2016-17. But the majority of that goes to the police, leaving immigration control only a small piece of the pie. Border Force's expenditure in 2016-17 was £503 million, while Immigration Enforcement's was £448 million.[26]

The bulk of Home Office money, around £13 billion, comes from the government's general tax revenues. The other £3 billion is income collected by the ministry itself. Most of that comes from two units, the only two to make a profit: UK Visas and Immigration and the Passport Office, which make money charging for visas and passports respectively.

UKVI received £1.18 billion in 2016-17 charging for visas and "immigration documents" – though it only cleared £350 million of that after covering its costs. Immigration Enforcement took in £194 million from collecting the Immigration Health Surcharge which visa holders pay to use medical services (see Chapter 10) – but it has to pass that on to the NHS. Its income from other sources, including charging penalties to businesses caught hiring illegal workers, was only £55 million.

Immigration Enforcement and Border Force officials often moan about being under-funded. But they are likely to stay that way. In fact, as the National Audit Office notes, their funding is set to go down in the next few years.[27] Their problem is that, despite all the media attention given to immigration, other parts of the Home Office are higher in the pecking order for the ministry's budget. The government has promised rises in overall police funding, counter-terrorism, and police and fire brigade pensions by 2020-1. But the overall Home Office budget remains constrained by the Conservative policy of austerity, which imposes tight spending limits on state funding.

The border regime may do better if Labour wins the next election. At the last one, leader Jeremy Corbyn and shadow Home Secretary Diane Abbot made promises of 500 – or possibly 1000 – "extra border guards".[28]

As we will see in the next few chapters, budget austerity has been having an impact on the Home Office's capacity to attack migrants. The number of detention places has been going down in the last five years (see Chapter 7), and so has the number of deportations (see Chapter 8). It is partly in this context of austerity that new hostile environment policies have moved to outsource Immigration Enforcement work to other government and private sector institutions.

3. **Sorting people**

At all levels, the border regime works by sorting people into categories. On one basic level, people are identified as citizens or migrants. Then, within the category of migrants, there is a host of further identities. For example, high-value investors and skilled professionals versus low-value "economic migrants". Genuine refugees versus "bogus" asylum seekers. And the vague but heavily political distinction between "legal" and "illegal".

In this chapter we will give a brief overview of the main categories and official routes in the UK immigration system. And we will touch on the issue of what it actually means to be "illegal".

Statistics and targets

But first we'll start with a glance at overall immigration statistics. These much-quoted figures play a big role in debates around migration, and we too will refer to them throughout this book.

There are two main sets of official figures on UK migration, both published every three months. One comes direct from the Home Office, its quarterly Immigration Statistics release. This includes a count of people Border Force have seen enter and leave the country, as well as the number of people claiming asylum or applying for different visas, the numbers of people detained and deported, and more.[29]

The other quarterly release, from the Office of National Statistics (ONS), includes figures on "long term immigration". This means not just people crossing the border, but people planning to stay for a year or more.[30] Note that these are very much estimates. By subtracting its estimates for people leaving to live abroad, the ONS then calculates the famous net migration figure.

The Home Office figures show that there were just under 140 million "passenger arrivals" into the UK in 2017. This does not actually mean individual people: many arrivals could be travellers crossing back and forth several times. The majority of arrivals, over 77 million, were by British people. Another 40 million were citizens of the European Economic Area (EEA – see definition below) or Switzerland. That leaves another 20 million "non-EEA nationals".

But the large majority are only short-term visitors. According to the ONS estimates, around 630,000 people came as "long term immigrants" in 2017. Some 350,000 people emigrated, leaving a net migration figure of around 280,000. As the ONS summarises: "Net migration has fallen following record levels in 2015 and early 2016, and has been broadly stable since." It remains much higher than the government's 100,000 target.

Citizens vs. migrants

The idea of citizenship is complex. For our purposes, the main point is that British citizens are free of any immigration controls. In legal terms, they have the *right of abode* in the UK: to "live and work in the UK without restriction", without needing permission from immigration authorities. Of course, citizens' freedom of movement may still be restricted by other authorities, for example by the courts or the police.

The legal details are complicated, but in general someone born in the UK before 1983, or who has a British parent, is entitled to citizenship.[31] Others can apply to become a "naturalised" citizen if they have lived in the UK legally for 5 years, are currently of "settled" immigration status, are judged of "good character", and pass language and "Life in the UK" tests.[32]

In the past, people from Commonwealth countries had wider access to British nationality and the right of abode. Much changed in the 1971 Immigration Act, which essentially classed Commonwealth citizens alongside other foreigners. The few remaining loopholes are gradually fading with the memory of empire.[33]

In 2017, around 123,000 migrants were granted citizenship. The majority of these grants (68,828) were on the grounds of long-term residency. Most others became citizens through family routes.[34]

Citizens can also be un-made. In recent years, laws have given the government increasing powers to take away citizenship. Since the 2006 Immigration and Nationality Act, the home secretary can take away citizenship and right of abode even from people who are citizens by birth or descent, if this is judged to be "conducive to the public good".[35]

In fact, citizenship is not one simple category: just as there are many categories of migrants, there are different classes of citizens, and for some people the right to abode is much more fragile than for others. In her book *Us and Them*, Bridget Anderson discusses in depth different figures of "Good Citizens", "Failed Citizens", "Tolerated Citizens" and more, and looks how ideas of citizenship are closely connected to ideas about migrants and other non-citizens.[36]

Times and rights

Not all migrants are equal. Different forms of *immigration status* carry very different rights. At one end are "settled" migrants with "indefinite leave to remain". This is usually granted after someone has been in the country for several years. For example, a 2016 Home Office report on the "Migrant journey" states that around 25% of people initially granted skilled worker visas go on to become residents after five years or more.[37] Refugees are now typically granted only temporary leave to remain for five years, and must later apply to extend.[38]

Other status categories give rights that are more limited: in terms of how long people are supposed to stay, and what they can do while they're here. For example, skilled workers, students, and rich investors can apply for visas lasting three years or more. But people on student visas are not allowed to work "in most jobs", and short-term "visitors" are not allowed to work at all. Most visas specify that holders have "no recourse to public funds" such as benefits.[39]

Although this is not a complete list, we can think of three main categories of "legal" migrants:

· European (EEA) citizens;

· non-EEA citizens with different kinds of temporary "leave";

· refugees and asylum-seekers.

EEA citizens

EU citizens, for the moment, generally have full rights to stay and work in the UK without a time limit. So do citizens of the other "European Economic Area" (EEA) countries which are not in the European Union: Iceland, Lichtenstein, Norway and Switzerland. After Brexit, they will all have to apply for some form of settlement status – the details of this are still unclear at the time of writing.

There are some limitations on these rights. For example, EEA citizens convicted of crimes can be stripped of their rights and deported, and those judged a risk to "public order" can be banned from entry. Also, to stay longer than 90 days citizens must be "exercising their treaty rights": which means being employed or self-employed, seeking work, studying, or being "self-sufficient".[40]

Since about 2012 – that is, in the run-up to the Brexit vote – EU nationals have been increasingly targeted by Immigration Enforcement, and now make up a large proportion of those detained and deported. The treaty rights clause provides the legal grounds for this. In particular, the recent policy of mass round-ups and deportations of homeless East Europeans (see Chapter 10) was justified by a Home Office decision that sleeping rough amounted to an "abuse" of treaty rights. This particular abuse argument was successfully challenged in the High Court in December 2017; but EEA citizens can still be illegalised on other grounds.

Non-EEA citizens: Visa routes

Citizens from many countries can enter as short-term "visitors" without the need for a visa. To stay legally beyond six months, or for other nationalities to enter at all, means applying for a visa. In most cases this must be done in advance, from outside the UK. The UKVI handles all visa applications, and charges handsomely for it – hence being one of two Home Office directorates, alongside the Passport Agency, to turn a profit. E.g. at the time of writing the standard skilled worker visa costs £610 for three years, plus another £200 per year for the "health surcharge".

There are numerous kinds of visa, but we can identify these main categories:

- *Visitors.* Visitors can only stay legally for up to six months, have no right to work, and no recourse to public funds. People from poorer countries will very often face a grilling by Border Force on arrival, demanding that they prove that they can support themselves in the UK and are not coming to work.

Entrants in 2017: 11.3 million. That number represents all non-EEA visitors; only 2.1 million of them needed visas.[41]

- **The rich.** "Entrepreneurs" or "investors" have their own rules. Currently, they are granted extendible three year visas, called the Tier 1 route. Investors can get a visa by investing £2 million in the UK; entrepreneurs must set up or run a business, and invest at least £200,000 (in some circumstances £50,000).[42]

Rich people visas granted in 2017: 5,127.

- **Workers.** There are some different types of work visas. The best known is the Tier 2 route, restricted to skilled workers employed by companies which are licensed as sponsors. There are two tracks for prioritised workers in "shortage occupations"[43], and others. With some exceptions for particular occupations (e.g. nurses), Tier 2 visas are only granted to people earning a high salary: the current minimum at time of writing is £30,000.

Another route, called Tier 5, covers some specific schemes for short-term workers, including sportspeople and artists, and the reciprocal youth transfer scheme under which young Australians, Koreans and a few other nationalities are able to work in the UK for up to 2 years.

Tier 3, for temporary unskilled labour, is currently closed: until recently, the UK could get all the cheap fruit-pickers it needs from Europe. What will happen to seasonal farm labour in future is one of the big discussion points for Brexit.

There is a special work visa category for "domestic workers in private households", allowing rich people to bring in their servants.

Work visas granted in 2017: 160,004. Of which 94,247 Tier 2; 40,864 Tier 5; 24,893 other.

- **Students.** International students are a major industry providing much of the income for British universities and other colleges. They are allowed in on Tier 4 visas. Institutions are licensed as sponsors, and then effectively given a quota of how many foreign students they can recruit. (See Chapter 10 for more on this.)

Student visas granted in 2017: 223,536. 88,456 were from China. This figure excludes short term student visas for less than a year.

- **Family.** There are various routes through which people can come to join partners, parents or children who are UK citizens, permanent residents, or refugees. One of the requirements is to prove a minimum household income. At the time of writing this is £18,600 to bring a partner. There are also separate visa routes for family of EEA citizens, and for dependents of time-limited visa holders.

Family visas granted in 2017: 134,857.

The "Tier" labels were introduced in a reorganisation of the visa system in 2008-10. This also brought in a points based system: i.e., within each category, applications are scored with points depending on various factors such as job type (for work visas), income, education level, or English language skills. But all of these details are constantly changing, and are constantly the focus of much debate and lobbying around Brexit.

Asylum seekers and refugees

NB: for a detailed guide to legal rights for asylum seekers and others see the Right to Remain Toolkit.[44]

The official definition of a refugee comes from the 1951 UN Convention. A refugee is someone who has left their country "owing to a well-founded fear of being persecuted for reasons of race, religion, nationality, membership of a particular social group, or political opinion".[45] Note how only certain kinds of persecution are covered. For example, people forced to move because of economic exploitation or environmental disasters are not generally counted. In some cases, states will grant a similar status of "humanitarian protection" to people who they do not accept as meeting the official definition of refugee.

To give a little bit of context, the United Nations refugee agency UNHCR estimates that there are currently 68.5 million "forcibly displaced people" in the world – the highest number it has ever recorded.[46] Many of these are internally displaced within their countries of origin, but 25.4 million are international refugees. Most of these come from just a few countries. At the end of 2017, the biggest refugee origin countries were:

- Syria: 6.3 million people

- Palestine: 5.4 million people

- Afghanistan: 2.6 million people

- South Sudan: 2.1 million people

- Myanmar: 1.2 million people

- Somalia: 986,400 people

The large majority of refugees, over 85%, are hosted in neighbouring countries. Turkey hosts 3.5 million people, Pakistan 1.4 million, Uganda 1.4 million, Lebanon 1 million, Iran 980,000. By comparison, the UK currently hosts 122,000 refugees. This is a tiny proportion of the world's refugees, and also a very small proportion of the UK's immigrants.

The asylum system

But what matters for immigration status is not whether people are refugees, but whether the system recognises them as such. There is a widespread "culture of refusal": around two thirds of cases are initially refused.

In 2010, Home Office whistle blower Louise Perrett revealed how asylum caseworkers in Cardiff who granted someone refugee status had a stuffed gorilla called the "grant monkey" placed on their desk as a mark of shame. Managers instructed them to automatically refuse difficult cases and "let a tribunal sort it out."[47] In her book *Borderline Justice*, barrister Frances Webber documents in depth the tactics used by the Home Office to deny people refugee status – and the endless legal struggle demanding refugee rights.[48]

People often wait many months for a decision. After the Home Office's initial decision, people are able to appeal to courts called the Immigration and Asylum Tribunals. They may also make a "fresh claim" if they can get new evidence to support their case. The Home Office's official target is to resolve "straightforward" cases within six months, and "non-straightforward" cases within a year. Like other Home Office targets, this is standardly broken, and the process often drags on for years. (Again, see the *Right to Remain Toolkit* for details on all of these procedures.)

During this time, asylum seekers are not generally allowed to work.[49] If they cannot support themselves, they are initially offered housing (in often dire conditions – see the next Chapter) and a small maintenance allowance (currently £36.95 per week). This minimal support may be taken away after claims are refused.

Before this process even begins, refugees have to manage to claim asylum at all. This can, in general, be done only on UK soil. The expectation is that people should claim asylum as soon as they arrive: either at an entry port or airport, or by making an appointment at Lunar House in Croydon. Not claiming immediately is often given as a reason for refusal.

Few refugees are able to simply board a plane to a UK airport. Some have no documents, some are unable to leave their countries legally or safely, many have no hope of getting a visa to be allowed on a flight. The majority thus have to take long and dangerous land routes, and avoid border controls.

Another pitfall for refugees is the Dublin Treaty. This states that people should apply for asylum in the first "safe" European country they reach – even if their family and other connections are elsewhere, they can't speak the language, or the country has a collapsed asylum system. The first thing that happens when someone claims asylum in the UK is their fingerprints are taken and checked against the EURODAC database, to see if they have already been encountered in another country.

A few figures:

- 26,350 people applied for asylum in 2017. 2,206 were unaccompanied children.[50] Asylum seekers are a small percentage of all immigrants – about 6% in 2016.[51]

- However the Home Office only made 21,290 initial decisions in 2017 (including on claims from previous years).

- In the middle of 2017 the Home Office had 84,190 asylum cases "in progress". 33,283 cases had been going on for over three years.[52]

- 32% of cases succeeded at the initial decision – that is, were either granted full refugee status or "humanitarian" leave to remain. Around ¼ of refused cases later win on appeal.[53] So just under half of all asylum-seekers are – eventually – recognised as refugees.

- The main nationalities of applications in the last two years were, in order of numbers: Iran, Pakistan, Iraq, Bangladesh, Sudan. (This doesn't include Syrians moved from other European countries under the EU "resettlement" scheme.)

- Asylum caseworkers decide cases largely on the basis of "country guidance" prepared by Home Office researchers who are meant to assess the risks for different countries. These assessments are notoriously arbitrary. But some nationalities get a much worse treatment than others. An indication comes from the appeal statistics. For example, in the year to September 2016, 87% of Eritrean cases which were initially refused by the Home Office were later granted by the courts on appeal. The same goes for 62% of Sudanese cases, and 51% for Afghan cases.[54]

- 314 people were deported under the Dublin regulation in 2017.

Legal vs. illegal

We have surveyed the various official routes for people to enter and stay in the UK. But of course, not everyone fits in these boxes. The standard media image of an "illegal migrant" is someone arriving on a boat or in the back of a lorry. But this is only a small part of the picture.[55] More generally, people may be "irregular" or "undocumented" migrants in a number of senses, including:

- people who arrive by official routes, but then stay longer than official papers allow ("*overstayers*");

- people who do work or other activities that their papers don't allow;

- people whose asylum claims are refused – and are then thrown into a limbo of destitution where they can't leave the UK, but are banned from working or claiming benefits;

- EEA citizens who are not "exercising their treaty rights";

- people born into "illegality" as the children of irregular migrants;

- people who are in fact long-term residents entitled to citizenship, but have no official documentation to prove this – as in the recent Windrush cases.

People in all of these categories, and more, may be targeted by Immigration Enforcement for arrest, detention, deportation, and other sanctions.

For obvious reasons, there are no reliable figures on numbers of undocumented people in the UK. The most widely quoted research on "irregular migrant" numbers in the UK remains a study carried out by the London School of Economics (LSE) in 2009. This gave an estimate of 618,000, with a range of 417,000 to 863,000.[56]

Who is illegal?

Politicians, media, and everyday speech often refers to all people on the fringes of the immigration system as illegal immigrants – or just, "illegals". But, to be clear, "illegal migrant" is not actually a legal term.

A few irregular migrants may be charged with the offence of "illegal entry" under the Immigration Act 1971. But the definition of this is strict, and probably applies only to a small minority: people who "knowingly enter the United Kingdom in breach of a deportation order or without leave". New hostile environment laws such as the Immigration Acts of 2014 and 2016 have escalated the criminalisation of migrants, particularly by adding the new offence of "illegal working".

But UK law still, for now, makes a distinction between the immigration system and the criminal justice system. Most people targeted for detention and deportation are not charged with any crime.

In particular, since the asylum panic started around 1999, it has become standard for major media outlets to equate asylum seekers with "illegals". But seeking asylum is not illegal in any sense. Many, though not all, refugees are forced to cross borders using clandestine routes, or with false or no travel documents. But, precisely because of this, Article 31 of the UN Refugee Convention makes it clear that states should not "impose penalties" on refugees "on account of their illegal entry or presence".[57]

Getting the UK (and other governments) to actually respect this principle is a continual legal battle – as Frances Webber relates in Borderline Justice.[58] Court challenges and campaigning eventually pushed the UK to introduce a "statutory defence" for refugees arriving without legal travel documents in the 1999 Immigration and Asylum Act. Even so, wilfully ignorant prosecutors and magistrates still send many refugees to prison just for arriving in the UK with a fake passport. These verdicts are regularly overturned on appeal – though often not until people have already spent months in prison.[59]

41

Official and unofficial categories

The question of "illegality" brings up an important wider point. All parts of the border regime involve labelling people with different categories. But not all these categories are defined in law or Home Office rules.

The "illegal" label is shaped not by official rules but by politicians, media outlets, and everyday speech. For example, although many media organisations have issued policies against it, this language continues to be widely used even by liberal outlets like the BBC or the Guardian.

Unofficial categories are widely used by officials too. For example, when ICE raid officers stop brown-skinned people in the street and let white people walk past, they are not using a legally sanctioned category. Indeed, what they are doing could well be illegal. But this is not unusual or exceptional: unofficial racial profiling is a basic part of Home Office operations at every level.

We can also think about how official and unofficial category schemes interact. On the one hand, official labels acquire whole new layers of meaning through informal use. For example, the term "asylum seeker" started as a dry legal category, but after two decades of tabloid coverage it has been turned into a term of abuse. On the other hand, "everyday" language in turn shapes official categories. For example, politicians, judges, and Home Office managers are continually responding to what they understand as "public opinion" when they write new laws, rulings and guidance.

4. **What is the border regime?**

The Home Office is obviously a leading player in trying to create a "hostile environment" for migrants. But it can't do it all alone. There is no way that 8,000 Border Force guards (or even the 8,500 Labour has promised) and 19 Immigration Enforcement raid squads can even begin to control the movements of many millions of people.

We use the term "border regime" as a shorthand to mean all of the many different institutions, people, systems and processes involved in trying to control migrants. For example, here are just a few more players besides the Home Office:

- airlines, ferry companies, coach and train companies, Eurotunnel, port authorities, lorry companies, travel agents, who all work closely with Border Force in different ways (see Chapter 9);

- security companies who run outsourced border searches, detention centres, or deportation "escorting" (Chapters 7, 8, 9);

- IT geeks developing new Big Data software, engineers inventing new surveillance systems and weapons (Chapter 11);

- big business organisations lobbying to keep down labour costs (Chapter 17);

- bosses who call Immigration Enforcement raids on workers demanding higher wages (Chapter 6);

- media moguls spreading anti-migrant propaganda to sell papers (Chapter 15);

- ambitious politicians posturing as tough guys (Chapter 16);

- far-right agitators trying to "push the window" of acceptable hate (Chapter 18);

- council and homelessness charity workers going out on joint patrols with Immigration Enforcement to find foreign workers or rough-sleepers (Chapter 10);

- NHS receptionists collecting personal data which they may never realise is passed on to Immigration Enforcement (Chapter 10).

It is the combination of all these people's actions, amongst many others, that makes the border regime. When they stop coordinating and collaborating, cracks emerge in the system.

Systems of control

In the next two parts of this book we will look further at who is involved in the border regime. But first, we want to think a bit about exactly what it does. We will start with this idea: it is a *system of control*.

In this world, we are controlled in many ways. We are controlled in obviously physical ways by police checks, razorwire fences, CCTV cameras, and cell doors. We are controlled in somewhat more subtle ways by credit approvals, glances of disapproval, or even our own internalised pangs of shame or desire. We are controlled according to the ID documents we carry, the tone of our skin, the way we speak or move, our bank balances, who we know or what we know. We are controlled in ways that prevent or allow us to move, eat, sleep, laugh, love, or feel safe from attack.

To give a drier definition: a system of control is a set of institutions and practices that determine what people can or can't do, what actions are possible or blocked. They govern, regulate, people. And also, they work together in a relatively stable and structured way – they form a *system*.

Many systems of control, including the border regime, work in a particular way. We can think of this in three steps:

· First, *identification*: we are labelled, sorted into categories.

In the last chapter we looked at many of the categories used by the border regime. As we noted, this goes beyond just official definitions of "immigration status". For example, we are identified and sorted when we apply for visas or asylum, or when e-passport readers or immigration officers scan our papers or fingerprints. But also when a landlord checks our accent or skin colour before deciding to call the "right to rent" hotline.

· Second, *control*: we are given different rights or abilities, different possibilities of life, depending on the category we are placed in.

Depending on our "status", we are able (or not) to enter the country, to stay for a certain period, to work legally, to rent a room, or to walk down the street without getting hassled.

- Third, *enforcement*: if we try to disobey, step out of our place, control may be enforced using threats and violence.

If we cross a border we're not allowed to, or exceed our rights inside the territory, we may risk arrest, beating, detention, deportation, etc.

Frontiers and interior

Although we have said the border regime is a "system of control", it would be still more accurate to see it as involving many interconnected systems. For example, just within the Home Office, different databases or units work separately, and may often clash with each other, even as they share many of the same objectives and resources.

Roughly speaking, we can think of two main kinds of controls in the UK border regime: controls at the frontiers of the national territory; and controls inside the territory.

Frontier controls came first. In Britain, governments have imposed forms of external border checks for centuries. However, until recently, they usually controlled taxable goods ("Customs and Excise") rather than people. As we saw in Chapter 1, it was only with the Aliens Act of 1905 that the UK state began to systematically sort people at the border into "citizens" or "aliens". It was only in 1919 that it became a legal requirement for travellers to show ID documents. And it was much later before the state had the resources or technologies to stop and search the bulk of border-crossers. And even now, of course, its control is far from total.

Internal controls are newer, at least in a systematic form. There was certainly a viciously hostile environment against Jews in 13th century England, with laws restricting their rights to work, to settle in different areas, and much more. But only in the 1970s did the government start to build the formal apparatus – the Immigration and Nationality Directorate (IND) – to systematically register, check, raid, detain and deport migrants in general.

Of course, frontier and interior controls overlap. Both largely work with the same official immigration status categories. Both come under the remit of the Home Office, although currently they are divided up into two directorates: Border Force, and Immigration Enforcement. These two forces share at least some of their "intelligence", and much of their culture, though there are also rivalries and miscommunication.

45

And both also overlap with many other systems of control. For example, Border Force works closely with Customs, with the police, with port authorities and their security, and with officials from other countries.

Officials and collaborators

Above we listed some examples of organisations and people involved in the border regime. It may be useful to group border regime actors into a few basic categories:

Officials. Paid specialists, working directly for the Home Office directorates.

Contractors. Paid specialists, working for corporations contracted by the Home Office. For example, private security guards run seven of the eight long-term detention centres, guard the fences at Calais and other ports, and "escort" shackled prisoners onto deportation flights. Other contractors build the computer systems and fingerprint scanners, book and fly the deportation planes, or demolish migrant camps in Calais.

Formal collaborators. Institutions and individuals who collaborate with the Home Office following laws and formal agreements. This includes officials in other government departments who, for example, share information or conduct joint operations with Home Office units. (As we will see in Chapter 10, some of these inter-governmental collaborations are governed by written agreements called "memoranda of understanding".) It includes private sector actors who are compelled to collaborate by laws: e.g. airlines are obliged to provide Advanced Passenger Information (API) and check passengers' travel documents. Or, e.g. colleges who check papers as a condition of keeping the sponsor licenses they need to recruit foreign students paying high fees.

(Informal) collaborators. For example: citizens of Calais encouraged by the Mayor to report "anything suspicious", or UK citizens grassing up their neighbours to the Home Office hotline, or bars or shops who refuse to serve migrants, or fascist gangs who take things further.

In short, there are a whole host of reasons why people collaborate with, or indeed work directly for, the border regime. We will come back to this topic in Chapter 12.

Legitimacy

One general point for now: the border regime, like many other systems of control, works best when many people think it is right – it has "legitimacy". Or, at least, when people just see it as something that is always there, that there's no point questioning – it seems natural, normal. To put it another way: people give it their *consent*.

But the border regime, like other systems of control, hasn't always been there. It has been introduced, bit by bit, over a hundred years and more, and at almost every step it has been questioned and challenged. It may seem totally natural now to queue up and show a passport, whereas just a hundred years ago it was bizarre and invasive.

Over time, things that first seemed strange may often become habitual, normal, and even feel "right". This seems a basic process of human psychology. But it can certainly be resisted – or helped along.

Powerful actors work to legitimise and win our consent for the border regime. As well as government institutions themselves, these include business lobbies, politicians, right-wing think tanks, and perhaps most of all, the big media outlets. We will look at this issue in Part 3 of this book.

Interwoven systems

The border regime interconnects with many other systems of identification, control and domination. For example:

Immigration controls work closely with other projects of state surveillance and repression. The same techniques and technologies developed to identify and control migrants are used against other excluded and criminalised groups. For example, young people, poor people, black people, homeless people, travellers, the unemployed, political dissidents, and more. The media's anxiety-propaganda cycles through groups of scapegoats as if they're largely interchangeable. Migrants are very often the front line, the testing ground, for tools that are later turned on citizens. For example, new ID schemes and data platforms are first developed for border control; immigration detention centres are used to pioneer prison privatisation.

Immigration controls work with capitalist projects of economic exploitation. Employers promote temporary work permit systems to keep down wages, or use the threat of raids to stop workers organising. Developers and local councils work alongside Immigration Enforcement to help "socially cleanse" and gentrify inner city neighbourhoods.

Immigration controls work with racism. On the one hand, immigration rules and status categories are rooted in racial identities. All the main laws that shaped the system derive from racist propaganda campaigns. The 1905 Aliens Act was drawn up against East European Jewish refugees; the 1971 Immigration Act against Black and Asian commonwealth migrants; the spate of 1999-2006 "Immigration and Asylum" acts against mainly Muslim "asylum seekers". On the other hand, anti-migrant laws and propaganda feed back to help create new patterns of racism, including what the writer A. Sivanandan called xeno-racism: "a racism that is meted out to impoverished strangers even if they are white."[60]

Immigration controls work with global projects of imperialism and neo-colonialism. Migration, and its control, is inextricable from the "mass displacement of impoverished and colonised communities" by the wars and economic and ecological devastations of "capitalism and empire". The wording here is from Harsha Walia, in her analysis of "Border Imperialism".[61] We don't have space in this book to go deep into these issues, but we will certainly come across many instances. For example, we will see how the UK government links deportation and trade agreements in negotiations with ex-colonial states such as Nigeria, Ghana, Pakistan, Sri Lanka.

Assemblage or monster

To use a technical term, the border regime is an "*assemblage*".[62] That is: it is a complex system made up of various different parts – like, say, a bicycle or a plumbing system. These parts are not necessarily or "naturally" bound together, and could be re-arranged in different combinations. The Border Regime hasn't always been with us, and it is always changing. Its components have been put together, assembled, over time. And they can also be dis-assembled, taken apart.

To put this more graphically, the diagram below illustrates the border regime as a monster, of the disjointed Frankenstein's monster variety.

THE BORDER
REGIME
MONSTER

POLITICIANS

MEDIA

CONSENT

COLLABORATION

COMMAND

DATA

SURVEILLANCE

HOME OFFICE ENFORCEMENT

DEPORTATIONS

DETENTION

RAIDS

REPORTING

BORDER STOPS

INFORMING

HOUSING

WORK

SCHOOLS

NHS

EVERYDAY REPRESSION

LEGITIMACY

INTERNATIONAL COOPERATION

FINANCE

TECHNOLOGY

RECRUITMENT

SORTING PEOPLE

Taking apart the Border Regime monster

The monster in our diagram is a vastly simplistic representation of the border regime. It has a few main component parts.

First, it has two big jaws, each with numerous teeth. This is the front line, where the system directly attacks migrants. The teeth include actual uses of force: border stops, raids, detention, deportations. But also less obviously violent controls: e.g. "right to work" or "right to rent" checks that deny someone a job or a place to live.

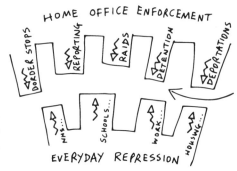

There are two jaws. The top jaw represents the professional specialists of the Home Office and its contractors, e.g. border guards, ICE raid officers, or private security guards.

The bottom jaw represents collaboration in direct control by other actors. E.g. police or council wardens, but also airline or NHS staff carrying out document checks, or maybe informal enforcement by shopkeepers or vigilantes.

The point of the two jaws is that one can't work without the other. The state can't operate effective immigration controls without help from "civil society". But nor can a monster be all jaws and teeth. It needs other parts to inform and supply direct enforcement.

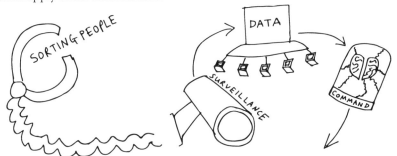

So the diagram also includes a clumsy robot hand which identifies and sorts people; surveillance systems (a giant camera-eye); databases; and a pickled brain which processes all this information and sends out orders.

Again, none of this can work without collaboration. This is represented by the big cog which operates the jaws, and also the tongue which stands for a constant stream of data from migrants themselves, from government agencies, from employers and colleges, from business rivals or neighbours informing on each other, etc.

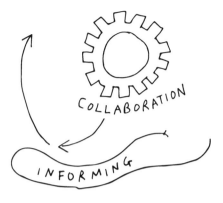

The monster's outlandish megaphone-ear represents the propaganda system and how it helps "manufacture consent".

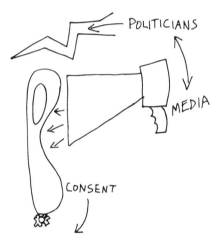

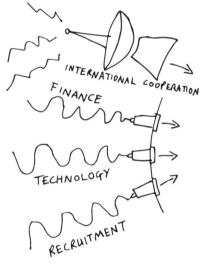

The monster cannot live all alone. It is plugged into other systems which fuel it and keep it alive. These include financing, developing technologies, and recruiting new employees or collaborators.

In technical terms, the monster picture is at the same time a *network diagram*. That is, it contains (i) a number of points or "nodes" and (ii) the lines which represent how they are connected. The nodes, here, stand for different actors involved in the Border Regime – e.g. Home Office units, or types of collaborator. The lines indicate relationships.

There are two kinds of lines in the diagram. Jagged arrows, like lightening bolts, indicate border regime actors attacking migrants. Straight arrows indicate relationships of support or supply between border regime actors. For example, informants supply (feed data to) the databases, which supply (give intelligence to) operational commanders, which supply (give orders to) the raid squads.

The crucial point is this: if a line is broken, an attack is blocked. If a zigzag attack line is broken or taken out, that means the attack is stopped at the cutting edge: e.g. a raid is blocked, a detention centre is shut down, a deportation is stopped, a hostile environment measure is paused. But attacks can also be stopped when supply lines are cut: e.g. people stop passing on information, airlines stop supplying planes, investors pull out of a company, hackers crash a database, or passers-by stop just passing by.

The border regime monster is made of many parts. A few broken teeth or supply lines may allow some people to escape its bite. But it will only be taken out of action altogether when breaks spread across the system, cutting off the power and leaving it toothless.

Part Two:
Control

Blockade of Iraq charter flight at Harmondsworth, 21 June 2011

5. In limbo: reporting, dispersal, destitution

We saw how the border regime divides migrants, granting some people forms of status and rights, while others are persecuted as "illegals". But another notable feature of the UK system is that keeps tens of thousands stuck in a strange limbo in between. Around 80,000 people queue up regularly at 13 *reporting centres* spread across the UK. These people, who include asylum seekers, have few rights, and always the threat of detention and deportation hanging over them.

At the same time, thousands of asylum seekers waiting for their claims to be processed are warehoused into squalid accommodation, scattered in "dispersal areas" around the poorest parts of the country. This housing is run by companies including G4S and Serco, who also run detention centres. But other migrants, including many refugees whose claims have been refused, are unluckier still: banned from working, but cut off from all official support and cast into destitution.

NB: for a guide to legal rights for asylum seekers and others see the Right to Remain Toolkit.[63]

The reporting system

Some 80,000 migrants in the UK are "subject to reporting requirements". They are "foreign nationals residing in the UK without permission", and so are considered liable to detention and deportation.

This includes all asylum seekers. Since 2002, one of the first things refugees receive when they claim asylum in the UK is a card informing them they are liable to be arrested at any time. Other people reporting include, for example, visa "overstayers" or other "irregular" migrants known to the Home Office. Reporting requirements may be imposed when people are bailed from detention, or on people arrested in raids and then released rather than detained.[64]

Typical requirements involve staying at a registered address, and signing on fortnightly, monthly or quarterly. 90% of signers travel to one of the 13 reporting centres. The other 10% sign at a local police station.

More than half of all signers report to the three London centres: Becket House at London Bridge; Lunar House in Croydon; and Eaton House in West London. In the busiest, Becket House, staff regularly see 1,200 people a day.

"Detained on reporting"

Reporting centres are intimidating and secure environments. On entering, people are typically searched, made to hand over mobile phones and other property, and may be fingerprint scanned. Interaction with staff is often minimal, simply to confirm name and contact details – in future, the Home Office plans to automate the basic process. But some people will then be called into another room for an interview. This may be a pre-detention interview as part of the process to obtain an Emergency Travel Document. In other cases, people will simply be detained and led to a cell.

Reporting centre buildings also hold cell complexes, called Short Term Holding Facilities. These are currently run by a private contractor, Mitie, as part of its national "escorting" contract which also includes guarding people on deportation flights. The same buildings are, in general, also the bases for Immigration Enforcement raid teams. The same cells thus hold both people detained on reporting, and people arrested in raids. In the evening, Mitie vans pick up detainees and take them to the main detention centres.

According to the Independent Chief Inspector of Borders and Immigration (ICIBI):

> Between 1 April and 30 September 2016, 2,646 individuals were 'detained on reporting'. As at 10 January 2017, 812 of those individuals had been removed from the UK, and a further 99 in detention on that date pending removal. The remaining two-thirds, 1,735 (65.5 per cent) individuals, had been released from detention as a barrier to removal had been identified.

"Barriers to removal" may mean the detained person has a legal case to stay in the country; others may be released on health grounds. Altogether, 14,774 people were detained in those six months.[65] So 18% of all people detained were picked up when reporting.

Reporting centre staff work to deportation targets. But, as ICIBI reports:

> Staff at the London Reporting Centres worked on the basis that to meet their removal targets they needed to detain twice the

number of individuals, as around half of those detained would later raise a barrier to removal and be released from detention.

So detention is clearly the main goal of reporting teams, alongside trying to persuade people to accept "voluntary return": that is, get on a flight themselves without a security escort. According to the ICIBI report, during early 2017 Immigration Enforcement was developing a "transformation programme" which set out its ambitions for reporting staff to be: "focussed on, and experts in, enforcing returns through detention or same-day returns, persuading offenders to return voluntarily and generating a hostile environment" so that reporting centres would become "the main source of volume returns for Immigration Enforcement."

When not locking people up, reporting staff also pass the time with other activities. For example, if they notice people have driven to the reporting centre they may try to get their driving licenses revoked under the new hostile environment powers. Or if someone doesn't report because of illness, staff may contact the NHS to get them charged for any medical treatment.[66]

Chasing absconders

About 9% of signers don't show up. The reporting staff then follow a three stage process. First, they try to get in touch by phone, or send out a letter with a new date. Second, they may ask ICE Immigration Enforcement teams to visit the home address and make contact. Third, and usually after at least two no-shows, the case is passed to a manager who may authorise "absconder action".

Once classed as an absconder, the person is flagged on the Police National Computer. The National Absconder Tracing Team (NATT) is tasked to track absconders, including working with other government agencies using data sharing agreements. Details may then be passed onto local ICE teams for a raid.

The logic of the reporting system

The UK has less than 3,000 detention places, and detention costs around £80 per person per day (see Chapter 7). So the state is not able to lock up all asylum seekers and other "irregulars" – even assuming this would be politically acceptable. The reporting system thus works alongside the detention system by keeping track of at least a part of the undocumented population. And it makes it very easy to arrest people, as they effectively hand themselves in every week.

To persuade people to keep coming to sign, there is both a carrot and a stick. The stick if the fear of being caught and detained if you go to ground – although in fact, the estimated population of reporting absconders is 60,000, almost as big as the number of people still reporting.

The carrot is the the that your may eventually win "status" if you keep following the rules. In this way, hope becomes a powerful weapon in the hands of the border regime. The UK government keeps people hanging on for years, always with the chance that a new appeal, a new fresh claim, a new lawyer, might be the key that opens the gates to a regular life.

The asylum dispersal system

As we saw in Chapter 3, just under half of asylum seekers are accepted as refugees. And some have to wait many months or years before their cases are settled.

People who apply for asylum and are destitute (without means to house themselves) are entitled to housing, as well as a small allowance (£36.95 per week at the time of writing). First off, refugees are usually placed in seven Initial Accommodation Centre hostels, or in private hostel rooms if these are full. Then they are moved to Dispersal Accommodation. This is usually shared rooms in "houses of multiple accommodation".

The dispersal system started in 1999. The stated aim was to spread asylum-seekers out of London and the South East, where most people arrive and claim asylum, into other regions around the country. So people are now concentrated instead in a few deprived areas, mainly in Scotland, the Midlands and the North of England.

Housing in these areas is dirt cheap. But also, Local Authorities must agree to have asylum-seekers housed in their areas, and many refuse. The government has a power to force councils to accept asylum housing, but does not use it. According to a 2017 parliamentary report: "at the end of September 2016 just 121 local authorities out of a total of 453 (27%) had Section 95 asylum accommodation within their boundaries".[67] Within local authority areas, too, asylum seekers are typically dumped in the poorest wards.

Housing contracts

In 2012, the Home Office reorganised the system so that all housing was provided by large private companies under six regional contracts. This arrangement was supposed to save £150 million over a seven year period.[68] Previously, there was a mixture of housing arrangements run by local authorities as well as private companies. The 2012 contracts were called "COMPASS", which stands for *Commercial and Operational Managers Procuring Asylum Support Services*".

The six contracts were awarded, two each, to three companies:

- **G4S:** North East England, Yorkshire and the Humber; Midlands and East of England.

- **Serco:** Scotland and Northern Ireland; North West England.

- **Clearsprings Group:** Wales and South West England; London and South East England.

However, as the Home Affairs Committee points out: "although the system of three Providers looks straightforward on the surface, below it lies a complex network of contractors, sub-contractors and hundreds of private landlords."

Basically: the three corporations take money from the Home Office; find and rent the cheapest houses they can; liaise with the local councils for authorisation; transport asylum seekers to the accommodation; and act as the point of contact for the refugees.

All three companies employ sub-contractors, either to source properties or to manage them day-to-day. In Scotland and Northern Ireland, Serco hires a sub-contractor called Orchard and Shipman to deal with the private landlords it rents from.[69] G4S has a number of sub-contractors including Live Management Group Ltd, Target Housing Association, UHS Ltd, Mantel Estates Ltd, Jomast, and Cascade.[70]

The COMPASS contracts are due to end in August 2019. They were initially scheduled for five years, plus an optional two year extension, which the Home Office took. The new contracts were meant to be awarded in Autumn 2018, but at the time of writing there has still been no announcement of who is taking over.[71]

In any case, the new arrangement looks set to be very similar to the old. It is based on the same model, with seven large regional contracts due to go to big corporate contractors. Again, there will be a whole load of other smaller companies and landlords profiting under them.

Losing money

The main contractors complain that they have made heavy losses on the COMPASS deals. G4S and Serco, in particular, seemed to have seriously messed up their preparations. Both had problems early on with sub-contractors and failed to source all the properties they had expected; both complained they hadn't anticipated the problems of negotiating with councils over properties; G4S took on properties without inspecting them. Then the mess got deeper as refugee numbers grew again in 2015 and the Home Office fell even further behind in processing claims, meaning the numbers of people to be housed swelled.[72]

Despite all this, G4S and Serco still both said they wanted to stay in the business – if they can get the Home Office to increase its fees. Whoever wins the deals, the signs are that the Home Office is willing to pump more money into the system so that its contractors can turn a profit. In March 2018, G4S' CEO Ashley Almanza explained to financial analysts how he expected the Government would offer better terms to keep them involved:

> Clearly the customer is very keen to have us in the process. There are only two other suppliers in the market who've got the expertise to manage a very, very, very complex contract. If the contract was offered on the same terms, clearly we would not participate. I'm going to guess that the other supplier would also not participate. We've both seen enough to know that that's not a viable model. I think there's every sign that the customer understands that, knows that. The discussions are constructive and positive.[73]

Slum conditions

Conditions in asylum housing are notorious. In 2016, one example got national media attention. G4S' sub-contractor Jomast painted the front doors of its Middlesborough and Stockton asylum houses with the same red paint, which then marked them as targets for attacks by racist gangs.[74]

South Yorkshire Migration and Asylum Action Group (SYMAAG) have collected numerous horror stories from people housed in Yorkshire and other areas. In Sheffield, a toddler with cancer is dumped by G4S in rat-infested accommodation.[75] In Manchester, Serco don't treat bedbug outbreaks but simply wrap infested mattresses in plastic covers.[76] These are not exceptional cases: water leaks, fire hazards, mould, rats, cockroaches and bedbugs appear standard.

In Birmingham, Migrant Voice published a survey of G4S-run housing in January 2017.[77] Its findings include:

- Over 50% reported accommodation was dirty when they arrived, and no cleaning equipment was provided. Many reported broken furniture, smashed windows, and other disrepair.

- 44% reported infestations including mice, rats and bedbugs.

- Only 11% had had positive interactions with housing staff.

- Only 16% felt physically safe in the housing.

- Others reported sexual harassment, abusive staff, and generally being treated with contempt or simply ignored.

Destitution

Asylum dispersal accommodation is available to all those whose asylum cases are still being considered. Once someone is granted refugee status they become eligible to work or to access social housing – but are also ordered to leave their existing home within 28 days.

For those whose claim is finally refused, with appeal rights exhausted, things can now get even worse. They can be allowed to stay in accommodation, and receive minimal financial support, for a short time under the Section 4 regime. This is temporary support granted while people "take all steps" to leave the country, or if they can show that there are medical reasons why they cannot currently travel.[78] But once caseworkers decide they have failed to "take all steps", the support is removed, and people are thrown out of accommodation – if they are not detained.

At this point, many refugees move from waiting in limbo to even greater misery: homeless, without any means of support, often with very limited access to healthcare, and risking imprisonment for "illegal working" if you try to earn money.

The logic of dispersal

The asylum dispersal system was first proposed in the Labour government's 1998 "Fairer, Faster, Firmer" White Paper, which led to the 1999 Immigration and Asylum Act. This gave the aim of helping "to relieve the burden on London, where the majority of asylum seekers are currently concentrated".

In practice, the main driver of dispersal has been cost. The Home Office and its private providers put people where they can find cheap housing. These Dispersal Areas are inevitably impoverished neighbourhoods with low housing demand and few resources.[79]

But this also means these are areas where existing residents usually have little economic or political power. Local authorities will avoid housing asylum seekers in more affluent wards where residents can cause trouble by resisting the development. So both cost and politics lead to the creation of dumping grounds, where the most alienated and stigmatised of all migrants are thrown into already oppressed communities.

The upshot in terms of racial and community tension is well known. But another point needs further thought: dispersing and isolating people helps stop them coming together to resist.

Resistance and solidarity

Undocumented migrants have formed strong movements of solidarity and collective struggle in many European countries. For example, the *Sans Papiers* movement in France has been a major presence on the streets of Paris and other cities since the 1990s, and similar forces have grown in Belgium, Spain, Italy and elsewhere. In Greece, where some 60,000 people were stuck in the country after the "Balkan Route" closed in 2016, refugees and local people in solidarity responded with a powerful movement of square occupations, squats, and "multi-racial rebellion".

The UK has never developed such a highly visible movement of undocumented migrants. We don't know all the reasons for this, but we can point to a couple of factors.

One is hope in individual solutions. Although only half of asylum-seekers are eventually granted refugee status, the UK system works well at persuading people to "keep playing the game" in the hope that their individual cases will eventually come through – even if this takes years. At the same time, people are given the message that collective organising may damage their individual cases. For example, in the book *Open Borders*, Teresa Hayter notes cases where asylum seekers who had spoken at demonstrations and on television were arrested and re-detained.[80]

Another is dispersal and isolation. In Paris, Brussels, Rome or Athens, migrants are often gathered together in large numbers, and also close to centres of economic, political, and media power. The UK's dispersal system scatters people and moves them away from the capital city and other power centres.

In spite of all this, it is certainly the case that migrants and supporters have built powerful solidarity networks locally in many of the UK's dispersal areas. Even if we knew all their stories, we wouldn't have space here to tell them. So we'll just point out one example.

Glasgow is the UK's largest dispersal zone: some 5,000 asylum seekers are currently housed by Serco in the city. The city is also home to notable resistance to the border regime. In 2005, residents on the Kingsway estate organised look-out patrols against dawn raids of asylum seekers housed in the tower blocks.[81] In the same year, national media gave attention to a group of Glasgow school girls who campaigned and stopped the deportation of a classmate.[82] And a local No Borders group began holding weekly gatherings outside the reporting centre and raid base on Brand Street.[83]

In 2006, the group rented a nearby shop, which became the Unity Centre.[84] People going to report sign in at the centre first; if they don't appear to sign out again afterwards, the network begins mobilising to get them out of detention. Over the last 12 years, Unity has not only helped countless people challenge detention and deportation, but become an organising hub for wider resistance. Other projects have included demonstrations, campaigning against Dungavel detention centre, night shelters for destitute people, anti-raid blockades, and coordinating support for struggles in Calais and beyond. Numerous groups in Glasgow have come together to fight the mass eviction of 300 people from Serco dispersal housing.[85]

Groups in other areas, from Croydon to Cardiff, have tried to replicate this model of organising around reporting centres. But we don't know any that have lasted and grown in the same way. It would be worth studying further the conditions that have made the movement in Glasgow so strong.

6. **Immigration raids**

Raids are the Home Office's basic terror tactic against migrants inside the UK. Nineteen raid squads across the country – called Immigration Compliance and Enforcement (ICE) teams – hit dozens of addresses each day.

First come dawn raids against residential addresses, to catch people while they're still sleeping. Later, the squads hit restaurants, shops and factories in "illegal working" raids: there are around 6,000 of these a year, arresting around 5,000 people. Or they join up with police and others in multi-agency operations against public transport, rough sleepers, street markets, and other targets.

Largely based on tip-offs and other "low grade intelligence", the squads hit easy targets – their great favourite is Indian takeaways. Yet they often come away with few arrests, and many people are released straight away as "not removable". What the raids do, though, is spread a climate of fear in migrant communities – affecting "legal" as well as "illegal" migrants.

In this chapter first we give a basic snapshot of some main types of raids and who they target. Then we'll look at a few issues in more depth:

- *Informing by "members of the public"*. Around 50,000 public tip-offs a year provide the bulk of initial intelligence.

- *Employer collaboration*. Standard ICE approaches include getting employers to hand over workers' personal details, including home addresses, or even helping arrange workplace sting operations or "arrests by appointment" – as in the infamous 2016 case of Byron Burgers.

- *Entry and interrogation without warrants*. Less than half of raids are sanctioned by court warrants. Immigration officers typically claim that businesses give so-called "consent" on the door.

- *The impact of resistance*. There has been significant resistance to raids in recent years. This has changed the way squads operate, and noticeably dented their arrogance.

Types of raids

The ICE teams carry out various kinds of operations, from crashing wedding ceremonies to linking up with ticket inspectors on buses and at train stations in working class areas. We do not have precise figures, but we know that most raids are of two types: residential raids, and workplace raids.

Until around 2015, high profile "street stops" – stopping and questioning people just walking in the street – were another common tactic. These have decreased in recent years, after provoking controversy as particularly blatant "fishing expeditions" based on racial profiling.

Workplace raids vary from routine corner-shop busts to operations against big factories or multiple premises, possibly involving a number of ICE teams alongside other state agencies. It would be good to do more research on residential raids. But the task is hard: they are highly secretive, happening well away from the public gaze, and with minimal reporting or oversight. And with rare exceptions (e.g. the Glasgow tower blocks that organised against regular dawn raids in the mid 2000s, discussed in Chapter 5) this means they have faced less coordinated resistance.

There is also a need to investigate raid activities linked to newer hostile environment policies. For example, the "right to rent" introduced in the 2014 Immigration Act requires landlords to check documents of prospective tenants. This may have led to new kinds of residential raids – e.g. ICE teams sourcing "illegal renters'" details from landlords or letting agents.

A snapshot in figures

One statistic the Home Office publishes is the number of arrests made every three months – but only from raids "where the intelligence source type is recorded as information received".[86] In 2017, 3,034 people were arrested in raids following "information received". Less than a quarter of them, 697, ended up being deported.[87]

For workplace raids, a good snapshot comes from a December 2015 report by the Independent Chief Inspector of Borders and Immigration (ICIBI).[88] According to this, the Home Office carried out a total of 36,381 illegal working "visits" across the UK in the six years from 2009 to 2014. That is roughly 6,000 workplace raids a year. From those, there were 29,113 arrests, just under 5,000 a year. More than two thirds of visits (24,621, or 68%) didn't lead to any "illegal workers identified" or arrested, but clearly others ended with multiple arrests. Although we don't have comparable figures since 2015, we believe the same patterns continue.

The raid squads

There are nineteen ICE teams in the UK. Five of them cover London areas. The Central and North teams are both based at Becket House, next to London Bridge station. The South team is based at the main Home Office headquarters in Lunar House, Croydon. You can see the full list of teams and their bases on the Home Office website.[89]

Each local unit is headed by an Assistant Director. Raid squads on the ground are usually headed by an Inspector or Chief Immigration Officer, and made up of a mix of Immigration Officers (IOs), and Assistant Immigration Officers (AIOs). New officers get just 25 days basic training, plus another three weeks taught by the College of Policing before they are "arrest trained".

Many recruits come from within the Home Office: junior office workers who take the chance of a more active life with slightly better pay. Others are recruited externally. Quite a few are ex-soldiers, a smaller number are ex-police. On the whole, there is not so much love lost between police and ICE: IOs are paid worse than real cops, and looked down on as ill-trained amateurs.

On the other hand, according to their trade union leader, the ICE team officer who makes the most arrests in a month does get "cake and possibly a box of Roses chocolates".[90]

Alongside the raid teams themselves, there are much smaller local Operational Intelligence Units (OIUs), staffed by Field Intelligence Officers (FIOs). ICE teams are meant to pass on more serious "organised crime" investigations to the Crime and Financial Investigation (CFI) teams. A separate central unit, called the Civil Penalty Compliance Team (CPCT), is in charge of chasing up penalties for employers found breaking immigration rules.

ICE culture and morale

Some insights into the culture of the ICE teams come from interviews carried out by the Oxford University research project called "Does Immigration

Enforcement Matter".[91] The overall impression is of rock bottom morale. Interviewed officers raised many specific complaints, including:

- *Confusing internal structures:* "the problem is we've got so many directorates and strategic, you know, teams, so many little enforcement units around the country" (words of an Immigration Officer); "it's this obsession with re-branding, even changing the names of units and acronyms" (a Chief Immigration Officer).

- *London bias:* "a very London-centric organisation" (an IO).

- *Stress and overwork:* "[we're told to] keep on nicking people, you just churn, churn, churn" (a former IO).

- *Budget cuts and low pay:* austerity means smaller teams, intelligence gathering is skipped, staff are moved around the country to deal with crises, and backlogs build up. Above all, officers complained about a ban on overtime: "management said no overtime, seniors said no budget. So what happens, we do unpaid hours" (an IO).

- *Outdated IT and an incoherent array of systems.* (See Chapter 11).

- *Bullying:* "bullying is quite a problem" (a CIO).

- *Leading to general low morale:* "my incentive to do the job is rock bottom" (an IO), "morale is very, very low" (a former manager).

Who gets raided?

The 2015 ICIBI report gives a snapshot of who is arrested in workplace raids. The number one targets are South Asian men.

Twelve times more men than women were arrested between September 2012 and January 2014. In the same period, 75% of all people arrested in workplace raids were from Bangladesh, Pakistan or India, in that order. The top ten nationalities, in full, were: Bangladesh 27%, Pakistan 27%, India 21%, China 10%, Nigeria 3%, Afghanistan 3%, Sri Lanka 3%, Nepal 2%, Vietnam 2%, Albania 2%.

The gender balance mirrors detention places, but the nationality breakdown is fairly specific to workplace raids. It reflects not just the history of British colonialism, but the types of businesses that offer easy targets. The ICIBI report sampled 184 visit files, and found:

> ... one hundred and seven of the 184 premises visited were high street restaurants and/or takeaways, mostly Indian Subcontinent or Chinese cuisine, with some fried chicken outlets.[92]

The high number of Pakistanis is also connected to the attempt to fill regular charter flight deportations to that country (see Chapter 8). On the other hand, Chinese people are seen as generally harder to deport – the Chinese government does not co-operate so readily with providing travel documents.

The ICIBI report suggests that Home Office bosses don't see the obsession with Asian restaurants as ideal: "some ICE managers told us that more attention should be paid to other sectors." But we still haven't seen much evidence of change.

In the ICIBI sample, 45% of people arrested were "overstayers", i.e. people who arrived in the UK on a valid visa but then stayed after it had run out; 20% were "illegal entrants"; 13% were "working in breach" of their visa conditions: e.g. asylum seekers or students working full time.

Timeline: from tip-off to detention

1. Gathering "intelligence"

Intelligence officers sort through tip-offs, add their own leads, and supposedly "research and enrich" them.[93] They then prepare "intelligence packages" on potential targets.

2. Picking targets

Each ICE unit has a weekly "tasking group" meeting to plan operations. This might consider 40 or 50 potential operations, though not all will be approved. It will look at:

· "packages" presented by intelligence officers;

· residential targets sent by case workers and reporting centres, e.g. "absconders" (see Chapter 5);

· monthly priorities set by national and regional commanders;

· priorities sent by the National Removals Command (NRC), e.g. to fill a charter flight;

- joint working plans with neighbouring ICE teams and with other agencies such as police and local authorities.

In the absence of special instructions, "removability" tops the criteria for deciding targets. Some nationalities are much easier to deport than others: e.g. Albanians and Pakistanis, the biggest charter flight nationalities. At the bottom are Syrians or Palestinians, or nationalities such as Iranians or Russians whose governments don't readily co-operate in issuing travel documents. The NRC, which is in charge of coordinating all deportations and also authorising detentions, plays a key role here. (See Chapter 8 on deportations.)

3. Planning and legal access

The tasking group will allocate an "officer in charge" for each raid. They should make a plan for the raid and co-ordinate with police or other agencies involved. They may carry out reconnaissance (a "recce") of the target. However, budget cuts mean nowadays recces are often just a quick look on Google Earth.

In theory, the officer in charge should also prepare a legal means to gain access to the target address. The three main options are: a court warrant; an "Assistant Director's letter"; or claimed "consent" from the legal occupier of the property. As discussed below, these procedures are systematically abused.

4. The daily grind

ICE teams typically assemble in the early hours (e.g. around 4 to 5 am) for morning briefings, then head out for residential dawn raids. The schedule may change if, e.g. major "joint agency" operations are planned. Raids continue through the day, and into the evening, on workplaces and other targets. Each ICE unit may have two or more teams working simultaneously. They may aim to carry out around five "visits" during the day – although this could also include other duties such as "compliance visits" on employers (see below).

5. The raid

Squads gain entry to the premises, with or without legal "consent". In theory, they should only question: individuals who have come to their attention through "prior intelligence"; their family members; or other people whose behaviour gives specific grounds to suspect them of "immigration offences". In practice, though, they just round up anyone who looks or sounds "foreign". They aggressively question people, and may use mobile fingerprint scanners. They may also search the property, e.g. for documents, money, and driving licenses (in order to prosecute people under the new "driving whilst illegal" law – see Chapter 10).

6. Arrests – "removability"

Arrested people are taken back to the ICE base. This is usually in a building shared with a "reporting centre" (see Chapter 5) and a cell block called a Short Term Holding Facility. Private Mitie security guards handle custody. But arrests also take one or more immigration officers out of action for several hours to process the prisoners.

That includes calling the National Removals Command, who have to authorise any detentions. This is a source of tension: officers get frustrated if they are instructed to release captives who don't meet current NRC priorities. Those who are detained will be collected in the evening by a Mitie transport van. Other people may be released with reporting requirements.

7. Aftermath

The proportion of removals following ICE "intelligence led" raids is extremely low. Only 23% of "enforcement visit arrests linked to information received" actually led to anyone being "removed".[94] Many others will linger in detention for weeks, months, or even years before being let go.

As for the employers, there is the chance of a criminal charge, but the most common outcome is a civil penalty of up to £20,000 per worker (see below). However, the Home Office's record in actually collecting these fines is poor. According to the 2015 ICIBI report, only "around 31% of debt raised was recovered and [...] it took an average of 28.4 months to recover it."

Allegations: where does "intelligence" come from?

In June 2014, ICE "intelligence" files for a two-week series of nationwide raids called Operation Centurion were leaked to the Anti Raids Network and other campaigners.[95] The files included "intelligence packages" on 225 targets – many of which were then successfully warned. They give a very handy glimpse of how Immigration Enforcement finds its victims. Our 2016 report "Snitches, Stings and Leaks" analysed the files. Here we recap some of the main points.

Debates around immigration raids have sometimes focused on the issue of "racial profiling". The question hit national media after the Operation Centurion leak, as Labour politician Keith Vaz, then Chair of the House of Commons Home Affairs committee, appeared on TV condemning the way raids appeared to be "fishing expeditions" for particular national groups, rather than being truly "intelligence led".[96]

And yet there certainly is "intelligence" behind the raids. In theory, all allegations received by Immigration Enforcement are processed onto a central computer system called the Information Management System (IMS).[97] The Home Office releases some basic statistics on this information.[98] For example, in 2017 IMS had 64,456 information reports. 26,830 were about people with "no permission to stay in the UK", and 12,538 about "illegal working". Other tip-offs concerned bogus marriages (6,626), fake or false documents (4,411), lying on applications (3,406), helping other people enter or stay in the country (1,983), smuggling goods (1,718), and human trafficking (985).

Where did the information come from? Another ICIBI inspection report on "The Intelligence Functions of Border Force and Immigration Enforcement", published in July 2016, helps here. In the twelve months between August 2014 and July 2015, 74,617 allegations were entered into the system. 49,109 came from "the public", including from calls to the Immigration Enforcement hotline, electronically via a form on the Gov.uk website, and in person to officers. Another 7,540 tip-offs were forwarded from Crimestoppers. 17,818 pieces of information were referred by "other Government departments". Finally, 150 tip-offs came from MPs – presumably passing on information from constituents.[99]

On this basis, it looks like the majority of ICE intelligence consists of snitching from "members of the public". But how much use does Immigration Enforcement make of these public tip-offs? Many are likely to be "low grade" to say the least. And what proportion of operations come from officers acting on their own initiative, rather than responding to allegations at all?

Public snitching in the Centurion files

The Centurion files give a few hints.[100] 30 of the leaked entries offer clues to where the initial lead came from. Eight mention "allegations". For example, one entry notes an "allegation of 30 illegally working students" at a cleaning company; in an import company an "allegation has been received that they are employing persons illegally"; a manufacturing company is "alleged to be employing [Brazilian] nationals".

Another seven cases are referrals from other agencies, including three from the police. After a worker contacts the police saying they have been trafficked and forced to work at a meat-packing plant, the police contact IE requesting involvement in a joint operation. In Glasgow, an "Immigration offender [is] encountered by police at Possible House of Multiple Occupancy [...] Others possibly residing there." Elsewhere, police propose a joint op also involving trading standards "during a series of test purchases at off licenses and pubs". Two cases involve the Security Industry Authority (SIA), which licenses security guards. In one, the SIA passes on a lead on a large security company in Luton; in another, ICE are planning to actually "attend an SIA test and check status of candidates".

Five cases recycle old targets, including two to firms that haven't paid old penalties, while another mentions "previous excellent results from enforcement visit". Two other cases dig up unspecified "old intel". In two cases, ICE has approached a company to provide information on its cleaning contractors, which then become targets.

If this sample is anything to go by, many ops do seem to start with a tip-off. There is just one mention in the documents of a team "cold calling" to do speculative intelligence gathering, in this case around hotels in South London. Although there is another reference to "markets being scoped/developed", which might involve teams starting from scratch in a targeted area.

This picture is also supported by the 2015 ICIBI report on Illegal Working. The inspector looked at a sample of 184 cases that had been evaluated according to the National Intelligence Model (NIM) "5x5x5" rating system – a standard model used by the police and other UK law enforcement agencies. In this system a piece of information is classified on three scales: the source is rated from A (always reliable) to E (untested); the particular information is evaluated from 1 (known to be true) to 5 (suspected to be false); and another scale from 1 to 5 indicates who can have access to the information.

In 127 cases, information is said to come from rated "sources". One fact leaps out: 98 of these are rated as E4: "untested source, information not known personally to source, and cannot be corroborated". Another eight were rated E3 "untested source, information not known personally to source, but corroborated." Only 20 were rated as B2 or B3, from "tested" sources, and none as A. In the other 57 cases the source evaluation was "not known, intelligence rating not shown or not clear in file".

And there is further confirmation from the ICIBI report on "Intelligence Functions" (para 6.11), which adds:

> In interviews and focus groups, staff commented that IE was overly reliant on allegations received from members of the public, and did not gather enough intelligence through enforcement teams and Field Intelligence Officers (FIOs). As a result, it was reactive rather than proactive.

In conclusion, there is substantial evidence that Immigration Enforcement "intelligence" does make heavy use of uncorroborated tip-offs from unknown "members of the public".

However, we should add one last point. Immigration Enforcement has strong political, and indeed legal, reasons to represent itself as "intelligence led", as not conducting "fishing expeditions". For this reason, we might expect that available data under-represent operations carried out on the basis of no allegations at all. This would also hold for the Operation Centurion files. If ICE teams are regularly "cold calling" high street takeaways, they are not likely to document this even internally.

So our general conclusion might be: a lot of ICE intelligence comes from uncorroborated public informing; some operations may not be based on any intelligence at all.

Employer collaboration

In July 2016 the restaurant chain Byron Hamburgers caused an outcry after setting up a "sting operation" with the Home Office to trap its own workers. Managers called in staff for early morning meetings, described as about "Health & Safety" or "a new kind of hamburger". When they arrived they were met by ICE officers, who made 35 arrests in different restaurants.[101]

As Byron was hit with pickets, boycott calls and an actual plague of locusts, mainstream and social media debated the morality and legality of its actions.[102] But was the Byron sting an exceptional case, or is this common ICE practice?

Just a few weeks before, on 2 June, ICE had raided the London training centre of Deliveroo, the food delivery courier company, whose workers had been protesting about a cut in wages.[103] The raid was a joint operation with police (focusing on drugs) and the Department of Work and Pensions, and ended with three arrests for immigration offences. Workers present said that Deliveroo management actively assisted the raid and, according to one online report, Immigration Officers arrived with "a list of names with photos of Deliveroo drivers they were looking for".[104] In a media statement the next day, a Deliveroo spokeswoman confirmed that: "we have worked with the Metropolitan Police to assist in a documentation check at our Angel office yesterday."[105]

Two earlier high-profile cases occurred in May 2007 and 2009, both involving contract cleaning companies: Amey and ISS. In December 2006, Amey took over the cleaning contract at the National Physical Laboratory (NPL) in Middlessex, and with it a workforce of 36 cleaners. The new contractor moved to "rationalise" staff numbers. The cleaners, who were seeking trade union recognition rights, resisted. Amey's next move, as told by union rep Julio Mayor, was as follows:

> they summoned all the workers to a closed area under the pretext of a training session. 15 minutes after we had assembled, about 60 police and immigration officials arrived and took away six people undocumented in the UK. Part of the policy of Amey was to get rid of the workers who were working there before they won the contract and they used every tool they had. All the workers were Latin American.[106]

In June 2009, ISS, the cleaning contractor for the School of Oriental and African Studies (SOAS) at the University of London, made a very similar move against its largely unionised staff.

> Cleaning staff were told to attend an 'emergency staff meeting' at 6.30am […] Within minutes the meeting was raided by at least twenty immigration officers. The cleaners were locked in the room and escorted one-by-one into another classroom where they were interrogated.[107]

How common are these kinds of operations? The Amey and ISS cases came to light because some of the workers targeted were active trade unionists and campaigners who raised a public outcry. The case of Byron, too, was initially reported in Spanish speaking media, then raised by Black activist groups on social media, and only picked up by mainstream UK press weeks later after the "#boycottbyron" hashtag went viral on twitter. We can suppose that there are more cases of this kind, which do not receive media attention.

In fact, we can read the following bare statement in the Home Office's official staff guidance on "Illegal Working Operations":

> The majority of reports about suspected illegal working come from employers.[108]

How does that square with the last section, where we saw that the bulk of information starts with "members of the public"? One possibility is that employers are also counted as "members of the public" in the figures, and so many of the 50,000 tip-offs come straight from bosses. Another is that, even if anonymous tip-offs are often the first lead,, ICE teams typically follow up by approaching employers and demanding more information.

Employer collaboration in the Centurion files

This picture is confirmed by the leaked Centurion files. 18 entries explicitly mention discussions between ICE and employers. For example, Midlands ICE teams plan to visit "markets and engage with managers there and do some intelligence gathering there". In London, "contact to be made with Berkeley Homes over a large construction site in Greenwich". In another case, "contact made with Holiday Inn [...], awaiting return contact from HR".

In other cases, the entries report that relationships have been established and the company is co-operating. The most common form of cooperation is handing over staff files and other information on workers. E.g.: "Contact made with Coral Bookmakers and William Hill bookmakers for sites across South London, 900+ staff files are being checked and it is conservatively anticipated there will be at least 5 offenders across the sites." Or in a care home: "staff list of 95 obtained and 8 offenders traced." One entry mentions the British Horse Racing Association "providing staff details (which we have not yet received)" on stable workers.

Three entries concern recruitment agencies. One case note reads as if the initial approach came from the company: intelligence officers are planning to visit the agency after "they noticed an increase in Africans submitting Italian ID cards and [passports]."

Another interesting entry refers to a visit by Field Intelligence Officers (FIOs) to a recruitment agency where "12 offenders were identified". It ends: "residential visits to be tasked". That is, it seems the agency is passing on home addresses of people on its books looking for work, so that ICE can then raid their houses.

As well as passing information on workers, employers may also point the finger at other employers. Two cases are mentioned in the files: in both, Immigration Enforcement is "contacting" or "in communication" with companies – a car auction site and a cinema chain – about their cleaning contractors.

Finally, two entries may indeed refer to Byron-style operations where arrests are set up "by appointment" with bosses. One from the South East team reads: "FIOs are liaising with cleaning companies with a view to arrests by appointment being made." The other is from the South Central team: "FIO looking at a mid size warehouse [...] which is owned by a Chinese national. FIOs are still liaising with cleaning companies with a view to arrests by appointment being made." Given the very similar wording, these two entries may indeed be talking about the same operation: apparently a large operation against a number of companies, and across at least two local ICE areas.

There is one entry in the documents about an employer, or in fact an employers' association, not cooperating. Officers contacted the association "to establish information flows however this is looking unlikely due to a reluctance to work with Immigration Enforcement". This is the only case of non-cooperation noted in the documents. Of course, other potential cases may not have made it into the files for precisely that reason.

The Centurion files suggest that it is very often Immigration Enforcement, acting on a prior tip-off, who initiate contact with employers. This seems to make sense: under most circumstances, why would it be in an employers' interest to "bring down heat" on themselves? After all, one of the perks of "illegal" labour is that it's not hard to fire workers.

But we can also think of exceptions. For example, an employer might be unwilling to do their own dirty work of firing workers, perhaps because of social or family connections to workers. Or some employers may be keen to have help in taking on a "difficult" workforce, perhaps where workers are organising. This, of course, is exactly the situation in which Amey, ISS, and possibly Deliveroo, set their stings.

"Educating" employers

In the second half of 2014, the Home Office ran a programme called Operation Skybreaker to pilot a new enforcement approach in the ten areas of highest "known" illegal immigration – all in London. The main change was the introduction of so-called "educational visits" in advance of raids.

> Before making an enforcement visit to a business to follow up information received about individuals suspected of working there illegally, IE would first visit the business to encourage them to comply with employment requirements.[109]

This scheme has since been rolled out nationwide – although, budget cuts mean teams may not always follow it. "Educational visits" serve a number of objectives. One is public relations, presenting Immigration Enforcement as a friendly service "encouraging" rather than punishing. Another is trying to scare workers into voluntary return, much cheaper than forced deportation. Another is to approach employers about collaboration, whilst gathering more intelligence.[110] The Home Office's evaluation of Operation Skybreaker specifically states that "intelligence generated" from educational visits in the pilot "led to 65 arrests".[111]

According to people involved in the Anti Raids Network, this is what typically happens: intelligence officers or ICE teams call into a business, or sometimes telephone. They ask for full staff lists, and may demand further information on specific individuals. The threat, made implicitly or explicitly, is that if firms do not hand over all information requested they will face a hostile raid.

In September 2014, the Anti Raids Network published a copy of a "consent form" Immigration Enforcement had asked a business to sign. This form was headed "Authorisation for Immigration Officers to review Staff Records". It gives permission to Immigration Enforcement to enter the premises and to check and copy staff records. The gathered "information may be shared by the Home Office with other government departments and law enforcement agencies".[112]

The form states clearly: "*I am aware that I am not obliged to provide consent. I can refuse to answer any questions and ask the officers to leave at any time for any reason*". As this makes clear, ICE are well aware that companies are not legally obliged to hand over personal information on workers. But they don't make a habit of explaining this to scared shopkeepers.[113]

Pressuring collaboration

This brings up an important legal question. In the Byron Hamburgers case, the chain's media defenders argued it was legally obliged to co-operate with Immigration Enforcement in setting a trap for its workers. This is not true. The choice was not legal but financial. Here are the basic points:[114]

- The 2014 and 2016 Immigration Acts – part of Theresa May's hostile environment drive – make it a criminal offence to employ someone if the employer "knows or has reasonable cause to believe that the person has no right to do the work in question".[115] For example, an employer could be convicted if the court finds they "deliberately ignored information or circumstances" about the worker's status.

- In addition, an employer is also liable to pay a civil penalty for employing someone who doesn't have the legal right to do the work. This is separate from the criminal matter: ICE can impose a civil penalty simply by issuing a notice, without having to go before a court and prove their case.[116]

- But the employer does not have to pay if they can show evidence that they have "correctly carried out the prescribed right to work checks using acceptable documents". (Legally, this is a "statutory excuse".) This involves checking the worker's ID documents, and not accepting these documents if it is "reasonably apparent" that they are false or do not belong to the worker.[117] This would apply if the documents are obvious fakes – but not, for example, if they are clever forgeries the company couldn't be expected to spot.[118]

- If the employer fails to show it has done the checks correctly, it faces a maximum penalty of £20,000 – or £15,000 if it has not been found employing an illegal worker during the last three years.

- But the penalty can be reduced on certain grounds. Crucially, these include: £5,000 off for reporting suspected illegal workers to Immigration Enforcement; another £5,000 off for "actively co-operating", which involves granting ICE access to premises and answering all questions and document requests.[119]

To sum up: there is no general legal requirement for companies to hand over any documents in advance of a raid. Companies may *choose* to show documents to prove they have correctly applied right to work checks.

On the other hand, while there is no legal obligation, there are financial incentives – *if* the company thinks it may get caught hiring "illegal" workers, it can reduce penalties by "co-operating". For example, in the Byron Burgers case, the company had already been caught in 2015, so less than three years before, employing at least one illegal worker.[120] But it could have got its penalties halved to £10,000 rather than £20,000 by reporting its workers and then "actively co-operating".

Two tier economy

Immigration Enforcement does not stop people working illegally – but it makes people work fearfully. It helps maintain a segregated "two tier workforce" in which hundreds of thousands of workers have no access to the rights or safeguards available to others. Fear of raids keeps workers in the lower tier scattered, unseen and unheard. The threat of Immigration Enforcement provides the ultimate human resources tool to stop workers becoming "difficult" and organising to demand improved rights or conditions – as seen in the cases of Amey or ISS.

It is important to see that this is not an issue just of a peripheral minority. Illegal workers are at the heart of the UK economy: building workers, office cleaners, food pickers and packers, warehouse lifters, drivers and couriers, the menials in every service industry. The "discount" on illegal workers makes a fundamental contribution to every business model.

But while every blue chip company relies on "illegal" labour this is not illegal – for them – so long as these workers are not directly employed. Only the base level contractors or sub-contractors who immediately hire cleaners or labourers are liable for "right to work checks" and penalties.[121] As we saw, one Immigration Enforcement tactic is to approach higher tier companies for information on contractors. Raids are usually kept at base level, leaving the "respectable" companies unscathed.

Fabricating consent

In many vampire stories, the undead can enter a building only when invited in by the occupiers. ICE teams often work on a similar principle.

There are currently four main ways they can legally gain access to a property. These are:

- **Warrant granted by a magistrate's court**

- **Assistant Director's (AD) letter**

A Home Office Assistant Director has a special power to authorise entry without a warrant. This is only meant to be used in urgent situations where it would be unreasonable to wait for a warrant.

- **"Informed consent"**

The legal occupier of the property can grant officers their consent to enter. According to Immigration Enforcement guidance, this means "a person's agreement to allow something to happen after the person has been informed of all the risks involved and the alternatives".[122] The ICIBI Illegal Working report clarifies that "the guidance requires 'fully informed' consent in writing by a person 'entitled to grant entry'".

- **Licensed premises exemption**

The Immigration Act 2016 gave ICE teams a new power, which came into force in April 2017. They are now legally able to enter businesses if these are "licensed to sell alcohol or late night refreshment". It does not apply to other kinds of "licensed premises" such as entertainment venues or members' clubs.[123] This will do nothing to halt ICE's habit of raiding curry houses.

In the 2016 ICIBI report on Illegal Working Operations (so before the new licensing power), the Inspector looked at how raids were carried out for the sample of 184 cases. This included how ICE teams gained entry to targeted premises. In 79 cases, the teams had court warrants. In three cases, the power of entry was not clear in the records. In the large majority, 102 visits, Immigration Officers entered without any warrant – claiming they had informed consent to do so.

An earlier ICIBI inspection from 2014 found widespread abuse of the AD Letter power: letters were used routinely, rather than only in exceptional cases.[124] Following that report, the use of letters seems to have gone right down.

As we noted, "informed consent" is meant to be in writing, and only "after the person has been informed of all the risks involved and the alternatives". According to people involved in the Anti Raids Network, this is what really happens: ICE officers turn up at the door and ask to speak to the manager, while other officers may already have sealed off other exits to prevent people from leaving the building; the officers then ask the manager (or an available worker) for verbal consent to enter the premises, or at best to sign a paper granting written consent on the spot.

As the ICIBI report notes, there is minimal recording of how consent was established. The inspector saw no records of how squads checked the person they spoke to was "entitled to grant entry". And, "in most premises visited, English was not always the first language of those encountered." "Files rarely documented how officers confirmed that consent was 'fully informed' as required."[125] There is no requirement for teams to keep signed consent letters on file and available for inspection. So there is no way for consent to later be proved or disproved, or for the officers involved in gaining consent to be held to account.

Questioning

Consent to enter is one issue; another is consent for questioning. The law and Home Office guidance allows Immigration Enforcement to enter premises in pursuit of specific named individuals suspected of immigration offences – again, this is key to the claim of "intelligence led" operations. Officers do not have a general power to question anyone else. They may only "invite" other people to answer "consensual questions" if "they had brought themselves to attention, such as by 'behaviour (for example an attempt to conceal himself or leave hurriedly)'."[126]

Once again, the ICIBI Illegal Working report shows that Immigration Officers routinely break the rules:

> In the 184 files we sampled there was no record of anyone being 'invited' to answer 'consensual questions'. The files showed

that officers typically gathered everyone on the premises together, regardless of the information known or people's actions.127

Even if raids are initially targeted based on some form of (low grade) "intelligence", once inside the building they become a general round-up.

Resistance and its impact

There has always been resistance to immigration raids. But in the last five years or so it has become substantially more visible, and this has had significant impacts on ICE tactics.

Here are just a few examples of recent resistance:

- February 2013: demonstration and anti-raids patrol of Old Kent Road, South London, which disrupts raid.128

- August 2013: Southall Black Sisters chase raid squad out of Southall, London.129

- June 2014: leak of "Operation Centurion" documents, after which nearly 200 targets across the UK are warned.130

- May 2015: a large crowd chases raid out of Peckham, South London, video "goes viral".131

- June 2015: over 100 people try to rescue arrested man on East Street, South London.132

- July 2015: locals chase major immigration raid out of Shadwell, East London, and sabotage vans – the Daily Mail spreads the story blaming a "Muslim gang".133

- 2016-17: after a wave of raids targeting the fast gentrifying Deptford Market in South London, raids are chased off and vans smashed, local traders organise a network to alert each other and resist raids together.134

These are just a few high profile stories that have spread, whether through national media, social media, or at street level through leaflets, posters, and word of mouth. There are many more smaller scale examples.

An initiative called the Anti Raids Network was formed in 2012 to spread information about raids and how to resist them. As its members point out, this is by no means responsible for "organising" the widespread local resistance against raids.[135] It helps circulate raid alerts, and stories of resistance. Local groups involved with the network have also run legal and practical workshops, held local information stalls, and more.

There was a noticeable shift in Immigration Enforcement approaches after the major episodes of Summer 2015. ICE teams were clearly nervous about growing resistance. Stories of "mobs" and smashed windscreens spread from London, and were talked about by anxious officers in Wales and Scotland. Numerous incidents were reported where raid teams now backed down and left after just a few people "stood up" to them. That could mean be as little as simply blocking entrances, handing out "know your rights" cards, or just shouting at squads to go away.[136] ICE teams also monitor social media to see if there are call-outs for people to gather and resist raids.

Our understanding is that, after resistance began to spread, ICE orders were as follows:

· If squads anticipate resistance when planning a raid, e.g. in areas known to be "troublesome", they should ask for police to accompany them.

· If during an operation squads think people are gathering to resist them, they should hold off and call a senior commander back at base.

· Very often, the commander will instruct them to quit the operation (make a "tactical retreat"). Back-up is limited, and senior officers do not want to take responsibility for giving the order if something goes wrong.

On the other hand, we have also heard of more recent cases (since 2017) where ICE commanders have instructed officers to arrest people (including UK citizens) for "obstruction". This may often backfire. Immigration Officers are not trained in "public order" tactics or law, and in the cases we have heard of, people arrested were later acquitted or charges were dropped as ICE bungled their procedures.[137]

It is important to remember that ICE have neither the powers nor the training of police officers. They are not used to serious resistance, the mainstay of their job is kicking down sleeping peoples' doors. They rely on police support for more difficult operations – but police commanders rarely see helping ICE as a priority. In addition, as discussed above, immigration raids may often themselves be unlawful due to the routine abuse of warrants or "consent", so squads may not want to draw attention to their own rule-breaking.

7. **Detention**

> I feel very isolated in here (Yarl's Wood). It's not like just a lonely feeling. It's a different kind of isolation. I feel like I have already been removed to a place with different laws, removed from my friends and family, removed from society, so far removed from every comfort.
>
> I find myself missing silly things like animals. I want to play with my dog. I have not seen a child in so long, do little people exist any more? I miss watching football with a cold Peroni. I wonder what happened in Game of Thrones? Silly things really.

Detained Voices, 24 February 2018[138]

As you read this, around 2,000 people are locked up without trial or time limit in the Home Office's immigration detention centres.

In theory, immigration detention is meant to be a short term measure while people are processed for deportation. In practice, only half of people detained are actually "removed". The other half are held for weeks, months, or even years before being released again, often into the limbo of the reporting system (see Chapter 5). Indeed, the UK is the only European country with *indefinite* detention. All others have a set time limit on how long migrants can be held: for example, the limit in France is 45 days.[139]

The UK is also exceptional in the scale of privatisation of its detention system – although other European countries are catching up fast. Of the eight long-term detention centres, seven are run by four private companies: Mitie, G4S, Serco, and GEO Group.

Detention is a very profitable business. Although kept secret on the grounds of "commercial confidentiality", the available information suggests these companies expect to make 20% and more profit from detention contracts. Companies keep costs down, and profits up, by systematic under-staffing, and by using detainee labour paid just £1 an hour. People rounded up for "illegal working" are put to work to clean their own prisons and make money for the likes of G4S.

This chapter gives a quick run-through of some key issues and trends in the detention system, followed by a list with details of the detention centres. There are mini-profiles of the four corporations in the Annex to this book (which summarise full length profiles on the Corporate Watch website).

The detention centres

The Home Office currently has eight long-term migration prisons, called "Immigration Removal Centres" (IRCs).[140] These are: Colnbrook and Harmondsworth near Heathrow airport; Brook House and Tinsley House (including the "family unit" where children are imprisoned) at Gatwick Airport; Campsfield House in Oxfordshire, Dungavel House in Lanarkshire, Morton Hall in Lincolnshire, and Yarl's Wood in Bedfordshire.

One key issue for the future is: if the third runway goes ahead at Heathrow Airport, Harmondsworth and Colnbrook will have to be demolished – and, unless there is some drastic change in government policy, replaced.[141]

There are another two stand-alone "residential short term holding facilities" (RSTHFs), where adults are held for up to one week. These are Larne House in Antrim and Pennine House at Manchester Airport. (There are also short term holding facilities within the Yarl's Wood and Brook House complexes.)

Finally, there are also more than 30 "non-residential" holding centres where people are kept for short periods.

A few figures:

- At the end of June 2018, 2,226 people were being held in immigration detention. 1,905 people were in detention centres, plus another 321 people in "immigration detention in HM [Her Majesty's] prisons".[142]

- There are in total around 3,000 available beds in long-term centres, plus more in short term holding facilities.

- 27,231 people were detained in 2017 altogether. The large majority (23,272) were men.[143]

- According to the Home Office, detaining someone currently costs on average around £86 per day.[144] That means the whole system costs roughly £170 million a year.

- 13,173 people were deported from detention in 2017.[145] That is, less than half of people detained were deported. Most are bailed, or released without conditions. Bail usually involves finding people to act as "sureties", and having to report regularly at Immigration Enforcement reporting centres.

- Detention numbers have fallen in the last two years, from a peak of 32,447 in 2015.[146]

- Only 44 children were detained in 2017; 20 of these were 11 or younger.[147] Only 11 of these children were actually deported. The other 33 were put through the ordeal of imprisonment without any departure at the end of it. Child detention numbers were down from 163 in 2015; but numbers may increase again now the new Tinsley House family unit is open.

- East Europeans are now top detention targets alongside South Asians. The top nationalities leaving detention in 2017 were Pakistan (2,565), Albania (2,288), India (2,252), Romania (1,879) and Bangladesh (1,385).[148]

- Most people are inside for less than one month: 63.4% in 2017, with 80% out by two months.[149] These proportions are very similar every year going back to 2010: the Home Office has not succeeded in speeding up detention-deportation "turnover" time. 225 people leaving detention in 2017 were imprisoned for over a year. One person had been in more than four years.

A little bit of history

The first detention centre, Harmondsworth, was opened near Heathrow Airport in 1970. It originally had space to lock up 44 people.[150] The next year, the 1971 Immigration Act formalised Britain's infamous system of indefinite detention: anyone without the right immigration status can be imprisoned indefinitely on the order of an Immigration Officer, without charge or trial. From the start, Harmondsworth was run by a private contractor: Securicor, which later became part of G4S.

By 1993, there were 250 detention places.[151] But fifteen years later, there were nearly 4,000. The detention system was rapidly expanded under Blair's Labour government.[152] This began with two makeshift centres, Lindholme and Oakington, opened in former RAF bases in 2000 (both have since closed); then Dungavel, a former hunting lodge, the next year. In 2001, two bigger purpose built centres came on line: Yarl's Wood, and a rebuilt Harmondsworth. (Although half of Yarl's Wood was permanently destroyed in a revolt just three month later.) Dover was converted from a young of-fender's institute to hold migrants in 2002, and the new Colnbrook opened in 2004.

In particular, Labour's detention regime targeted asylum seekers: they were 83% of people detained in 2001, the first year for which we have records.[153] Since 2011, asylum seekers have been around half of detainees every year.[154] In 2000, the official name of these prisons was changed to Immigration Removal Centres.[155] This was meant to indicate the fact that, legally, they are only meant to hold people being processed for imminent deportation. Although, as the figures above show, this is far from true.

In recent years, several detention centres have closed and the overall number of places has gone down – it is currently just over 3,000. Two detention centres, Haslar and Dover, were shut in 2015. Another one, The Verne, in Dorset, closed in December 2017.[156]

The Home Office also planned to close Dungavel in Scotland: the idea was to replace it with a "short term holding facility" near Glasgow airport, with detainees moved quickly down to the main English centres.157 However, this plan was scrapped after campaigners succeeded in blocking planning permission for the airport site, and Dungavel is still open.[158]

The future: government strategy

Detention centre places have reduced in the last few years, and the proposed Dungavel closure would have meant further cuts. This is not because Theresa May's conservative government suddenly developed a soft heart. Rather, it is a result of financial austerity: depending on size, detention centres cost between £5 and £10 million to run each year, or an average of over £20,000 per "bed" (see below). And Home Office budgets are squeezed (see Chapter 4). The basis of current detention policy, then, is to try and slash costs.

One way would be to speed up the flow of people through detention to deportation flights. This has long been the Home Office's stated objective – but there is no sign of success. The statistics on how long people stay in detention have been essentially unchanged since 2010.

Another way is increased privatisation. All the recently closed centres were publicly managed, leaving all but one now outsourced. Although it is questionable how much the government actually saves this way: as we see below, the private contractors are still making extremely healthy profit margins.

Finally, the basic thrust of recent strategy has been to concentrate people into the two main detention centre complexes at Gatwick and Heathrow, while closing down smaller regional centres.

However, it looks like any new government plans are on hold for the moment. There has been increased attention on detention after recent negative publicity around abuse by G4S guards in Brook House. And there are now a number of inquiries taking place into the detention system.

One of these was the second "Shaw Review" into immigration detention. Commissioned by the Home Office, this was led by Stephen Shaw, former Prisons and Probation Ombudsman. Back in 2004, Shaw published the government's official review of the 2002 Yarl's Wood uprising (discussed below). More recently, he was commissioned to make an extensive review of "the welfare of vulnerable people in detention", published in January 2016.[159] His second follow-up report was published in July 2018.[160] Shaw's reports usually make some broad criticisms of detention conditions, and recommend small reforms such as ending the detention of people over 70 or people born in the UK. They do not call for any major changes to the detention system overall or its management.

Following the Panorama revelations, G4S and the Home Office also commissioned a so-called "independent investigation" into conditions in Brook House – which is being carried out entirely behind closed doors.[161] However, in May 2018, the High Court ruled in favour of two former detainees calling for a formal public inquiry into the centre.[162]

Meanwhile, the House of Commons Home Affairs Select Committee is also conducting its own inquiry into the detention system.[163] This began by looking at Brook House but has since expanded its remit to cover the system as a whole, including the issue of detention time limits.

Abuse revelations

Detention is a form of violent abuse, even in the best possible conditions. But there are certainly more and less vicious ways to treat people locked up. Occasionally, small glimpses of the violence of detention reach the national media. The most recent scandals have focused on the widespread sexual abuse of women detainees in Yarl's Wood[164]; and on systematic humiliation and abuse by G4S guards in Brook House – revealed by a whistle blower who filmed numerous scenes undercover, working with the BBC's Panorama programme.[165]

2017 was the deadliest year yet in UK immigration detention, with six people dying.[166] The Institute for Race Relations (IRR) keeps regular track of deaths in the system.[167]

There have been numerous studies by NGOs and advocacy support groups into the harms done to detainees. In particular, we should mention the work by Medical Justice documenting the treatment of torture victims, and the physical and mental health impacts on all detained people.[168] One good place to keep track of latest news and resources is the Detention Forum website.[169] Another invaluable website project is Detained Voices, which records and spreads messages from people currently inside.[170]

Child detention

In 2010, the Conservative – Liberal Democrat coalition government promised to "end child detention". In 2011, they announced they had done it. This was a lie. In fact, the Home Office had just opened a new dedicated detention centre for families with children, in a former hotel now named Cedars, near Crawley and Gatwick Airport.

Child detention had simply been rebranded, with Cedars described as "pre-departure accommodation". Families were meant to be held for no more than three days, but this could be extended for up to a week with the Home Secretary's consent. G4S was the main management contractor at Cedars, but "children's services" were run by the charity Barnardo's. The children's charity was condemned by many for helping to legitimise this new form of child detention. No other charity would take the job, but Barnardo's was in major financial trouble at the time.

In October 2016, Cedars was closed, and replaced with a new "family unit" built inside Tinsley House. The reasons for this were purely financial: it was not cost effective to run a separate family site, and its "suites" were often under-occupied. Barnardo's lobbied for[171] the bigger children's prison to stay open, but was unsuccessful.[172] G4S won the contract to run all aspects of the new family unit, including "welfare services".[173]

Although child detention continues, numbers reduced significantly under the Coalition and Conservative governments. In 2009, more than 1,100 children were locked up; in 2012, only 242. And numbers have fallen since: only 71 children entered detention in 2016. However, this latest fall may be to do with the closure of Cedars and the switch to the new unit at Tinsley House: numbers are likely to have increased since this unit became fully operational.

Slave Labour

Outside detention, it is a criminal offence for most asylum seekers and other irregular migrants to work. Inside detention, the same people arrested for illegal working can be put to work.

A Corporate Watch report in 2014 showed that all four detention profiteers were saving large sums of money by paying detainees to do cleaning, cooking, and building maintenance inside their own prisons. The standard pay rate was £1 an hour, well below the legal minimum wage outside. The companies were estimated to be saving around £3 million a year this way. Detainees are supposedly not forced to work, but this may be the only way they can get money to buy basic supplies inside.[174]

According to a January 2018 report by Phil Miller, in Dungavel detention centre 64 detainees were working up to 30 hours a week on jobs including cleaning, hairdressing and gardening. GEO Group had paid detainees £130,919 for 128,742 hours worked between November 2014 and April 2017. Paying the minimum wage would have cost them around £727,607 more.[175]

Private Contractors

With one exception, detention centres are run by private companies. Mitie is now the biggest contractor: it runs the Heathrow centres, Colnbrook and Harmondsworth, and also Campsfield. G4S runs the Gatwick centres, Brook House, and Tinsley House. It also has a separate contract to run the family unit in Tinsley House. Serco runs Yarl's Wood, and the US prison giant GEO Group runs Dungavel. Only Morton Hall is currently run by the state, contracted by the Home Office to Her Majesty's Prison Service, HMPS.

The recently closed detention centres (Dover, Haslar, Verne) were run by the government. Presumably, it would be harder for the Home Office to shut a privatised centre unless its contract had come to an end.

Mitie also runs the two stand-alone Residential Short Term Holding Facilities (RSHTFs). It also runs the large majority of over 30 non-residential SHTFs, where people are usually (but not always) held for less than 24 hours. This is as part of the overall contract for "escorting and travel services", which Mitie took over from Tascor (subsidiary of Capita) in May 2018.

As well as the main management contracts, private companies also have smaller contracts for healthcare services, cleaning, and more. Some of these are detailed in the detention centres list below.

NB: the detention centre contracts can be downloaded from the government's Contractsfinder archive website – although in heavily redacted forms.[176]

Contracts on hold

A number of big detention centre contracts should now be up for renewal. However, it looks like the government is putting off re-tendering the deals until the various inquiries take place and, it hopes, negative publicity has died down.

The G4S contract to run Tinsley House and Brook House was due to expire at the end of April 2018, and a tender process began in November 2016.[177] However, immediately after the May 2018 local elections, it was quietly announced that the tender process had been suspended.[178] Instead, G4S was given a temporary two year extension of the existing contract.[179] The Home Office stated that the tender would be relaunched after the "independent review" of G4S' running of Brook House. Effectively, then, the exposure of G4S' abuses in Brook House has led to the company being rewarded two more years of fat profits.

Two other contracts are also coming to the end of their terms: Mitie's contract to run Campsfield is meant to end in June 2019; GEO Group's Dungavel contract in September 2019. Usually, re-tendering of such big contracts would start well over a year in advance. And yet, as we write this there have been no tender announcements for these deals.

Detention centre profits

Detention centres make big profits for the contractors. Although profits are kept secret on the grounds of "commercial confidentiality", the information that has emerged suggests that profit margins on detention contracts are usually at least 20%.

A recent Corporate Watch report on detention centre profits investigated this issue in detail, looking at the accounts published by detention subsidiaries of GEO Group and G4S, and at internal G4S documents.180 The 2017 accounts of GEO Group's UK subsidiary suggests it makes a profit of up to 30% on the Dungavel contract. Internal G4S presentations show the company boasting of over 20% profit rates at Brook House, and even over 40% in one year at Tinsley House. We have not seen similar information for the other contractors, but have no reason to believe their profits are any lower.

These extreme profit levels are certainly well above the expected profit margins set out in the Home Office contracts, which are in single figures. For example, the Brook House contract specifies a "profit contribution" of 6.8%. If companies manage to make above these levels through "cost savings", the excess profits are supposed to be split with the Home Office. However, we have not seen any details of such profit sharing agreements, and do not know to what extent the contractors actually pass on savings – if at all.

Other government "outsourcing" contracts are not doing nearly so well. As we saw in Chapter 5, the COMPASS asylum housing contracts have hit G4S and Serco hard. Healthcare and construction are other areas where many have struggled. Mitie, for example, sold off all its home care business at a loss in 2017, while the collapse of outsourcing building contractor Carillion made shockwaves in the industry. But detention remains very much profitable, and all four companies currently in the market continue to seek out and compete for new tenders.

And as we have seen, funding for the Home Office's immigration work is relatively low. So why do detention contracts remain so lucrative? We can think of a number of reasons. One is the savings from slave labour we discussed above. Another is that there is very little scrutiny of detention contracts, so contractors can cut costs further by under-staffing and stripping facilities to a minimum. As we reported in 2015, detention outsourcers are allowed to "self audit" their own performance, with minimal checking by the Home Office.[181] Meanwhile the voices of those in detention themselves are rarely heard.

Another reason is that a small handful of specialist corporations have an effective oligopoly in the detention market. There is not the same competitive pressure on margins as in, say, a general "facilities management" contract where many businesses are able to apply.

Also, these companies know the business very well. Again, the very first purpose built immigration detention centre, Harmondsworth, was already run by Securicor (now part of G4S) on opening in 1970. The rash of new PFI-funded detention centres opened during the Blair government were handed straight into private management. Headline loss-making deals tend to be ones where outsourcing companies push into new areas they haven't tried before – like asylum housing.

In general, while many other service contracts are being squeezed in today's austerity conditions, locking people up remains good business, as does security more generally. This is ultimately why outsourcers who focus just on security and imprisonment like G4S and GEO Group are growing and turning a healthy profit. Prison and immigration control industries are fuelled by insecurity, inequality, and xenophobia – and recent trends suggest the rush to lock up society's unwanted is not going away. Or as Serco's latest Annual Report puts it:

> ... we can be very confident that the world will still need prisons, will still need to manage immigration ... a prison custody officer can sleep soundly in the knowledge that his or her skills will be required for years to come.[182]

Resistance and its impact

Detention centres have always been amongst the most active sites of migrant struggle in the UK. Inside, resistance takes numerous forms: small everyday acts of refusal and solidarity, sit-in protests and hunger strikes, escapes, and sometimes major outbreaks of revolt. The most famous of these was the Yarl's Wood uprising in 2002, which permanently destroyed half of the new centre just a few months after it opened.

On the outside, detainees' struggles have been supported by numerous visitors' networks, vital legal and medical support groups such as Bail for Immigration Detainees and Medical Justice, solidarity demos, and more. Recently, political campaigns have particularly focused on the introduction of a time limit. It is hard to assess the impact of reforming campaigns. What we are sure of is that solidarity from the outside plays a vital role in sustaining people struggling individually and collectively inside detention.

Campsfield in the 1990s

Some basic patterns of detention struggle are clear from the first few months of Campsfield's history, as documented by the Campaign to Close Campsfield. In February 1994, three months after the centre opened, eleven mostly Algerian detainees started a hunger strike which was supported by demonstrations on the outside organised by the Algerian Community Association and others. All eleven won their release.

Then on 11 March 175 detainees started a mass hunger strike, which spread to 400 people in detention centres across the UK. On 12 March, detainees occupied Campsfield's roof for the first time. The authorities came back hard, transferring nine of the occupiers to prison, and starting a wave of unannounced deportations of hunger strikers and other detainees.

On 4 June, 600 people held a solidarity demonstration outside the centre. Some stayed to form a "camp for human rights" outside the gates. The next day, 5 June, guards grabbed Ali Tamarat, a vocal former hunger striker who had been released then arrested and detained again, and took him to be deported. This sparked the first mass revolt. Detainees set fires and occupied rooftops, and eleven people managed to escape. Riot squads retook the centre, and 22 people were transferred to prison.

Protests, hunger strikes and riots continued at Campsfield throughout the 1990s. A revolt in 1997 led to the first case in which detainees were put on trial for rebelling – nine West African men were charged with "riot". Supporters organised a significant solidarity campaign, and a solid legal defence team that exposed numerous examples of abuse and false testimony from Group 4 guards – the case was withdrawn by the prosecutor before the end of the trial.[183]

The 2002 Yarl's Wood revolt

As the new rash of centres opened from 2000, resistance grew rapidly as thousands more people were dragged into the detention system. Yarl's Wood, opened November 2001, was the centrepiece in Labour's expansion programme. It was designed to hold 900 people, far bigger than any other detention centre before or since. Security was outsourced to Group 4 (now part of G4S). Managers and guards were without experience in running this new kind of experimental facility, and detainees say that guards were particularly brutal and arrogant. Any complaints or protests were ignored and typically led to people being locked in their rooms. Anyone continuing to resist was sent to the segregation unit – this included people who had self-harmed or attempted suicide.

We'll quote from Harmit Athwal's summary of how the revolt began on the night of 14 February. This gives a taste of the petty disrespect of everyday life in detention, and of how people's tolerance gets pushed to the limit.

> it was the treatment by Group 4 officers of Eunice Edozieh, a 52-year-old Nigerian detainee called 'Mama' by other detainees, that sparked the disturbance. Eunice had been asking that day to see a doctor as she was suffering from haemorrhoids (and has now been diagnosed with an uterine prolapse). She became agitated and this was 'dealt with' by a supervisor distracting her by sending her a bogus message implying she had an outside phone call. DCO Suzanne Roadnight hearing one of Eunice's requests to see a doctor told her to 'Shut up and get out of my office'.

> Later, Group 4 supervisor Gloria Bates and shift manager Alan Hughes decided that Eunice would not be allowed to attend church because of the 'scene' she had caused earlier. A notice was put up banning Eunice from church that night. Officers failed to tell Eunice of their decision, but when Eunice tried to attend church, she was refused access. Eunice became angry and upset and at least four Group 4 officers restrained her. [...]

> When other detainees caught sight of what was happening, they attempted to stop it and disorder broke out. In the ensuing m l e, Group 4 staff lost control and fires broke out. Eunice and the female asylum seekers with her were then locked into the stairwell of the burning building [...]

Group 4 ordered its guards to evacuate the building, leaving detainees locked inside. But not before some detainees had managed to take keys and free other prisoners. Prison service Tornado riot squads re-entered the centre at 2 am. By this time one half of the complex had burnt to the ground. The Home Office had decided not to install sprinklers. Thankfully, no bodies were found in the rubble. 23 people are believed to have escaped.

Eleven men, all asylum seekers, were put on trial for "violent disorder" and "affray". Four were convicted, including two who pleaded guilty. But three were found not guilty by the jury, and four had their cases dismissed by the judge. In a common Home Office move, many key defence witnesses had been deported before the trial. All the acquitted defendants were re-arrested and put back in detention under immigration powers.

The destroyed half of Yarl's Wood was never rebuilt. No doubt this was largely due to cost: the damage was estimated at £40 million. The Home Office also paid out to upgrade Harmondsworth and the remaining half of Yarl's Wood with "millions of pounds worth of remedial investment", while Colnbrook, which opened in 2004, was built "to a far more robust (concrete) specification".[184]

An official inquiry was commissioned, led by the Prisons Ombudsman Stephen Shaw. His report, published in 2004, recommended many new security procedures, as well as reforms such as improved food and medical care, cheaper phone calls and allowing detainees internet access. But it also found that the centre was simply too big for Group 4 to control. According to Shaw, the "decision to open an institution so much bigger than anything that had gone before" was the result of a rush to meet Jack Straw's target for 4,000 detention places to facilitate 30,000 deportations. As Shaw concluded in 2004, this target was "now accepted to have been unrealistic."[185] By then, too, the tabloid fever around asylum-seekers had died down, and with it the government's urgency to expand the detention system.

Later revolts

The next few years saw a number of other major revolts including at Harmondsworth in July 2004 and November 2006; and Campsfield in March 2007.

The 2006 Harmondsworth revolt began on the day the Chief Inspector of Prisons published what it called "undoubtedly the poorest report we have issued on an immigration removal centre". That evening, after word of the report spread, people began breaking cameras and set fires. Kalyx (a subsidiary of Sodexo) security guards withdrew and called in the Tornado riot teams. Detainees gathered in a courtyard used sheets to spell out "SOS" and "Freedom" to the media helicopters buzzing overhead. All of the four people later charged with "violent disorder" were acquitted by the jury. Even the judge commented that "one might feel sympathy" with the detainees.[186]

In the weeks after the Harmondsworth revolt, there were also riots in Oakington[187] and Lindholme. Then in Campsfield, on 14 March 2007, inmates tried to stop "Control and Restraint" teams grabbing an Algerian man for deportation. The prisoner was taken, but riots and fires broke out.[188] Since 2007, there have certainly been many protests, and occasionally small riots, in UK detention centres. But there have been no revolts on the scale seen in 2002-7, and none have caused enough damage to put centres out of action.

Why is this? On the one hand, there is perhaps not the same level of pressure as in the mid-2000s, when the government's rush to detain large numbers of people was at its height. On the other, the Home Office and its contractors have learnt lessons. Private sector detention managers and guards were in-experienced newcomers in 2002, but now this is a well-established business. The physical structures of detention centres have become more secure – and more fireproof. Brook House, Colnbrook, and Harmondsworth are effec-tively now Category B prisons. (This is the second highest of four security categories in the main prison system). As Stephen Shaw writes in his 2016 official review of the detention system:

> It is relevant to the physical conditions in which detainees are now held that the early years of the century witnessed a num-ber of serious disturbances, the most significant of which (Yarl's Wood in 2002, Harmondsworth in 2004 and 2006) resulted in the near total destruction of the buildings.

And Shaw's 2018 follow-up report adds that for any new detention centres: "what I do not think is in any doubt is that the houseblocks and perimeter security should be to category B standards."[189]

The last ten years

The absence of major revolts does not mean struggle has gone away. Resistance is a constant of life in detention, taking many forms. Some nota-ble recent examples include the struggle by women inside Yarl's Wood who formed a Movement for Justice group in 2012, resisted deportations inside the centre, and held numerous protests and occupations.[190] These actions were given considerable support by regular demos on the outside – by 2016 these were sometimes thousands strong.

Hunger strikes remain a major tactic of detainee resistance. In 2014 and again in 2015, mass hunger strikes spread through most of the UK's detention centres. The Detained Voices website, set up in 2015, is an important resource broadcasting stories of resistance and calls for solidarity from inside detention.[191]

It is hard to assess the impact of this continued resistance. Revolts which cause serious damage lead to official enquiries, recommendations and sometimes reforms. Hunger strikes and solidarity demos do not get the same public attention, but that doesn't necessarily mean they don't have an impact behind the scenes. (It could be useful to make a thorough study of hunger strikes through the years, and see how and when they have been successful – unfortunately we haven't had time to do that for this book).

The Home Office's standard approach is, in public, to ignore all protests. But more experienced managers will try to see off struggles before they grow into a major threat. Sometimes this will mean stamping down hard – but other times quietly meeting people's demands.

Campaigning on the outside

On the outside, there have been numerous groups and movements since the 1990s campaigning for detention closures and reforms.

Unfortunately, there are no successful examples of outside campaigns closing detention centres. The Campaign to Close Campsfield, started in 1993, has held monthly demos at the centre since it opened. Members say the campaign came close to succeeding in its first few years; it also helped win the acquittal of all nine West African prisoners accused of rioting in 1997.

It seems easier to stop centres being built or expanded than close them once they're open. In 2015, campaigners stopped plans to expand Campsfield.[192] According to someone involved:

> It was a broad-based campaign mixing community organising, legal tactics, planning arguments (but not "Not In My Back Yard" (NIMBY) ones!), lobbying of local politicians and councils, and media-based campaigning. The straw that broke the camel's back was the threat of legal action against the council for ignoring our argument that they should consider our principled case against detention as part of the planning decision, since the government had argued that the necessity for detention was a factor which made it possible to build on protected greenbelt land.

When the council decided not to consider the planning application, the government withdrew it.

In 2017, the Stop Detention Scotland campaign stopped the opening of a new Short Term Holding Facility at Glasgow airport. Although there was an unintended consequence: the government kept Dungavel open instead. One person involved told us:

> We did extensive research, consulted with the councillors who were to make the decision, created petitions and had the public submit hundreds of letters of objection to the planning committee. We went door to door around the community generating local resistance to the proposal and held protests at the council meeting and in Glasgow. The plan was unanimously rejected by the council and the Scottish National Party pledged that there would be no more detention centres in Scotland.

Recently, various detention campaign groups have united around the demand for a 28 day time limit. The present government is highly unlikely to budge on this, and a parliamentary amendment calling for a 60 day limit was soundly defeated in 2014.[193]

Things might change if Labour get elected. In May 2018, shadow home secretary Diane Abbot not only agreed with a 28 day limit, but talked of shutting Brook House and Yarl's Wood (though not the others), and added that "private firms have no business in detention."[194]

But so far, it is fair to say that political campaigning against detention has not yet brought significant reverses at a national level. Recent falls in detention numbers have been due to government austerity cuts rather than any political shift.

The power of solidarity

On the other hand, we believe that solidarity campaigns from outside have given considerable strength to people inside, empowering both their personal and collective struggles. We know how much detention managers hate solidarity demos, because they fear how prisoners become fired up by feeling passionate support from without. And there are untold statements from prisoners themselves testifying to the power of solidarity across the walls. (Take a look at the Detained Voices website for some examples.[195])

It is also worth noting how many of the revolts mentioned above began with acts of solidarity between people inside: for example, other prisoners trying to help Ali Tamarat or Eunice Edozieh when they were attacked by guards. Both inside and outside, solidarity is central to resistance. Struggle comes alive when when people feel they are not lone individuals isolated and crushed by the massive power of the system. When an attack on one is felt as an attack on all. These same patterns play out again and again in detention resistance – as they do in all prisons, and in our "prison society" on the outside too.

> A manager told me last week that I should concentrate on my case and be more selfish as I might feel better if I stop taking on people's problems. He might have a point but I can't help but have empathy and maybe that's why I could never do a job like his. I empathise with people regardless of the colour of their skin, sexual orientation, religious beliefs, and political beliefs. To me people are people, and we all want the same things on a human level. We want to feel safe, we want to love and be loved, and we want to feel accepted.

Detained Voices, 26 February 2018[196]

Detention Centres list

Heathrow centres:

Colnbrook IRC

A4 Bath Road/Colnbrook by-pass, UB7 0FX

Opened in August 2004. Colnbrook is a high security detention centre built to the same standards as a Category B prison. Capacity of 312 males and 27 females.[197]

Currently run by Mitie. The contract, which covers both Heathrow centres, runs from September 2014-22.[198] The total contract value at award was £240m, or £30 million per year – roughly £28,000 per bed.[199]

Previous contractors: Serco 2004-14, the original contractor when the centre opened (then under the name "Premier Detention Services" or PDS.)

Healthcare: Central & North West London NHS Foundation Trust (CNWL).[200]

Harmondsworth IRC

A4 Bath Road/Colnbrook by-pass, UB7 0FX

The first detention centre, Harmondsworth was originally opened in 1970. It has been substantially rebuilt since then. With a current capacity of 726 male detainees, it is the largest UK detention centre.[201]

The older part of the centre (359 beds) is "hostel type accommodation" with lower security; a newer part (367) is run on similar lines to a Category B prison.

Currently run by Mitie. The contract, which covers both Heathrow centres, runs from September 2014-22.[202] The total contract value at award was £240m, or £30 million per year – roughly £28,000 per bed.[203]

Previous contractors: Securicor (now G4S), 1970-1988; Group 4 / GSL (now G4S), 1988-1999; Burns International, 1999-2001; Sodexo (at first under the name "UK Detention Services UKDS", then rebranded "Kalyx" in 2006), 2001 –2009.

Healthcare: Central & North West London NHS Foundation Trust (CNWL).

Gatwick centres:

Brook House IRC

Perimeter Road South, Gatwick airport, RH6 0PQ

Opened 2009. Current capacity of 508 male detainees – expanded by 60 places in 2017 by putting extra beds in existing rooms.[204] The £1.7 million construction contract for expansion of both Gatwick centres was awarded to Wates Construction.[205]

Run by G4S since opening. The contract[206] for the management of the Gatwick detention centres began in May 2009 and was due to end in 2018, but has now been extended until May 2020. The total contract value at award was £90.4 million; £10m per year, or roughly £18,000 per bed.[207]

Healthcare: G4S Medical.[208] Cleaning and catering are sub-contracted by G4S to Aramark.[209]

Tinsley House IRC

Perimeter Road South, Gatwick airport, RH6 0PQ.

Capacity of approximately 178 (after expansion by 40 places in 2017).[210] This includes the "family unit" with 34 beds (8 suites), which is run under a separate contract by G4S.[211] Tinsley House first opened in 1996.

Currently run by G4S. The contract for the management of the Gatwick detention centres began in May 2009 and was due to end in 2018, but has now been extended until May 2020. The contract's total value at award was £43.6 million; £4.8 million per year, or roughly £27,000 per bed.[212]

Previous contractors: it was run by the US security firm Wackenhut on opening in 1996. Group 4 bought Wackenhut's prisons division in 2002, incorporating it into its prisons company GSL. In 2004 Group 4 merged with Securicor, forming G4S. At the same time, to satisfy competition regulators it also sold off GSL to a venture capital partnership. G4S then bought back GSL in 2008. So the same management has been in charge since the start under different names.

Healthcare: G4S Medical.[213] Cleaning and catering are sub-contracted by G4S to Aramark.[214]

Elsewhere:

Campsfield House

Langford Lane, Kidlington, Oxon, OX5 1RE

Capacity of 282 male prisoners.[215] Campsfield opened as an IRC in 1993, before that it was a young offenders' prison.

Run by Mitie. The contract started in May 2011 and is due to run until June 2019, including a three year extension – although this could be extended, as with the Gatwick contracts.[216] Total value at award was £42 million; value per year £5.25 million, roughly £19,000 per bed.[217]

Previous contractors: Group 4 / GSL (now G4S), 1993 – 2006; GEO Group, 2006-11.

Health services run by Care UK.[218]

Dungavel House

Strathaven, South Lanarkshire, ML10 6RF

Capacity of 249: 235 male, 14 female. Originally an aristocratic hunting lodge, later a prison, it opened as an IRC in 2001.

Run by GEO Group. The contract[219] began in 2011 and is supposed to expire by September 2019[220] after a maximum of three annual extensions. However, as with the Gatwick contracts it might get extended further. Total contract value £45.2 million; £5.65 million per year, or roughly £23,000 per bed.[221]

Previous contractors: PDS (Serco), 2001 – 2006; G4S, 2006 – 2011.

Healthcare is provided by NHS Lanarkshire.

Morton Hall

Swinderby, Lincolnshire, LN6 9PT

Capacity of 392 males. Opened as an IRC in 2011, it previously served as various other kinds of prison for men, women and youth since 1958.

Run by Her Majesty's Prison Service (HMPS).

"Facilities Management", which includes responsibility for works, maintenance and stores, has been contracted out to Amey PLC since June 2015. Healthcare is by Nottinghamshire Healthcare NHS Trust. Education services are provided by Lincoln College. A charity called Children's Links runs the visitor centre.[222] Food is provided by Bidvest (formerly called 3663), which has a nationwide contract with HMIP for prison food.[223]

Yarl's Wood

Twinwoods Business Park, Thurleigh Road, Milton Ernest, Bedford MK44 1FD

Purpose built as an IRC, opened in 2001. Originally designed to hold 900 people, three months after opening half of it was burnt down in a major revolt by inmates. Current capacity 410.[224] It mainly houses women and adult families. There is also a "residential short term holding facility" where 38 males can be held for up to a week.[225]

Run by Serco (contract 2014-2023).[226] Total value £69.9 million; value per year £8.7 million – or roughly £25,000 per bed.[227]

Previous contracts: Group 4 / GSL (G4S), 2001-2008 – as part of a PFI joint venture with building contractor Amey; Serco 2007-2015.

Healthcare is run by G4S under a separate contract, with an annual fee of £1.2 million.[228]

Residential Short Term Holding Facilities (RSTHFs)

In these short-term detention centres, adults can be held for up to one week: seven days if removal directions issued, otherwise five days. Technically, there are three such facilities: one for male prisoners, which is part of the Yarl's Wood IRC complex; and the two stand-alone facilities described below.

- **Larne House**

2 Hope Street, Larne, Antrim, BT40 1UR

Formerly a police station cellblock.

Capacity of 19, male and female.

Run by Mitie.

- **Pennine House**

Room 1506-1510, Terminal 2, Manchester Airport, M90 4AG

Capacity of 32, male and female.

Run by Mitie.

8. **Deportation**

For some, the journey ends with a deportation flight out of the UK: either handcuffed by private security "escorts", or pressured to accept "voluntary return". The Home Office deports over 12,000 people each year in "enforced returns". Over 20,000 more are officially pushed into so-called voluntary departure.[229]

The majority of deportations take place on standard scheduled flights, like the 2010 British Airways flight on which Jimmy Mubenga was killed by three G4S guards in the back seats of the plane. But perhaps the most brutal face of the UK border regime is the practice of mass deportation charter flights. Up to 2,000 people a year are loaded onto these secretive night flights, which may leave from Stansted airport or from smaller airports and military bases. Often shackled in "waist restraint belts" or "leg restraints", deportees are manhandled by private security "escorts" onto aircraft hired from charter companies such as Titan Airways.

In this chapter we'll give a short overview of deportations as a whole, then look in more depth at charter flights in particular. In 2013, Corporate Watch published a report titled "Collective Expulsion: the case against mass deportation charter flights"[230], which argued in depth that these charter flights are unlawful. We summarise and update some of those points here, but the original report is worth looking at for the legal details.

Deportations: an overall snapshot

The UK Home Office "removes" tens of thousands of migrants every year. We prefer to use plain language and call all of these "deportations". Officially, though, they are classed in a number of categories:

· The Home Office uses the word "deportations" only for people being deported on "public policy" rather than "immigration" grounds. Usually, this means Foreign National Offenders who have been convicted of crimes.

· The large majority of cases, which don't involve any crime being committed, are called "returns". These include, for example, people whose asylum claim has been refused, or people found to be overstaying their visa. "Enforced returns" means that they are taken to the airport by Home Office staff – usually, contracted security guards.

- "Voluntary returns" are where people leave by themselves under the threat of enforced removal. The Home Office may pay their fares under the "Assisted Voluntary Return" scheme and other programmes. Coerced would be a more accurate description than voluntary. For example, often people agree to voluntary return as a way to get out of detention, knowing they could be locked up for months waiting for bail if they don't agree.

There were 12,229 "enforced returns" in 2017. At least another 19,896 people agreed to "voluntary return"[231]. So 32,125 people were "returned" altogether.

Media often make out that people deported are dangerous foreign criminals. In fact, only 5,865 "foreign national offenders" were "returned" in 2017, either by "enforced" or "voluntary" deportation. That is, only 18% of people deported had been convicted of any crime.

The number of forced deportations has been gradually declining since its peak in the early 2000s. There were 14,395 "enforced returns" in 2014, 14,854 "enforced removals" back in 2010, and as many as 21,425 back in 2004.[232]

The Home Office says that its aim is to increase the number of voluntary, as opposed to enforced, returns. This is for cost reasons: it is much cheaper if people leave without a security escort. And indeed there was a marked increase in "voluntary" deportations in the early years of this policy shift. Only 3,566 people left "voluntarily" back in 2004, but the number rose every year from then to reach 32,178 in 2013. However, it has been declining since then. As with the drop in detention places, this is for cost reasons rather than due to any change of heart.

The official rationale of Theresa May's "hostile environment" approach is precisely to push people to leave "voluntarily" by making life unliveable in the UK. The official figures do not show this working. We will look at this point further in Chapter 13.

Who is deported?

One obvious shift in the last few years is the increased deportation of Europeans, including EU and other European Economic Area (EEA) nationals. In 2017, 6,931 European nationals were deported by force from the UK, 57% of all "enforced returns". 41% of all forced deportees were EU citizens.

In both 2016 and 2017, the three main nationalities targeted for deportation were all Eastern European: Romania, Albania, and Poland. 1,715 Romanians were deported in 2017, 1,599 Albanians, and 1,213 Poles.

Albanians have long been a prime target for the Home Office, and of course for the UK anti-migrant media, since the fall of the Soviet bloc and the Balkan wars. Albania is not part of the EU or EEA, and so its citizens have fewer international rights than most other Europeans. A newer development is the move to detain and deport large numbers of citizens of EU member states, including Romania and Poland. Until 2011, EU citizens never made up more than 10% of forced deportees. The proportion has been rising rapidly each year since then.

The Home Office clearly switched to a deliberate policy of targeting East Europeans after this time, using the legal argument that they are "not exercising their treaty rights" (see Chapter 4). This started some years ahead of the Brexit vote, but was no doubt linked to attempts by the government to address media panics about East European immigration numbers. In November 2017, the High Court ruled against one form of the targeting of EU migrants (see Chapter 10) – but we have not yet seen this affect detention and deportation numbers.

East Europeans have been replacing Asians as the main target groups. Between 2005 and 2014, people of Asian and Middle Eastern nationalities were the main targets of enforced deportation in every year. They still made up 28% of the total in 2017. Above all, this means people from India, Pakistan and Bangladesh – the nationalities who are most hit in Immigration Enforcement raids. 876 people from India were forcibly deported in 2017, 829 from Pakistan, and 424 from Bangladesh.

Other nationalities targeted in large numbers were Lithuania (649), Nigeria (391), China (318), Jamaica (250), and Vietnam (215).

Charter Flights: the basics

Mass deportations on chartered aircraft are only one small part of the deportation system. Many more people are "removed" on standard scheduled flights. But in many ways charters are the system's most brutal and terrifying instrument, taking place away from the public gaze in secretive night flights.

Target countries

The UK began using charter deportations in 2001. From the beginning, they have targeted a handful of countries, mainly those symbolically identified with the "refugee crisis", and with the UK's war machine. But also, the countries involved in charters are just those the UK has been able to strike mass deportation deals with, often embedded as part of wider trade and "aid" negotiations.

The first flights were to Kosovo and Albania – and Albania is still the number one charter destination, with 15 flights to Tirana in 2017, and at least eight more in the first half of 2018. Romania and the Czech Republic soon followed, with Roma people the main targets of these deportations. In 2003, charters began to Afghanistan, newly declared "safe". For the next nine years, the majority of flights were to Kosovo / Albania and Afghanistan.

More recently, Pakistan has taken over as a main charter "partner", since a landmark trade deal was struck with the Pakistani government in 2011. The Home Office flew 11 deportation flights there (to Islamabad) in 2017, six in the first half of 2018.

African countries have also now became regular destinations, notably Nigeria and Ghana (Lagos and Accra): nine planes went to one or both countries in 2017, four in the first half of 2018. September 2016 also saw the first charter flight to Jamaica since 2014, and there was another charter to the island in 2017.

Flights have ceased, at least for the meantime, to Iraq and Sri Lanka, after successful political and legal campaigns involving refugee movements from these countries. In the case of Iraq, organised opposition in the destination country was a major factor, which led to the Iraqi parliament and Iraqi Kurdish authorities refusing to accept deportees.[233] In May 2017, it appeared that the Home Office was attempting to renew Iraqi charters, after more than 30 Iraqi Kurds and others were rounded up and detained. Vigorous campaigning again helped win the release of most of them; although a few were deported on scheduled flights run by Royal Jordanian, Turkish Airlines and Qatar Airways.[234]

Flights to Afghanistan and the Democratic Republic of the Congo (DRC) have also stopped for the moment, although they continue from other European countries. Back in 2014 there were nine charters to Afghanistan, then three in 2015. But many fear they Afghan charters will also soon resume from the UK.

Dublin flights

One new development, in February 2017, was the introduction of regular "Dublin" charter flights deporting asylum seekers to other EU countries. The Dublin regulation states that refugees can be sent back to claim asylum in the first "safe" European country in which they are recorded. 314 people were deported under the Dublin regulation in 2017, almost half of them on charter flights. There were five such charters to Germany (Frankfurt and Leipzig) in 2017, and one flight that stopped in France, the Czech Republic and Bulgaria (Toulouse, Vienna and Sofia). In the first half of 2018 there were two flights stopping in France, Switzerland and Bulgaria.

There is a different chain of command for the Dublin flights: they are overseen by a separate Home Office department called the "Third Country Unit" (TCU). The security guards are the same. However, inspection reports reveal that a higher level of physical force is used on these flights, including all prisoners being automatically placed in waist restraint belts (see below).

Home Office Charter Flights in 2017[235]

Total 42 flights, 1,664 people (1,565 male, 99 female)

Albania 15 flights, 681 people

Pakistan 11 flights, 489 people

Nigeria/Ghana 7 flights, 261 people

Germany 5 flights, 120 people

Nigeria 2 flights, 57 people

Jamaica 1 flight, 32 people

Bulgaria/Czech Republic/France 1 flight, 24 people

More charter flight figures

The UK government does not routinely publish data on charter flight deportations. However, it does release some information on the numbers and destinations of people deported on these flights in response to Freedom of Information (FOI) requests.

1,644 people were deported on charter flights in 2017, and 1,571 people in 2016.[236] Thanks to an earlier Freedom of Information request submitted by Thomas Avery, we know that 1,877 people were deported on charters in 2015, and 2,364 in 2014.[237] So, as with enforced deportations overall, numbers appear to be generally going down over recent years.

As with deportations in general, media reporting of charters presents them as being laden with "criminals". Only 31% of people sent on charter flights in 2017 were criminal "deportations" (in 2016 it was 33%, and below 30% in 2015 and 2014).

Campaigners have highlighted the particular torture of the "reserve" system, in which many more people are booked on flights than are actually deported. Sometimes dozens are taken on coaches from the detention centre, still waiting news from lawyers or officials about their cases, before being sent back or released at the last minute.

This remains standard practice. In 2017, in fact 4,314 people were given "removal directions" for charter flights (3,771 in 2016). So only about 40% of people who are told they are going to be on the plane are actually taken.

What are charter flights for?

Every now and then, right-wing media run stories slamming the exorbitant cost of charter flights. And, indeed, they are expensive. In 2015, then Immigration minister James Brokenshire stated in parliament that they cost over £5,000 per person deported.[238] The precise figure for 2017 was in fact £5,345.56.[239]

Corporate Watch's 2013 "Collective Expulsion" report analysed the expenses of charter flights, and considered some of the reasons why the UK Home Office chooses to use them even so. Our report highlighted a number of possible factors.

1) **Meeting targets.** Charter flights are a quick way to organise mass deportations of particular nationalities, so helping meet Home Office headline targets. A 2002 government White Paper explained: "Despite the cost of charter flights, this is a very efficient way of enforcing the volume departure of those who have no right to stay here."

2. Stifling rebellion. This aim was very clearly put in 2009 by David Wood, then UKBA head of Criminality and Detention, who explained that the charter flight programme is:

> ... a response to the fact that some of those being deported realised that if they made a big enough fuss at the airport – if they took off their clothes, for instance, or started biting and spitting – they could delay the process. We found that pilots would then refuse to take the person on the grounds that other passengers would object. So although we still use scheduled flights, we use special flights for individuals who are difficult to remove and might cause trouble.

3. Deterrent dogma. As with other aspects of the UK border regime, the Home Office views charter flights as a terrorising deterrent for those who remain or who might yet arrive. (See discussion of the "deterrent dogma" in Chapter 13).

4. Foreign policy tool. Charters only go to a select number of countries where the UK has specific agreements with partner governments. Charters have a particular symbolic value in international relations, perhaps in a number of respects. For example, they may be used to demonstrate that a country is now "safe" after British military intervention: as in the cases of Kosovo and Afghanistan, and less successfully Iraq. In the Sri Lankan case, Tamil campaigners argued that charters also served as an instrument of the Sri Lankan state in both "normalising" its post-war regime and terrorising the Tamil diaspora.[240] In the cases of Nigeria, Jamaica, Pakistan and other charter destinations, these agreements may play other complex material and symbolic roles within wider trade, aid, and "security" negotiations with Britain's former colonies.

How charter flights work: the mechanics

Step 1. High politics

Charter flight routes are agreed between the UK and other states at the highest political and diplomatic levels. For example, the first in the new wave of charters to Pakistan took place in November 2011, not long after a visit by the then prime minister David Cameron to negotiate a new "Enhanced Strategic Dialogue", which included an objective of increasing bilateral trade to £2.5

billion per year as well as a £650 million "education aid" programme. The flight itself took place on the same day of a visit to Pakistan by the then home secretary Teresa May. The first flight to Ghana took place in the same month, just a few weeks after a visit by the then immigration minister Damian Green.[241]

Step 2. The routine is fixed

For the main destinations – Albania, Pakistan, and Nigeria / Ghana – flights are scheduled at more or less regular intervals. So in 2017, there was at least one flight to Albania each month; a flight to Pakistan in most months; and flights to Nigeria and/or Ghana roughly every six weeks.

In the first six months of 2018 there were again flights to Albania every month, with two in April and two in June. There was one flight to Pakistan each month. There were flights to Nigeria and Ghana in January, February, March, and May, each time at the end of the month.

Altogether, flights are spaced out so there is no more than one a week. In all cases we have seen, they take place in the middle of the week: Tuesday, Wednesday or Thursday. (This has been the case since 2014).

Flights to the longer distance destinations, are scheduled to take off at night: e.g. 22.30 for Pakistan, and 23.30 for Nigeria. Albanian and other European flights tend to be scheduled for the morning: typically 07.45 for Tirana flights in 2017, and around 10am for Germany. The two Jamaica flights in 2017 were both scheduled for 6.30 am. Of course, flights often don't take off on time.

Step 3. Filling up the flights: the "National Removals Command"

In July 2013, the Home Office set up a central unit called the "National Removals Command" (NRC) within Immigration Enforcement. This unit, based in Croydon's Lunar House, is in charge of arranging detentions and deportations, as well as running the "assisted voluntary return" scheme. To do this it liaises with the Immigration Control and Enforcement (ICE) teams who carry out raids and arrests on the ground.

The official procedure is basically as follows. First, "illegal migrants" are picked up when reporting at signing centres (see Chapter 5), in ICE raids (see Chapter 6), or sometimes by the police. The arrest team contacts NRC, who give the order as to whether or not the person should be detained. Once in detention, NRC decides how and when to deport the detainee, including whether they should be put on a charter flight.[242]

In reality, we know that NRC has spaces to fill on the charter flights, and this will affect how they decide about which people to target and detain. We believe it likely that:

- ICE teams have standing instructions to find and arrest quotas of migrants from the regular "charter nationalities", i.e., at the present time, Pakistanis, Albanians, Nigerians and Ghanaians. Home Office statistics show that these nationalities are particularly hit by deportations, although it is hard to show whether the existence of regular charter routes is the cause or result – or both – of this.

- If a specific less regular charter flight is planned, e.g. the occasional flights to Jamaica, ICE teams may be given specific instructions to round up people of these nationalities in the weeks running up to the flight. There is plenty of anecdotal evidence of this pattern.

The Home Office has repeatedly denied the practice of targeting particular nationalities to fill planes. However, there is written confirmation of it in an official document that was released on the order of the Information Commissioner after Corporate Watch won a Freedom Of Information legal battle in 2015.[243] This is an audit report by the director of Harmondsworth detention centre written in 2014.[244] He writes:

> Figures rising and falling [in the detention centre] can often be attributed to the amount of charter operations in progress by DEPMU [a Home Office unit] and other pick up operations in effect from the Home Office enforcement teams. In certain circumstances these two departments may work together **to focus on a specific nationality to fill a charter** [...]

Step 4. Booking the plane

Much of the logistics of running charter flights is outsourced to a private company called Carlson Wagonlit Travel (CWT). This company has been the Home Office's "travel services" contractor since 2004. Its initial contract was renewed in 2010, and again in 2017, and is now scheduled to last until 2024.[245]

According to the "Independent Chief Inspector of Borders and Immigration", CWT's job covers: "management of charter flights and ticketing provision for scheduled flights for migrants subject to enforced removal and escorts, where required, and the management of relationships with carriers to maintain and expand available routes."

I.e. it is Carlson Wagonlit that deals with the airlines and books the planes, rather than the Home Office directly. This includes both charters and scheduled deportations. The cost of the contract is around £30 million per year – about half of that goes on scheduled flight tickets, and more will be passed on by CWT to the charter companies it sub-contracts. Carlson Wagonlit itself is expected to be paid £5.7 million for its administrative services over the current seven year deal.[246]

The Home Office has repeatedly refused to release information on the companies that lease the planes, citing "commercial confidentiality". And, unlike other large government contracts including even Ministry of Defence charters, the contracts do not appear in public tender databases. This may just be because they are all sub-contracted through Carlson Wagonlit. Corporate Watch has contacted CWT in the past about its contract, and been told that the company is "prohibited" from speaking.[247]

One company that has provided charter planes on many occasions is Titan Airways. This is testified by multiple deportees and supporters as well as press reports.[248] We do not know at this time whether other charter companies are also involved.

Step 5. Notice period

If the Home Office plans to deport someone, it should give them notice. For people deported on normal scheduled flights, the usual notice period is 72 hours, including two working days. For charter flights (and also for "third country" "Dublin" cases in general) it is five working days.[249]

People on scheduled flights are usually given exact flight details, including the airline and departure time. But since spring 2017, this is no longer the case for charter flights. Standard practice now is to just give people a letter informing them of a "removal window": i.e., that they will be deported any time after the end of the five day notice period, and within 21 days.

In practice, that usually means people booked on a charter flight are given a removal notice letter the week before. In the cases we have seen, notices are issued from Monday to Thursday, and the actual flight is from Tuesday to Thursday the next week. Occasionally, flights are rescheduled for a few days later, in which case further warning must be given.

The reason for the notice period is to give people a chance to make legal appeals against their deportations. For scheduled flights, deportations are *normally* stopped if the deportee can get in an application for Judicial Review. (Note "normally": see the latest Home Office guidance for full details.[250]) Things are not so simple for charter flights: in many cases, the Home Office will not let someone off the flight without an injunction from the courts. This is why the notice period is longer.

In practice, these notice periods give very little time to get a case through the legal system to stop a flight. Particularly as the majority of detainees' only access to legal representation is queuing up for the few sessions run by the handful of legal aid lawyers with contracts to work inside the detention centres.

Even so, some do manage to get last minute injunctions to stop their deportations. Often that really means the very last minute, when people are on the way to or waiting at the airport. For this reason the Home Office routinely issues removal directions to more people than will actually fit on the flight, and takes extra coach loads of these "reserves" to the airport, in order to fill up the spaces of those whose lawyers are successful.

Step 6. Detention centre to airport

Until 2016, deportation charters typically left from Stansted Airport, east of London. More recently, though, the Home Office has been using smaller airports such as Biggin Hill, south east of London[251], and also military airfields such as Brize Norton.

In the days before the flight, people held in faraway detention centres (e.g. Dungavel in Scotland, or Morton Hall in Lincolnshire) may be transferred to the main London centres near Gatwick and Heathrow (Brook House, Tinsley House, Harmondsworth and Colnbrook). According to the Unity Centre, detainees are typically put into cells alone the night before the flight, and may be moved to a separate wing for this purpose.

On the day of the flight itself, detainees are boarded onto coaches, usually many hours ahead of the scheduled departure time. For example, for the flights scheduled to take off at night, coaches can begin boarding at the detention centres in the early afternoon. For flights leaving in the morning, deportees are woken in detention centres in the middle of the night. For example, on an Albania flight observed by the Independent Monitoring Board (IMB), "the discharge process at one IRC started just after 01:00", and at 3 am for a Germany flight.[252]

Shortly before boarding the coaches, guards will come to people's cells, tell them to gather their belongings, and take away their mobile phones. The prisoners are gathered in a hall or stairwell, then walked onto the coaches accompanied by "escort" guards. They may spend many hours penned on the coach. On 2017 flights monitored by the IMB, people taken from Brook House were often picked up first and spent longest on the coaches: "from five hours to seven hours forty minutes."[253]

The HMIP inspection of the flight to France, Austria and Bulgaria gives further detail on timings (although this one seems to have gone more quickly than others):

> The first detainee boarded a coach at Brook House at 1.15am and the last at 3.35am (all times GMT). The Brook House coach arrived at the airport at 4.30am. At Colnbrook, the first detainee was placed on the coach at 2am. The coach left Colnbrook at 4.20am and arrived at the airport at 5.27am. Detainees started to be taken from the coach on to the aircraft at 5.45am. By 6.40am, all detainees had boarded the aircraft and it took off an hour later at 7.40am.

Both escorts and coaches are provided by private contractors. Under the Home Office's current arrangements, the same big security contract covers escorting for both charter and scheduled deportations, and also moving detainees between detention centres and running "short term holding facilities". The current contractor is Mitie, who won the job from Tascor, a subsidiary of Capita, in May 2018. Before Tascor, the contract was held by G4S until 2010, the year in which three of their escorts killed Jimmy Mubenga.

Various coach companies have been used. One of the best known is WH Tours, based in Crawley, not far from Gatwick Airport. Hallmark Coaches is another recent firm.[254]

Recently the Home Office have had big troubles with their coach contractors. In May 2017 an elderly coach overheated and had to pulled off the road, where deportees and guards waited until a new vehicle arrived. According to the IMB: "there was something fundamentally wrong with a coach used in September; a lot of noise and juddering during the journey. The driver was reluctant at one point to turn off the ignition in case the engine would not then re-start."

Then on 14 February 2018, a coach caught fire on the M25 not far out of Harmondsworth. According to detainees on the coach interviewed by the Guardian, guards spent minutes handcuffing everyone before taking them off "just minutes before the vehicle exploded and as fumes filled the cabin".[255]

Detainees often arrive at the airport before the actual flight. In Stansted, deportation planes have been seen to leave from the private aviation area at the western side of the airport, which is clearly visible from the perimeter. On arrival, coaches may head for the "Inflite Jet Centre" building.[256] Escorts may get off the coaches to use facilities or stretch their legs, while detainees are kept on the coaches until boarded onto the plane.

Step 7. On the plane

On the plane itself, deportees are generally outnumbered at least two to one by escorts. Waist restraint belts, in which people's arms are shackled to their sides, are common. On two 2017 "Dublin" flights inspected by Her Majesty's Inspector of Prisons (HMIP) and the Independent Monitoring Board (IMB), waist restraints were automatically used on 100% of detainees. On other inspected flights, a minority were restrained.[257] Leg and head restraints are also used. Pain compliance techniques are used to put unwilling people into restraint, and those who continue to struggle are carried onto the plane. We'll quote just one example from the IMB report:

> A young woman did not want to go. She refused to stand up and leave the coach to board the aircraft. She was cuffed to get her off the coach. She stood on the tarmac weeping. She was asked whether she was willing to walk and allowed a matter of seconds in which to decide. She did not appear to make a decision. She was put into a WRB, then into leg restraints as she continued to weep and say "You cannot take me this way" and then carried on board. She was not fighting, just weeping.

Official inspections by HMIP and IMB note some guards showing "empathy", but others who appear to enjoy intimidating, abusing and humiliating their prisoners. And this is in the presence of an inspector. Personal accounts by people being deported without any such oversight are more harrowing still.[258]

Step 8. Aftermath

What happens once the plane lands? There is little or no official information on this: the Home Office washes its hands of people once they're deported. Some may be simply dumped in an airport, perhaps in a "third country" they have no connection with. Others are met by authorities from the arrival country, and may then be arrested, interrogated, imprisoned again, and in some cases tortured or "disappeared".

Resistance and its impact

> I had put in a Judicial Review and I had support form Black Women Against Rape and Movement for Justice and Yarl's Wood Befrienders as well. They had got support for me on the internet to stop the flight. When we arrived at the airport I could hear people screaming. They said 'Stop! Don't take her on the flight'. I didn't see them, but I could hear them screaming 'Stop Stop' and the air crew told me what they were saying. I felt really great I was so happy. I felt really powerful. Before I was helpless but then I was powerful, I was excited.
>
> I went in the plane and sat between the two officers. I was thinking about ways to misbehave. Then suddenly another escort came from behind said 'Stop Stop Stop'. Everything happened quickly. They said 'get off, quickly, quickly'. I couldn't believe it.

Detained Voices, 9 October 2015[259]

Resistance against deportations is extremely widespread. Firstly, many people avoid deportation through legal challenges. One basic, and often successful, form of solidarity is helping people threatened with deportation find decent legal support. Since the 1990s, the Right to Remain network (formerly called National Coalition of Anti Deportation Campaigns) has been supporting people campaign against and stop deportations. Their *Toolkit* is a crucial guide on the legal routes to do so.

But also, direct resistance by deportees is very often successful. We personally know numerous people who have got off deportation flights on scheduled aeroplanes through direct action. This point cannot be emphasised enough: it is very common for either security managers or airline staff to cancel individual deportations due to relatively low level resistance. Successful cases include:

- Deportees physically resisting their escorts in the airport – managers will often then instruct guards to give up the deportation attempt. (Of course, there are serious risks here: as in the infamous case of Jimmy Mubenga who was killed by G4S guards restraining him. But in many cases, guards are very wary of using serious physical violence in public sight.)

- Deportees "kicking up a fuss" by, e.g. shouting and screaming in waiting lounges or on planes, until either escorts' managers instruct them to give up, or pilots order them off the plane.

- Deportees taking off their clothes, and in some cases smearing themselves with bodily substances, so that guards refuse to touch them or airlines to fly them.

- Other passengers complaining to the pilot, or refusing to sit down until deportees are removed. (For a recent example see Elin Erlsson's video: in August 2018 she refused to sit down on a flight from Sweden where an Afghan man was being deported. After several minutes other passengers including a whole football team joined her in standing, and finally the pilot stopped the deportation.260)

- Supporters leafleting passengers and airline staff in the airport, e.g. asking passengers to complain and refuse to be seated, and asking pilots and cabin crew to refuse to take the deportee.

- Campaigners phoning and emailing airlines, occupying their offices, etc., asking them not to fly deportees.

- One basic form of solidarity campaigning has been just to spread the word of successful resistance, e.g. by distributing leaflets through migrant solidarity networks or at reporting centres.

Resisting charters

Charter flights are much more difficult. Deportees are heavily outnumbered by guards, pilots have no qualms about "passenger safety", and no one is watching. Indeed, as we saw, one of the main reasons for charter flights is specifically to avoid successful resistance.

We know three cases of successful campaigning against specific charter routes. In the cases of Afghanistan and Sri Lanka, regular charters have been halted by legal challenges winning court injunctions. In both cases, legal action has been backed up by political lobbying and media campaigning – although we are not able to assess how much impact this has had.

A court injunction also stopped the last charter to Iraq in June 2011[261], but this decision was later overruled. The flights did not resume because the Iraqi government then refused to continue with the charter agreement, after a vote in the Iraqi parliament in July 2012.[262] Campaigning co-ordinated by the International Federation of Iraqi Refugees (IFIR) played an important role in this.

There have been several examples of people supporting charter deportees by blockading coaches leaving detention centres on the way to the airport. Blockades against Iraq flights took place at Tinsley House in March 2009, and at Harmondsworth/Colnbrook in May 2009 and then in June 2011. There were blockades at Harmondsworth/Colnbrook against Sri Lanka flights in November 2011 and September 2012, and against a Ghana flight in February 2012.[263] These actions were organised by the No Borders and "Stop Deportations" networks working closely with Iraqi and Tamil refugees.

In all these cases, the blockades managed to delay flights for several hours, which enabled numerous people to get court injunctions through and avoid deportation. That is, they effectively worked as delaying tactics in conjunction with legal action. We are not aware of what longer term impact, if any, they had on deportation procedures. Most of the blockades led to people being arrested – but, except for people who pleaded guilty to a minor offence on one occasion, no one was convicted. Every time, the prosecutors dropped the charges, or the cases were thrown out after police "forgot" to bring evidence or messed up technicalities. Possibly the Home Office did not want to draw attention to charters by going to trial.

On 28 March 2017, campaigners from the "End Deportations" collective blocked a plane itself on the tarmac in Stansted Airport, by chaining themselves to its wheel.[264] (NB this is a new group, distinct from the earlier "Stop Deportations" network). The flight, destined for Nigeria and Ghana, was rescheduled for 30 March, when it took off without incident. Again, delaying the flight – this time for 48 hours – allowed numerous people to get legal challenges through and avoid deportation. Eleven months later, 11 of the 60 people booked on the original flight were still in the country.[265]

The Stansted blockade seems to have prompted changes in charter procedure: e.g. deportees are no longer informed of precise times of flights, and recent charters have left from smaller airports and military bases. The action has received substantial media coverage, probably drawing more attention to charter flights than ever before. As we write this, people involved in the blockade are about to stand trial in October 2018.

Blockade of Iraq charter flight at Harmondsworth, 21 June 2011

9. **Calais**

This chapter is a shortened version of information compiled on the Calais Research website, which is a collaboration between Corporate Watch, Calais Migrant Solidarity and other friends.

Calais is the main port on the south side of the Channel that separates Britain and France. In the early 1990s, as the Channel Tunnel was being dug, the governments of Britain and France made an agreement to shift UK border controls onto French soil, and vice versa. This is called the "juxtaposed controls" arrangement: its aim is to stop refugees reaching the UK shore, where they would have the right to claim asylum. It has killed more than 100 people in the last 10 years, and caused misery and trauma for thousands more.[266]

Calais plays a special role in the UK Border Regime for several reasons:

· First, it is the number one crossing point to the UK, not only for human beings but for trade. Actually shutting the border here would crash the UK economy, and threaten essential food supplies from mainland Europe.

· Second, Calais has unique importance as a symbol in anti-migrant propaganda, the scare stories that drive the border regime.

· Third, juxtaposed controls in Calais pioneered the "externalising" of border controls to partner countries. The UK now has border posts across Europe, Africa and Asia. Similarly, the EU frantically cuts deals with Turkey and North African states to export its borders.

· Fourth, Calais is a testing ground for border security and technology, and a goldmine for the private contractors who profit from this. The UK has spent millions in an unending escalation of security around the port, the tunnel, and the highways and railways.

· Finally, for twenty years Calais has been the ultimate "hostile environment" experiment. It is a place of state-imposed misery, as thousands of people get stuck trying to cross the narrow waterway to England. Aiming to deter people from arriving or staying, the authorities conduct the "Chasse à l'Homme" ("hunt for humans"): arresting, beating, gassing, destroying dwellings, and otherwise harassing migrants.[267]

And yet, as with the hostile environment on the mainland, the deterrent dogma has never worked. People keep coming, and people keep crossing.

While Calais is a key part of the UK immigration system, it has some particular features of its own. The Calais border regime is its own strange kind of monster, based on tense alliances between actors with quite different goals. The British state wants to keep migrants in France, but needs the co-operation of the French state which wants rid of them. Both need to work with big commercial interests whose concern is to keep trade flowing.

Background

The Strait of Dover (or in French, "Pas de Calais") is the narrowest point in the Channel between England and France, just 20.7 miles (33.3 kilometres) across. Calais, Dover, the smaller neighbouring ports, and the Channel Tunnel, together make up the "Short Straits" trade route – one of the busiest and most valuable in the world.

More than half of Britain's imports, and in particular the bulk of food imports, come from the EU. And more than half of EU trade passes through the Short Straits. In 2017, the Port of Dover handled 2.6 million lorries, over 17% of *all* UK trade with the world.[268] The Channel Tunnel claims it runs one quarter of UK-EU trade.[269]

The straits are also one of the main crossing points for human traffic. Millions of people with papers cross through the car ferries and the Eurostar passenger trains. For undocumented migrants, this short span of water presents a much greater barrier.

Refugee crossing

Calais has an ancient refugee history, but recent events begin with the fall of the Soviet bloc in 1989, and the vicious Balkan wars that followed. In 1988, less than 4,000 refugees claimed asylum in the UK; in 1991, 44,000 people did. Ethnic cleansing in the Balkans pushed people to move, and modern cross-European transport links made travel much easier than in past generations. Older Calais residents sometimes still refer to refugees there as "Kosovars".

The large majority of the world's refugees stay close to their home countries: currently the biggest refugee populations are housed in Turkey (3.5 million), Uganda and Pakistan (1.4 million each). Much smaller numbers try to reach countries in Europe, including a few thousand heading for the UK. This is very much a product of Britain's colonial legacy. Refugees aiming for the UK do so because they have friends and family here, because they speak English, or because Britain's reputation for "fairness" lingers after generations of imperial propaganda.

Work on the new Channel Tunnel began in 1988, and was completed in 1994.[270] States generally accept asylum claims only from people actually on their territory. So now the UK government worried about a rise in asylum seekers arriving through the tunnel. To address this, it agreed the "juxtaposed controls" system with France in the 1991 Sangatte Protocol.[271] The UK would run border checks on French soil (Coquelles) to stop refugees reaching British territory, while France started border controls in Cheriton, Kent.

The juxtaposed control system has continued to expand. In 2000 the "Additional Protocol" included Eurostar passenger trains; in 2003 the Le Touquet treaty included the ferry ports at Calais and Dunkerque; in 2004, Belgium signed up too, bringing UK border checks to Brussels Midi train station.

Sangatte and on

The result was a bottleneck at the border, with increasing numbers of refugees stuck in sight of the white cliffs of Dover. Numbers grew further in the late 1990s. Now the biggest groups were Afghans fleeing civil war and Kurds fleeing Saddam Hussein's repression in Iraq. In September 1999, the Red Cross opened the Sangatte refugee camp to house at first several hundred, but eventually well over 1000.

The UK media, led by the Daily Mail and the Express, began a hysterical campaign against refugees in Calais. Repeated headlines about asylum seekers causing chaos and plotting to storm the tunnel were accompanied by endless photos of "gangs" of hooded young men.[272] In response, the first fences went up at the port in 2000, then at the tunnel in 2001. The media campaign then focused on calling for closure of the Sangatte camp. The authorities obeyed: Sangatte was shut in December 2002, by order of the French state on the demand of the UK state.

Of course, this did not "solve" the problem of Calais. What it did was make it less visible: migrants became scattered into precarious squats and camps. By September 2008, the governments were spending €12 million a year on security measures, including "530 policemen ... dedicated exclusively to fighting illegal immigration while the number of exiles in town varies from 200 to 600."[273]

Then numbers started to rise again, with new waves of refugees from Afghanistan and Sudan (particularly Darfur). A major new major settlement developed, called the Pashtun "Jungle". (The word "jungle" derives from the Farsi and Pashto word "zhangal", which means forest – it later became widely used by refugees of all backgrounds.) Unlike the Sangatte camp, this was an informal camp self-organised by over 1,000 Afghan refugees.

Again, the UK media took notice and a new run of tabloid horror stories began, focused on the Jungle. And again, the UK state responded, demanding and funding new French security measures, and extended policing to Dunkerque and Boulogne sur Mer along the coast. France evicted and destroyed the Pashtun Jungle in September 2009.[274]

The refugee summer

After that eviction, people once more scattered into smaller camps and occupations of Calais' many deserted ex-industrial buildings. In 2013 and 2014, a number of more permanent occupations were opened and defended by members of the Calais Migrant Solidarity network with the support of many local residents. This included the first dedicated house for women and children on Boulevard Victor Hugo.[275]

This growth of solidarity initiatives pushed the French government to create the first official facility since Sangatte. This was a complex including women's accommodation and other facilities at the old Jules Ferry sports centre. It was six kilometres out of town: the strategy was to keep migrants invisible and segregate them from the "native" population. Any settlements in the town were continually evicted, while people were told to camp around the Jules Ferry site. This led to the creation of a new tolerated Jungle, which would grow bigger than any seen before. Later, the government also authorised some official accommodation in repurposed shipping containers on the site.

After the vicious repression of the Arab revolutions came the European "summer of refugees". Around 8,000 migrants were stuck in Calais by the end of 2016. Set against three million Syrian refugees in Turkey this is nothing; but on the front pages and TV screens it was presented as a mass invasion. The Jungle at Jules Ferry became the new focus both for media hysteria – though also for an unprecedented show of solidarity from many British and other European people. Again, it was shut down, in a massive police operation in October 2016.

After the Jungle

Calais seems to be running on a seven year cycle, with big media frenzies and clearances in 2002, 2009, 2016. After each clearance, some people are imprisoned, some given asylum, and the majority dispersed across France without any permanent resolution to their asylum cases. Then people gradually trickle back to Calais.

As we write, in late 2018, there are again several hundred migrants stuck in Calais trying to cross. Police numbers remain escalated, with orders to break up any growing settlement. Due to the increased security measures, the channel crossing is harder than before 2016. But it is still there, and people will keep coming.

Securing the border

To get past juxtaposed controls, refugees need to find ways to reach British soil "clandestinely". In Calais, this often means hiding in cargo containers carried by lorries or freight trains. To try and stop this, the UK government has spent millions making the area around Calais into a militarised zone. This security project has two main strands:

Fortifying the ports and tunnel

Starting in the 1990s, the key crossing sites have grown ever higher, longer, and more advanced fences. The main fortified zones are at the ports of Calais and Dunkerque; the entry to the tunnel at Coquelles; and, more recently, spreading along the roads and train lines leading to these. The main system now comprises two lines of four-metre high steel grille topped with coiled razorwire, and sandwiched in between these a line of electronic motion sensors. Along the highway near the port there is also a solid concrete wall, dubbed the "great wall of Calais".

Besides fences, a whole range of technologies guard entry points, including dogs, drones, and heat and CO_2 sensors used to detect people in vehicles and containers. All this also needs human guards and operators. Private security guards patrol inside the fences. Outside the fences, the roads are patrolled by French riot police. All this is largely paid for by the UK, with contributions from the European Union. Policing arrangements, funding agreements, and private security contractors are detailed below.

Creating an ultra hostile environment in the surrounding area

The second approach is to try and chase migrants away from the Calais area altogether. The mechanics of this were analysed in a June 2011 report by Calais Migrant Solidarity, entitled "This Border Kills". After the brief interlude of the tolerated Jungle in 2015-16, the situation is again very similar today – only with an even bigger police presence. CRS riot police companies are stationed on rotation in the Calais area, largely working under direction from Police aux Frontieres (PAF) border police. Besides guarding the fences they patrol the streets of the town and the surrounding countryside, engaged in the "*chasse à l'homme*", the hunt for humans.

"This Border Kills" identified three main forms of attack:

- *Crude violence*. Police beatings, violent arrests, and chases which lead to injuries and deaths. In recent years, there have also been greater waves of "extra-state" violence by fascist vigilante groups.

- *Systematic harassment with ID checks and arrests*. Anyone looking like a migrant is profiled, stopped and made to show ID papers. Dozens of people every day are arrested and taken to the PAF station at Coquelles. Most are let go within a few hours or days, perhaps with a document called an "Order to Quit the French Territory" (OQTF). A minority are transferred to the longer term detention centre in the same Coquelles complex, and held for deportation. Particular nationalities are periodically targeted for mass charter flight deportations.

- *"Making life unliveable": raids and attacks on shelters, food, water, sleep and dignity*. CMS and other groups continue to document hundreds of examples include poisoning water supplies with CS gas, tear-gassing charity food distributions, urinating on bedding, and most commonly systematic theft of possessions and destruction of shelters.

The "chasse à l'homme" tactics in Calais are largely unlawful, and have been repeatedly condemned by courts and the French state's own Human Rights Defender. Occasionally, after atrocities are exposed in the media, the violence diminishes for a short while. Then it resumes. Both governments know they will have minimal come-back from using extreme brutality against transient migrants in this emergency zone. It is the "hostile environment" taken to another level.

Key Actors

The Calais border regime involves a number of major actors, whose agendas sometimes coincide but sometimes clash. The Calais Research website profiles them in some detail; here is a summary.

UK government

The UK is the only main actor with a direct interest in border controls in Calais. France wants migrants to leave; the port, Eurotunnel, and freight companies simply want trade to flow freely. The UK tries to secure the border in two ways: directly running its "juxtaposed controls"; and paying other actors to do its dirty work.

· *Direct UK controls*

Border Force oversees border controls itself within the Port. Officers are based in the directorate's South East region command base in Martello Tower, Folkestone (they travel to Calais daily through the tunnel, on coaches operated by a company called Buzzlines travel.)[276] In Calais port, they run passport control and vehicle checks. Border Force, the French PAF, and port security liaise as a "Joint Operations Taskforce" sharing a central control centre. Other Border Force officers work with Eurotunnel inside their complex. UK authorities have also led on building security fences and other infrastructure in and near the Calais Port.

Passport checks are run by BF officers, but searching vehicles is largely contracted out to a company called Eamus Cork Solutions (ECS), as well as a dog handling company called Wagtail. Eamus Cork supply a constant presence of

40 "authorised search officers" (24 hours a day, 365 days a year). Trucks and cars first pass through a Border Force line where documents are checked, and then reach a second line where ECS and Wagtail conduct searches. ECS guards are also in charge of "short term holding facilities" to hold undocumented people found inside the ports and Eurotunnel complex. After processing, prisoners are handed over to the PAF.

- *Funding French authorities*

Britain is not directly responsible for controls and "hostile environment" measures outside the ports. But Britain picks up much of the bill for French police operations through continual funding arrangements (some are listed in the next section). Besides money, Calais is just part of the broader diplomatic relationship between the two states and we can suppose the UK also repays its "debt" to France in other ways.

- *Other relationships*

The UK pays Eurotunnel for the costs of border-related security in the tunnel.

French government

Calais is a problem for the French government: it would rather let migrants pass to the UK, but is caught in its diplomatic relationship with the UK. And, as in the UK, Calais has become a media spectacle. It is used to represent a zone of lawlessness, where the state is failing to control the territory. The far right Front National party and the local right-wing mayor (see below) played this up to undermine François Hollande's Socialist Party government (2012-2017), and now Emmanuel Macron's centrist regime.

In response, government leaders occasionally visit to announce new tough control measures. The rest of the time, officials quietly carry out the UK accords and chase migrants.

In the French system, much of the central government's authority in the area is delegated to a senior local official called the Prefect, who is in charge of police operations and more in the "department" around Calais. There are three main police forces involved:

- *Police aux Frontières (PAF)*. Border police, coordinate most migrant-related operations in Calais, including anti-smuggling intelligence, work with

UK Border Force, process arrested migrants for detention and deportation. The PAF have a base and detention centre complex near the tunnel entrance in Coquelles.

- *Compagnies Républicaines de Sécurité (CRS)*. Notorious French riot police. Calais is one of a few "emergency" zones in France where CRS have a constant presence. Companies are brought in from around France, typically rotating on three week shifts. They are known for brawn not brain, and generally act as "muscle" for PAF operations. They also patrol on their own in their distinctive white vans, picking up migrants on the roads for arrest or beatings.

- *Gendarmes Mobiles*. More riot police, better trained than CRS, technically part of the army. Until 2015 they were only brought in for major one-off operations, but recently have been used alongside CRS to guard the security fences.

Besides policing, the Prefect exercises considerable power through:

- *The asylum system*. Refugees come to Calais in the hope of reaching the UK, but a fair proportion give up and claim asylum in France. France accepts about the same proportion of asylum claimants as the UK. However, waiting times are long, and accommodation and support even worse than in Britain: e.g. many asylum seekers have preferred to stay in jungles and squats rather than official hostels ("foyers"), and in any case there are often no places available. The NGO "France Terre d'Asile" has a major contract to give asylum advice.

- *Ownership and control of land:* The government has direct control over much of the area around the town, including the security zone around the port and tunnel, and the highways. The site of the 2015-16 Jungle was effectively controlled by the state through an environmental quango.

- *Funding and regulating NGOs*. The state funds approved NGOs who distribute food and manage "solidarity". In the Jungle, the prefect used major charity contracts to control the space. One charity, La Vie Active ran the Jules Ferry centre facilities. Another, Acted, became a proxy for the prefecture in the Jungle, advising migrants not to resist evictions, and organising a "council of migrants" made up of pacifying "community leaders". Migrants and solidarity groups who didn't accept this framework were identified and targeted for repression.

The Mayor

The Mayor has considerable power over the town of Calais, and important influence on the port, landowners, NGOs, businesses, and pretty much anyone who wants to operate in the town. Calais was once a Communist Party stronghold, but since 2008 has been run by right-winger Natacha Bouchart (of the Les Republicains party, once headed by former president Nicolas Sarkozy). In 2011 she also became a national Senator. In 2016 she stepped down as senator to become vice president of the Regional Council, in charge of "the sea, ports and coastal policy".

The Mayor heads a sizeable Town Hall infrastructure, which includes a municipal police force – although this is not directly involved in anti-migrant operations. Another key figure is Philippe Mignonet, the deputy mayor for security.

- *Political platform*. Bouchart has used her office as a platform to attack the government and launch crackdowns on migrants in the town, presenting herself as the one with the real answer to the "migrant problem". She has occasionally called for reversal of the juxtaposed control agreements (as did her political ally Sarkozy), and got attention threatening to shut the port.

- *Directing police raids*. Although patrols and raids are carried out by national police forces, the Town Hall collaborates closely. Mignonet has often been present personally leading larger raids, where town hall workers accompany police to demolish structures, clear migrants' belongings, and spray chemicals.

- *Apartheid policy*. The Mayor has implemented measures to stop migrants using football pitches, swimming pools, the library, and other facilities in the town.[277]

- *Targeting squats*. The Mayor has tried to implement a "zero tolerance" approach to squats and other settlements inside the town.[278] Dwellings on municipal land are swiftly cleared. Where the Town Hall does not have direct control over property, it uses influence over land owners: e.g. organisations such as the OPH (French housing agency) that owns many of the empty buildings in the town.

- *Encouraging fascist gangs*. In October 2013, Mayor Bouchart set up an email account for citizens to report migrant settlements in Calais.[279]

This call was swiftly followed by the establishment of an anti-migrant citizens group called "Sauvons Calais", which initially claimed to be supported by the Mayor.[280] The Town Hall later distanced itself from the group, however, after its main spokesperson Kevin Reche was revealed to be a swastika-tattooed Neo-Nazi.

· *Supporting anti-migrant demonstrations.* In 2016, Bouchart supported so-called "apolitical" demonstrations organised by a group called "Agir Ensemble Pour Sauver Calais", which was fronted by a local shopkeeper and included representatives of the port management, ferry companies, and a port trade union.[281]

· *Blocking solidarity.* Bouchart has banned pro-migrant groups and events from using municipal property, e.g. shutting down the "A l'Uni Son" 2013 festival which was due to take place in the "Maison de Tous" community centre.[282] She has also used the Town Hall's regulatory powers, such as around "health and safety" regulation, to shut down pro-migrant solidarity spaces opened in private buildings, e.g. the "Centre Zetkin" set up by Calais Migrant Solidarity in 2013.

Eurotunnel

Eurotunnel is a private stock-exchange listed company with the concession to run the channel tunnel until 2086. It is owned by major international investment funds. It has a heavyweight board of directors with politicians from both sides of the channel, including disgraced British ex-ministers Patricia Hewitt and Tim Yeo and local heavyweight Philippe Vasseur, alongside the likes of arms industry fixer Lord Levene (chair of General Dynamics UK, and former UK National Armaments Advisor), and the infrastructure boss of Goldman Sachs.[283]

Eurotunnel has its own 300-strong private security force to guard the tunnel zone, managed by a former French police chief and an ex-military police colonel. Eurotunnel has played a key role in the militarisation of the border from the start: the treaties that originally exported the UK border to France emerged from negotiations around the tunnel.

Mitie has had a major security contract with Eurotunnel. Mitie won a four year £12 million security deal with Eurotunnel in 2010, which was extended in 2014.[284]

Eurotunnel's costs related to border security are paid for by the UK and French governments, under a legal agreement which goes back to the 1989 Treaty of Canterbury. The amounts are not disclosed, but are multi-million. Eurotunnel claimed it spent €29 million on security overall in 2015, substantially more than €12 million in 2014 and €11.3 million in 2013.

In 2007, Eurotunnel won a case in the Hague Court of International Arbitration against the two governments, ordering them to pay €24 million for costs due to "lost business" in 1999-2002. This was only the second ever judgement against the UK under the Investor State Dispute Settlements (ISDS) procedure, which allows corporations to sue governments in secretive closed tribunals. In 2015, Eurotunnel said it was again taking the governments to court demanding compensation for the "migrant crisis".[285] Despite the fact that in 2015 Eurotunnel's profits were its highest ever.

Port of Calais

Technically, the port is owned by the Conseil Regional (regional council, a regional government body currently controlled by the right wing Les Republicains party). But it is run under a 50 year concession by a semi-private company called Société d'Exploitation des Ports du Détroit (SEPD). The concession also includes the smaller Boulogne port nearby.

SEPD is a majority state owned "Public Limited Company". 73% of its shares are owned by the regional Chambers of Commerce (CCI Nord de France and CCI Cote d'Opale). These are quangos run by local businesses, which are more powerful in France than the UK. 11% is owned by the state investment fund CDC (Caisse des Dépôts et Consignations); another 11% by a private infrastructure investment fund called Meridiam; and 5% under an employee shareholding scheme.

The Port is currently in the midst of a major five year expansion project (called "Calais Port 2015"). French construction multinationals, among them Bouygues and Vinci, have multi-million euro contracts in the expansion scheme.

The port and Eurotunnel are major competitors. In the 2015-16 security "crisis", managers from the two companies often spoke out against the other, criticising the support each was getting from the state, which they saw as redirecting migrant incursions towards their own site. In 2015, Eurotunnel initiated court proceedings to challenge the state subsidy of the Calais Port 2015 expansion.[286]

The port company has no direct interest in attacking migrants: it is border controls, rather than the migrants they target, that disrupt the flow of trade. But as the UK is not about to lift border controls, the port must actively co-operate in security.

In 2015-16, migrants made repeated large-scale incursions into both the port and the tunnel, and an arms race developed as the two sites built ever tougher fences. Some of the measures the port has recently pursued have included: the construction of more fences and the 'Great Wall of Calais'; the installation of infrared barriers providing real-time notifications to security officers about potential break-ins; and the employment of increasing numbers of private security guards. The largest private security contractor is Eamus Cork (ECS) – the same company which also works checking vehicles for Border Force.

Some recent funding agreements for the Calais Border Regime

2009: After a new 'Arrangement' agreed in the France-UK Summit 2009, the UK agrees to provide £15 million, largely for new border control technology.[287]

2014: The European Union's "Asylum, Migration and Integration Fund (AMIF)" is set up with a total of €3.137 billion to spend across Europe in a seven year period (2014-2020).[288] It includes: "€266 million earmarked for France" and "over €370 million earmarked for the UK". This is not only for Calais, but "both of these programmes will, amongst other things, also deal with the situation in Calais."[289]

2014: UK spends £3 million on upgrading vehicle scanning.[290]

2014: The European Commission grants €3.8 million in "emergency funding" to co-finance the creation of the "Jules Ferry" day centre.

September 2014: A €15 million "Joint Fund for Calais" is announced by Bernard Cazeneuve (then French prime minister) and Theresa May. This is largely used on port security, including €5.1 million on fences; €3.1 million on extending the coach hall controls and offices, €2.5 million on "secure freight queuing", €2.45 million increasing Border Force controls in the port "tourism zone"; and €500,000 on cameras. Another undisclosed amount, but possibly many millions, was spent on new tunnel security.

July 2015: UK announces a further £9 million Calais funding. £2 million to be spent on a "secure zone" in Calais for UK-bound lorries, and £7 million for other security measures.[291]

August 2015: In a joint declaration on "Managing Migratory Flows in Calais", the UK pledges an extra £3.5 million per year over two years. The statement explains there will be an extra 500 police from the UK and France, as well as additional freight search teams, dogs, and UK funding for French deportation flights.[292]

31 August 2015: The European Commission announces €5.2 million in "emergency assistance" for work on the area around the Jules Ferry centre and to fund the "transport" of refugees and migrants from Calais to other locations in France.[293]

March 2016: A France-UK Summit announces another £17 million for Calais security.[294] The same statement also announces a €2 billion Anglo-French collaboration on a military drone programme called the Future Combat Air System. The funding will go to arms companies including Britain's BAE Systems and Rolls-Royce (UK) and Dassault Aviation, Safran and Thales (France).[295]

October 2016: Another £36 million UK funding is announced to cover the jungle eviction, further boost port security, and more.[296]

Calais border profiteers

With all this money flowing around, Calais has become a honeypot for border security profiteers. Here are just a few highlights – see the Calais Research website for more names and more details on each.

Eamus Cork

Also known as Eamus Cork Solutions or ECS. The Dunkirk-based company was created in 2004 by a former Calais policeman. It is Border Force's main security contractor searching for migrants in Calais and neighbouring ports. ECS first won a £7.1 million three year Border Force contract in 2011, which was later extended for a further two years. Then in 2016, it won an expanded £27 million Home Office contract for both checking vehicles and running detention facilities in Calais, Dunkerque and Boulogne ports. This is due to last until at least 2020, with extension clauses for up to another two years.[297]

Wagtail

Wagtail provides dogs and dog handlers who work alongside ECS in port searches. Its current £9.3 million contract was awarded in 2014 and runs until 2020. On its website, Wagtail claims to be "the ONLY private UK Company that provides Body Detection Dogs (to detect illegal immigrants) for the UK Border Force".[298]

Mitie

Mitie, which has major detention and deportation contracts inside the UK, has also been a security contractor for Eurotunnel since 2010. (See Annex 2 of this book for more on Mitie.)

Biro Sécurité

Biro is a local security company close to Mayor Bouchart, which has won numerous municipal contracts. It supplied biometric technology, guards and dogs for the Jules Ferry container camp. Biro has also provided secure parking for lorries near the motorway, and further afield secures the Saint-Laurent rest stop at Steenvoorde, Belgium, which has also been the site of migrant Jungles.[299]

Vinci

Vinci is one of the biggest French multinational building and concession corporations. It makes most of its billions from a highly profitable concession to manage French motorways. It has been involved in numerous international scandals, from slave labour allegations in Qatar to ecological devastation and corruption in Russia, and union blacklisting in the UK. Three of the companies initially involved in building and owning the Eurotunnel are now part of Vinci. In 2016, Vinci subsidiary Eurovia worked on the £2 million contract to build the "great wall of Calais", a £2 million 4 metre high wall to secure the highway near the port. In the same year, another Vinci subsidiary,

Sogea, carried out the Jungle demolition. (See our in-depth company profile on Vinci.[300])

Fencing contractors

A Kent fencing contractor called Jackson's fencing won the 2015 contract to install new security fencing around the Eurotunnel.[301] A French company called Clôtures Michel Willoquaux (Groupe CW) built the fences in the "Jules Ferry" container camp.

Thales

The massive French arms multinational Thales designed and installed much of the security tech at Calais port. Its installation includes:

> equipment to control access, such as revolving doors for pedestrians and badge readers for personnel authorised to enter the port zone. 50 IP (Internet Protocol) cameras monitor the 8,000-metre long fence, the single public entry point to the site and various crucial locations.

Thales also provides "spycoptor" drones to Eurotunnel. Beyond Calais, Thales is one of the biggest beneficiaries of government and EU funding for border security technology across Europe.[302]

Scanners, drones, x-ray technology

Besides Thales, many more companies build, install, and maintain high-tech surveillance equipment for Border Force and Eurotunnel. Here are just some of their names – see the Calais Research site for further details. FLIR systems (thermal cameras); Smiths Detection (X-ray and CT scanners for Eurotunnel); AMG Systems (Eurotunnel CCTV); Clearview Communications (Eurotunnel CCTV); Rapiscan (Calais port X-ray scanners); Scan-X security (maintenance of X-ray scanners); Chess dynamics (night vision for Border Force boats); Sorhea (infrared detectors in the port and highway fences).

Teargas and other police weapons

The following companies manufacture tear gas used by the CRS and Gendarmes: Nobel, SAE Alsetex, Etienne Lacroix. Enormous quantities of tear gas are used against migrants in Calais. Other weapons include tasers (manufactured by Taser France) and "flashball" grenades (SAPL, Verney Carron). One new weapon available to French riot forces, and which they announced would be deployed in the 2016 jungle eviction, is a blinding "laser cannon". Although it is not confirmed who supplied the laser cannon, a weapon of this kind is made by a French company called GEIM.[303]

Struggle and solidarity in Calais

In other chapters we have talked about migrants' fight against the border regime as "resistance". But there is a danger with this term: it could suggest that migrants are always *reacting* to attacks by the state, rather than taking the initiative themselves. In fact, particularly in border situations like Calais, it often makes more sense to think of migrants as *protagonists* – people who lead the way.

Every year, thousands of people come to the border following their own needs and goals, their own dreams of safety and a better life. The border regime tries to block them with its razorwire fences, tear gas, and other weapons. These attacks cause great suffering, but never manage to totally stop movement. Even now, with thousands of police around Calais and millions spent on security measures, people still get across the channel every day.

Crossing the border in these conditions involves great creativity and resourcefulness. For obvious reasons, we are not going to talk about this here in any detail. We should note that there certainly are "mafia" groups involved, and there certainly is exploitation and violence. But also many people cross without paying smugglers, and many smugglers are far from the vicious stereotypes.

And we should mention the times in 2015 and 2016 when hundreds of people joined together to cross the border in large coordinated groups.[304] This movement was beyond the control of any mafias, and was certainly not instigated in any way (as French authorities alleged) by European "No Borders anarchists".[305] Some European anarchists, and others, went to support these actions, most often in basic ways such as bringing water and first aid. But the crossings themselves were entirely self-organised by people without papers, and were powerful and inspiring examples of large-scale collective direct action.

Dwelling, living

For the weeks or months many people spend stuck in Calais, the struggle to cross is also the struggle just to stay alive and keep your strength up. To find somewhere warm and dry to sleep, to feed yourself, to avoid injury and police violence. Again, this involves great creativity, resilience, and co-operation.

The most obvious examples of this have been the large settlements created by migrants in Calais: the Pashtun Jungle of 2009, the big Jungle of 2015-16, and long-running squats such as the several Africa House occupations of 2010-12. But there have been many more smaller settlements and shared spaces, and there still are today.

The 2015-16 Jungle was the first and only time the state and its funded NGOs provided some basic facilities such as water, electric lighting, minimal rubbish collection and (horrific) toilets to a migrant settlement in Calais. But everything else was self-organised by migrants under extremely harsh conditions. It was certainly no paradise, and there were all the tensions and abuses you would expect in any human settlement under pressure. But there was also very effective solidarity and self-organisation at work.

Solidarity across borders

While undocumented migrants are the main protagonists of the struggles in Calais, people with papers have played important supporting roles. In 2015-16, the massive influx of volunteers, donations and funds from the UK and across Europe was an unprecedented display of welcome from many citizens, which helped offset the brutality of the governments and corporations. Unfortunately, this humanitarian surge was also short lived.

But away from the headlines, there have been many people consistently standing with migrants in Calais. There are plenty of racists and fascists in the town, but also many others who have hosted migrants in their homes, stood up against police brutality, donated food and clothing, and organised shared spaces and events. The Calais Migrant Solidarity network has played one part in this since 2009. Activities have included:

· helping provide basic infrastructure including first aid, translation, legal support, information resources;

- opening and defending squats with migrants, including the first women's only space in the town;

- documenting and challenging police violence (the "This Border Kills" dossier, regular media releases since then);

- opening social centres (Hangar Kronstadt, Centre Marie-Noel "Zetkin", Fort Galloo squat, "Le Locale") in the town to help bring together migrants and local Calaisiens;

- supporting and joining migrants' protests and direct action against the border.

How do we assess the impacts of these actions? First, there are those that have led to government reforms. For example, we have found that exposing state violence has prompted temporary reductions in brutality – but it always resumes once the outcry dies down. Similarly, the women's squat pushed the state to open its first provisions for "vulnerable people" in the Jules Ferry centre – but these were shut again within two years.

At least until recently, French politics and media have been less resolutely anti-migrant than in the UK, with more of an equal split between xenophobic and liberal voices. Yet no amount of political campaigning has made any long-term difference to the state's hard line in Calais. Reforms have created breathing spaces which are welcome, but always temporary. This will stay true as long as the underlying economic and political imperatives that drive the border remain.

Housing and other basic infrastructure helps sustain people and keep up strength to fight the borders. Nor should we ever underestimate the basic power of a friendly welcome. Self-organised solidarity structures have also always been temporary: every squat and jungle is evicted, whether it lasts days or years. What matters is not particular spaces or structures, but a culture of solidarity that keeps bouncing back and making new ones.

Ultimately, the most powerful solidarity "work" involves making new relationships of common struggle between people with and without papers. While Calais is usually seen as a place of crisis and despair, it also has another side. It is a meeting place, a place of encounters, where many strong relationships have formed between people from different backgrounds.

Marginalised Calais youths make friends with migrants in the parks, and find they have a common enemy in the arrogant police. In the "Zetkin" social centre, opened in a warehouse in a run-down neighbourhood, builders from Palestine and Sudan worked alongside unemployed Calaisiens to construct a space for all. The Fort Galloo squat became a regular meeting place visited by hundreds of people sharing meals, concerts, stories, and developing projects together.

Unsurprisingly, riot police closed the Zetkin centre after a few weeks. Galloo was harder to shut down. But its success helped prompt the state to develop the Jules Ferry centre and encourage a tolerated Jungle kilometres away – the aim being to keep migrants and locals well apart. The authorities know what we know: if migrants have to face repression alone, they are easily segregated and targeted. When people with and without papers join and fight together, we can turn the tables.

Africa House, Calais, 2011

144

10. The "hostile environment": making a nation of border cops

In 2012 Theresa May, then Home Secretary, announced a new approach to immigration. She would make Britain a "really hostile environment" for people who have "no right to be here".[306] This would work by cutting off their "access to services, facilities and employment".[307]

Of course, hostility to migrants is nothing new. And in the last chapters, we have seen how the UK government ramped up violence and control towards scapegoated asylum seekers and "illegals" since 1999. This has involved both the militarisation of Calais and other border crossings, and the expansion of immigration enforcement inside the country.

In the measures we have looked at so far, the enforcers are paid specialists: border guards and ICE raid squads, or contracted private security guards working for G4S, Mitie, or Eurotunnel. But also, the Labour governments had begun to take the first steps along another road: demanding collaboration in Immigration Enforcement from institutions and "partners" beyond the Home Office. For example, airlines were legally obliged to check travellers' documents, bosses were pressured to help catch "illegal workers", and colleges made to monitor foreign students.

The hostile environment strategy didn't begin these measures, but it ramped them up to a new a level. It kicked off in 2012 when then prime minister David Cameron set up an "Inter-Ministerial Group on Migrants' Access to Benefits and Public Services". This brought the Home Office together with up to ten other ministries, to develop ways government departments could work together to attack migrants. Proposals led to two new sets of laws: the 2014 and 2016 Immigration Acts. And alongside these, a host of new rules, protocols, "memoranda of understanding" between government departments, and more informal practices.

We can see three themes running across all these different measures:

- *Collaboration*. Hundreds of thousands of citizens are co-opted as civilian border cops, including landlords, bosses, bank clerks, doctors, college lecturers, and many others. People in a wide range of roles are required to check documents and control or refuse access to homes, jobs, bank accounts, healthcare, education.

- *Information*. Even more of us are co-opted as immigration informers. Teachers, nurses, civil servants of all kinds, through to taxi drivers and charity workers, collect personal data on migrants and pass it to the Home Office for use in targeting raids. Often, the informing is unwitting: many people collecting this information don't know where it goes or what it is used for.

- *Criminalisation*. Simultaneously, new laws introduce offences such as "illegal working" and "illegal renting", which turn many more migrants into criminals.

The open objective is to increase the misery of migrants in the UK. It becomes ever tougher for people without the right immigration papers to get a job, rent a flat, use a bank, drive a car, get medical treatment, send their kids to school, or otherwise live a normal life. As with older immigration enforcement approaches, this is supposed to deter people from coming to or staying in the UK. Although, there is no evidence that it does so. (We will look at that point in Chapter 13).

But these policies also have other, perhaps even more sinister, impacts. By involving so many more citizens in the work of immigration enforcement, they tear at bonds of trust and solidarity in our neighbourhoods, workplaces, streets. They sow suspicion. They help make informing, surveillance, and big data gathering by the state and its corporate partners into a normal part of everyday life.

Yet the Home Office has not had everything its own way. In recent months, there has been push-back against a number of the hostile environment policies. Some have been dropped after court challenges. Others have been watered down or put on hold. There is still all to play for.

The dirty dozen: 12 hostile environment policies

In this chapter we will outline 12 main attacks on migrants that form part of the hostile environment approach. Many of these policies have met increasing opposition in the last year. We will look at what the government has tried to do – and where it has been forced to retreat, or at least put plans on hold. Here are the dirty dozen:

- *Healthcare charges:* making "overseas visitors" pay for NHS care. Starting with "non-emergency" hospital treatment, the government hopes to extend charges to all forms of medical care including emergency and GP treatment.

- *Healthcare data sharing:* using hospitals and GP surgeries to collect patient details, which are passed on to Immigration Enforcement.

- *Schools:* collecting and passing on details of migrant families through the "Schools Census".

- *Higher Education:* intensive monitoring of foreign students by their "sponsor" institutions.

- *Housing:* the "right to rent" banning undocumented migrants from renting and criminalising landlords.

- *Homelessness:* the round-up of mainly East European migrant rough sleepers, coordinated by local councils and homelessness charities working together with ICE squads.

- *Work:* escalation of "illegal working" controls with new criminal offences.

- *Driving:* confiscating migrants' driving licenses, and collecting driver licensing data.

- *Bank accounts:* closing migrants' bank accounts, and using the banks to gather data, organised through private credit databases.

- *Marriages:* collaboration by registry offices.

- *Police Liason:* the "Operation Nexus" agreement, under which police hand over foreigners they "encounter" to ICE – not just arrested people but also victims and witnesses of crime.

- *Local Councils:* encouraging local authorities to launch immigration enforcement schemes, often targeting migrant housing, with money from the "Controlling Migration Fund".

So far, there have been notable reversals on four policies:

- *Homelessness:* in November 2017, the High Court ruled that the key policy used to target East European rough sleepers was unlawful. The government announced that it was ending these raids.

147

- *Healthcare data sharing:* in May 2018, the government announced it was dropping most of this scheme.

- *Schools:* in May 2018, the government announced it was dropping two controversial Schools Census questions asking about nationality and country of birth. However, the rest of the data sharing operation continues, including passing on migrant families' addresses to Immigration Enforcement.

- *Bank Accounts:* in May 2018, the government announced a "temporary suspension" on requiring banks to check existing customers' immigration status.

Other policies, such as the roll-out of health charges, have at least been delayed or slowed down. More legal challenges, including on the "right to rent" and Operation Nexus, are in progress.

1. Healthcare: hospital charges

From 23 October 2017, hospitals in England have been required to ID check all patients and make people who are not legal "residents" pay for their treatment.[308] The new NHS regulations do not initially apply to emergency treatment (A&E) or to GP surgeries (primary care) – but the government has said it wants to extend charging to both in future. Further down the line, it aims to also look into charging for hospice care for dying people, which is part-funded by the NHS alongside charities.[309]

NHS charges for migrants are not wholly new. They were first introduced in 1982, when the Thatcher government introduced a distinction between people classed as "ordinarily resident" in the UK, entitled to free health care, and "overseas visitors" who could be made to pay. But previously charging was at the hospital's discretion, and was not widely put into practice.

The hostile environment approach set out to change this. In 2014, alongside the new Immigration Act, the Department of Health set up what it calls an "Overseas Visitor and Migrant Cost Recovery Programme" to encourage hospitals to charge, with a target of making £500 million per year from NHS charges. At first, charging was still down to the hospitals' discretion. Then new 2017 NHS regulations made charging a "statutory requirement" forced on hospitals.

Health Surcharge

The 2014 Immigration Act also introduced a "health surcharge". Non-EEA citizens applying for a UK visa for six months or more (e.g. for work or study) must pay this fee before entry, and are then exempted from charges while the visa lasts. At the time of writing, the fee is £200 per year or £150 for students. But the government has said these figures will double by the end of 2018.[310]

Who has to pay?

The Immigration Act 2014 redefined who counts as "ordinarily resident". Citizens of the European Economic Area (EEA) – the EU countries plus Iceland, Lichtenstein, Norway and Switzerland – are still included so long as they are "exercising their treaty rights" (see Chapter 3). Other migrants must be "living lawfully in the United Kingdom voluntarily and for settled purposes". For example, people who have been granted "indefinite leave to remain" are okay; but people on temporary student or work visas are not "settled", and people without any valid papers are not "lawful".

There are a few exemptions: e.g. refugees with temporary leave to remain, or asylum seekers who have not been refused asylum or who are receiving "Section Four" support (see Chapter 5), do not have to pay.

As well as immigrants, these measures can also affect British citizens residing abroad. Within this group, anecdotal evidence suggests Black people or people with foreign-sounding names are more likely to be impacted.

What must be paid for?

For the moment, accident and emergency (A&E) care and GP services (primary care) are still free for everyone. So is treatment for many contagious diseases, including sexually transmitted diseases and plague; pregnancy care; and treatment to "victims of violence", including, e.g. torture survivors – so long as they have not "travelled to the UK for the purpose of seeking that treatment."

But the Department of Health has said that it wants to extend charging further, eventually covering almost all areas of care. The thinking was set out in a document published in February 2017, called "Making a Fair Contribution", which followed a consultation exercise carried out in 2015-16.[311] In the consultation, the government sounded out health professionals, migrant charities and "members of the public" on its proposals.

The consultation proposals included charges for all A&E care, to ambulance and paramedic care, and to primary care. The one area exempted was initial consultations with GPs or nurses. There are strong "public health" arguments against charging for these, as it may mean people don't report symptoms of contagious diseases.

The government claims that over 50% of those consulted agreed with all the proposals except for two: charges for A&E and for ambulances. On these, more than half disagreed or "strongly disagreed". So the conclusion was to introduce some changes immediately, then phase in the less popular ones more slowly, whilst working to try and get professional bodies such as the Royal College of GPs and the British Medical Association (BMA) on side.[312]

How the system works

For less urgent cases, patients are supposed to be ID checked and charged upfront before treatment. If treatment is urgent, patients may not have to pay in advance, but should be presented with a bill after.

Routine document checks on patients mean a massive shift in NHS procedure and culture. Just who is responsible for performing the checks and demanding the charges? How can staff be made to comply?

Designated bureaucrats called Overseas Visitor Managers (OVMs) play a key role in the scheme. The basic procedure is often that "front line" staff, particularly nurses and admin staff, should flag potentially chargeable patients to OVMs for assessment. However, hospitals only have small OVM teams, who do not have the capacity to check all patients themselves. They thus rely heavily on participation by front line staff.

Another part of the policy is to deter people from asking for treatment in the first place. Intimidating posters warning people they may be charged are now a common site in NHS hospitals. OVMs are also responsible for these propaganda efforts.

In the modern NHS, hospitals are run by semi-independent structures called NHS Trusts or NHS Foundation Trusts, the latter being the "better performing" ones that are rewarded with more autonomy and funding opportunities. They are subject to continual assessment and financial rewards or penalties. To ensure compliance with the hostile environment, trusts could also in future be scored on performing ID checks and collecting charges. Such incentives were proposed in a House of Commons Public Accounts Committee report in January 2017.[313] It is notable that one of the first hospitals to pilot ID checks back in 2013 was Peterborough and Stamford: it was in the midst of an acute financial crisis, owing to massive PFI debt, and receiving special government bail-outs.[314]

The government is well aware that ID checking and charging patients does not sit easy with many health professionals. It recognises that it needs to create what it calls a "cultural change" where doctors and nurses will become happy immigration enforcers. In Chapter 12 we will look further at how it tries to achieve this.

Rationale

The charging policy has a dual rationale: as well as attacking and deterring migrants, it is supposed to save money for the NHS. Actual evidence of cost savings, however, is extremely weak. The government has not provided clear estimates of the supposed burden of "health tourism". As the fact checking charity Fullfact writes, it has only published "incredibly rough figures". According to those rough figures, the high-end estimate of "deliberate health tourism" is a cost of £300 million per year, or 0.3% of the NHS budget.[315]

And it is not clear, either, how much it costs to carry out the ID checks and chase people for payment.

Implementation and resistance

NHS charging has been one of the most controversial of all hostile environment policies, particularly amongst health professionals themselves. The campaign group Docs not Cops[316], has organised amongst medics, held demonstrations at hospitals, and been visible in the media. The charity Doctors of the World, which has long provided free healthcare without ID checks to excluded people in its clinics, has been a loud voice against anti-migrant health policies.[317] The charity Medact has also been campaigning, including organising an open letter against the policies signed by 150 health professionals in June 2018.[318]

Opposition within the health sector has slowed the policy's implementation. Obligatory checks and charges were initially due to start in April 2017.[319] But the Department of Health delayed the scheme and instead launched further pilots across 18 hospitals in Autumn 2017, including 11 in London. 8,894 people were asked to show ID in London; only 50 were found to be eligible for charges.[320]

The system is now officially in place across England and Wales. But, as ID checks necessarily rely on cooperation from front line staff, it is not clear yet how thoroughly they are being carried out. Just possibly, if resistance keeps up, they could prove unworkable. And, for the moment, there is no further news on plans to extend charging to A&E and GP surgeries.

2. Healthcare: NHS Digital intelligence gathering

The hostile environment's NHS policy was a double attack. Alongside charges, the second part involves passing patient data from the NHS to Immigration Enforcement. The NHS collects data on millions of individuals who willingly hand over addresses and phone numbers, details of family members, and other personal information when they register with a GP. This information is gold dust for Immigration Enforcement, who can use it to locate and arrest "illegals".

The data is automatically fed by GP surgery computer systems to a national database called the Personal Demographics Service (PDS), run by an "arms length" business unit called NHS Digital (previously the Health and Social Care Information Centre). A Freedom of Information disclosure showed that, in the first 11 months of 2016, the Home Office made 8127 information requests from NHS Digital; 5854 of these led to people being traced.[321]

Then, on 1 January 2017, a new "Memorandum of Understanding" (MoU) came into force between the Home Office and NHS Digital. This was a formal agreement between the two organisations that standardised data transfer (we will look more at data sharing procedures in Chapter 11). It meant that patients' addresses and other personal information could be handed over without GPs' permission.

In May 2018, after opposition from MPs, the government announced it was suspending the Memorandum of Understanding – except for cases of "serious criminality" or "risk to the public". So, at least for now, most of this part of the policy appears to be on hold.

NHS Digital's data goldmine

The Personal Demographics Service (PDS) database is one of the most complete collections of personal information on people in England and Wales.[322] Anyone who has ever used NHS services in England and Wales and been given an NHS number is recorded, and records are updated and synchronised every time you access another NHS service.[323] It is widely accessible by NHS staff across the country.

The "demographics" collected include name, date of birth, gender[324], current and previous addresses, place of birth, "ethnicity category", details of GP practice and preferred pharmacy, and details of relatives and other close contacts, cross-referenced to their own database entries. It also carries alerts about individuals flagged as "violent". The NHS number is the key element of the system, acting as a unique identifier for individual patients.

The PDS does not contain medical records but is used as the basic identification tool that underpins the NHS Care Records System (CRS). The whole system of identification and care records together is often called the "Spine".

Sharing of NHS medical records has been controversial. In 2013, the *care.data* project to centralise patients' clinical records was hit by worries about private companies access to the information.[325] In response to these concerns, patients are given some (rather vague) "opt outs" on sharing of medical data. This is reflected by a field in the PDS which records if patients have said they "express dissent" to their Care Records being shared. But there is only an opt out from sharing medical records, not non-medical personal data.[326]

Implementation and resistance

In May 2018, the government announced that it was suspending the Memorandum of Understanding under which this data sharing was taking place. According to a Home Office statement, data will now only be requested "to locate foreign national offenders we intend to deport who have been given a prison sentence of 12 months or more and others who present a risk to the public."[327]

The immediate push to drop the policy came from MPs, following campaigning from health professionals including Doctors of the World. In January 2018, the chair of The House of Commons Health select committee called for an immediate end to the agreement.[328] Then in May, two MPs – one Conservative and one Labour – tabled an amendment to the Data Protection Bill suspending the memorandum. The government backed down and accepted the amendment.

This does appear, for now, to be a genuine climb-down. But to sound a couple of notes of caution: (i) data sharing went on for some years, unpublicised, before the formal memorandum of understanding was signed; and (ii) "others who present a risk to the public" leaves a lot open to interpretation.

3. Education: the Schools Census

Three times a year, each term, school teachers collect personal data from parents and children in a survey called the "Schools Census". The information collected includes: name, date of birth, address, family members, ethnicity, and first language. Schools and other bodies such as social services also feed in further data to pupils' records, for example test results, and records of absences and exclusions. All this is stored on a central database called the National Pupil Database (NPD).

As with NHS data, this is a treasure trove of information for Immigration Enforcement. For example, a family that has moved from an old address and dropped off the Home Office's radar can be traced through their children's schools.

In December 2015, the Department of Education (DfE) also signed an agreement ("Memorandum of Understanding") with the Home Office to pass over an anticipated 1500 pupil records every month for immigration enforcement purposes.[329] The memorandum's aim is written in plain language: to "create a hostile environment for those who seek to benefit from the abuse of immigration control."[330]

Every month, the Home Office sends a list of names they want to trace. These may be names of children or of their family members. The DfE searches its National Pupil Database and sends back information including the family's latest address, within a target of 10 days.

It is a legal requirement for schools to complete the census – but not for parents or children to answer the questions. The census is collected on one given day each term: e.g. in 2016-17 on the third Thursday in October, January and May.[331] The DfE unit responsible for replying to Home Office requests is called the National Pupil Database and Transparency Team.

The memorandum anticipated about 1500 requests each month. In practice, the numbers seem to have been lower. In response to a Freedom of Information request by Jen Persson, the DfE said it had received 599 trace requests from Immigration Enforcement in September through December 2016 - so more like 150 a month. In those four months the DfE only found matches in its database for 151 of these.[332]

The new census questions

In September 2016, two new questions were added to the Schools Census asking for pupils' nationality and country of birth. Education ministers at first denied that data from these questions were being shared with the Home Office.[333] But it was then exposed that a new clause had been added to the Memorandum of Understanding agreeing to share nationality data too.[334]

The guidelines on the new questions state that schools should record the answers as given by the pupil or guardian. Pupils or parents may refuse to answer, in which case schools should mark "refused", not put their own answers down.[335] The guidance explicitly states that schools are not allowed to ask for ID to check the answers.[336] Leaked cabinet papers published in December 2017 show that the Home Office had indeed wanted to introduce ID checking in schools but this was resisted by the Department for Education.[337] Despite these instructions, there are plentiful reports of schools demanding ID documents or passport numbers; and of racial profiling where "non-white British" children were specifically targeted.[338]

Implementation and resistance

In April 2018 the Government backed down on one part of this policy: it said that it was removing the questions on nationality and country of birth from the Schools Census. This came after campaigning by the Schools Against Borders for Children group, amongst others.[339]

Schools ABC and the human rights charity Liberty attempted a judicial review of the policy in December 2017. When this was denied by the High Court, they started an appeal process in March 2018.[340]

Alongside the legal challenge, campaigners attempted to mobilise both parents and teachers to boycott answering the nationality questions. There are signs that this had some impact: in December 2017, the government revealed that it had only managed to collect nationality data on three quarters of the 8.1 million registered pupils so far that year. In 2.1% of cases, children or parents were explicitly recorded as refusing. Another 23.5% were "not known" or "not yet obtained".[341]

However, the victory is only partial. The government still collects a wealth of other personal information in the Schools Census – including up to date home addresses, the key piece of "intelligence" sought by Immigration Enforcement. There is no indication that it has stopped passing this information to Immigration Enforcement. The Schools Census is still being used to gather intelligence for immigration raids.

4. Higher Education

Higher Education was one of the first areas where the Home Office outsourced border control to other agencies, making universities and colleges responsible for vetting non-UK students.

Student visas are currently known as Tier 4 visas, under the wider "points based" visa system which was first introduced in 2009 (see Chapter 3). To get a Tier 4 visa, a student must show that they have sufficient funds for their study and living expenses, and must be sponsored by an educational institution which holds a Sponsor Licence.[342] The government's rhetoric is that education is a route for illicit migration where "bogus students" either enrol at a sham college or drop out of their courses after arriving: their real interest is in entering the country to work – or even to prepare terrorist plots.[343]

Foreign students are now central to many universities' and other institutions' income, so they are anxious not to lose sponsorship status. To keep it, they must commit to collaboration with Immigration Enforcement. This includes agreeing to "support immigration control" and to:

... co-operate with the Home Office by allowing its staff immediate access to any of its sites on request (whether or not visits are pre-arranged) and complying with requests for information[344]

Students details, including addresses and other personal information, are entered on an online system called the Sponsorship Management System (SMS), and must be kept continually updated. The Home Office team in charge of this database, and of the Tier 4 visa system in general, is the UK Visas & Immigration (UKVI) Sponsor Management Unit (SMU), based at Vulcan House in Sheffield.

Sponsoring institutions are required to continually monitor foreign students, including their attendance. In general, they are expected to withdraw sponsorship and report to the Home Office if a student misses "10 consecutive expected contact points", e.g. lessons, lectures, tutorials, supervisions, exams, or coursework submissions.[345]

The Home Office does not specify just what internal monitoring procedures institutions must be put in place. A certain amount of vagueness seems to work well for the Home Office: the burden is on institutions to prove that their systems are satisfactory, and precisely because the requirements are not spelled out colleges are likely to go well beyond the basics. For example, according to a 2012 article by the then National Union of Students international student officer:

> At Coventry University 'all undergraduate students are required to Check-In on 3 days per week.' Checking in is done by 'present[ing] your Student ID Card to the member of staff at any monitoring station.' The University of the Arts London and the University of Glamorgan requires all its international students to 'check-in' once a week. The University of East London has introduced a 'three-strikes' system where if a student misses '3 compulsory elements of a module' or 'whose overall attendance falls below 75' will be de-registered from the module. Other universities have introduced similar physical checks albeit not of the same quantity. Greenwich and UWE require monthly check-ins.[346]

In August 2012, the Home Office made a show of suspending London Metropolitan University's "highly trusted" status. It regained the license in April 2013, but this served to scare institutions into tightening up their surveillance.

In many institutions, the front line role of monitoring attendance is mainly carried out by lecturers and teachers taking class registers. Attendance registers will often be taken for all students, not just foreign students, which helps avoid the appearance of discrimination. So surveillance of one target group in fact leads to increased monitoring of everyone.

Teachers may not even be aware that a main reason for taking registers is to comply with Home Office sponsorship requirements: instead, the university may say that the main aim is to help with "pastoral care".[347] Many institutions will have dedicated "international student" teams in charge of assessing this data and liaising with the Home Office.

However, there are also other cases where monitoring demands are more blatant. In July 2018, University College London (UCL) was exposed telling lecturers to perform "spot checks" on students' documents. And academics in UCL's Bartlett architecture school were warned they could be fined £20,000 from their research and conference expense accounts for "inadequate compliance" with monitoring international students.[348]

Implementation and resistance

Heavy monitoring of foreign students pre-dates the main wave of hostile environment policies introduced with the 2014 and 2016 Immigration Acts. It has certainly escalated in recent years though, particularly as the government has used crackdowns on students to help get down overall net migration figures.

The main university teachers' union (UCU), and the students union (NUS), have both produced statements against elements of this policy since it began. But neither have campaigned very actively on the issue. For all the wealth of academic writing and theorising about border controls, this sector has seen little actual resistance to its own place in the border regime. It seems that immigration controls are now fully "normalised" in higher education culture.

That said, resistance to the hostile environment in other areas such as health and schools might give academia an organising jolt. Some have started new groups such as Unis Resist Border Controls.[349] And international academics have started to realise that they can become targets too: for example, lecturers taking part in industrial action have been warned that "time off" striking could be against the terms of their work visas.[350]

5. Housing: no passport, no home

The Immigration Act 2014 banned people who are not British or European citizens, or who have not been granted "leave to remain", from renting a home. In the government's language, they do not have the "right to rent".

The law requires landlords to check prospective tenants' ID documents, or call a Home Office hotline to check people without the necessary papers. Renting to someone without the right immigration status can mean a civil penalty of up to £3000 (£1000 on the first occasion) for the landlord. The penalty will not apply, though, if the landlord can show evidence that they made the checks correctly and have kept copies of the documents.[351]

The Immigration Act 2016 made things heavier still. As well as civil penalties, landlords can also be charged with a criminal offence punishable by up to five years in prison. In this case, the prosecution will have to prove that they had "reason to believe" the tenant was illegal. The 2016 Act also allows landlords to evict existing tenants who do not have a "right to rent", without any court order, and the Home Office can order them to do so.

Landlords can delegate their responsibility to letting agents, and landlords or agents are allowed to charge prospective tenants fees for checking their papers. The law also applies to lodgers in someone's home, so long as money changes hands (the civil penalties for renting to lodgers are smaller, between £80 to £500). A few types of properties are exempt from the checks, including hostels, refuges, and student halls of residence.

Landlords need to check documents of all prospective tenants, not just those they suspect of being foreign (as that would break discrimination rules). A wide range of documents can be presented and small landlords are unlikely to be familiar with the procedures.

Impacts

As with other hostile environment policies, the government has provided no evidence of the "right to rent" actually deterring any "illegal migrants". But it clearly does have an impact on people's opportunities and quality of life. And this is felt not only by undocumented people, but by anyone who may be perceived as "foreign".

The Joint Council for the Welfare of Immigrants (JCWI) is monitoring the "right to rent" policy and its impact on migrants. In a report published in February 2017, one year into the scheme, it found:

- "51% of landlords surveyed said that the scheme would make them less likely to consider letting to foreign nationals."

- "42% of landlords stated that they were less likely to rent to someone without a British passport as a result of the scheme. This rose to 48% when explicitly asked to consider the impact of the criminal sanction."

- "An enquiry from a British Black Minority Ethnic (BME) tenant without a passport was ignored or turned down by 58% of landlords, in a mystery shopping exercise."[352]

On the other hand, some people are clearly gaining from the new regime. It is a boon for letting agents, who can profit by offering landlords their experience in document checking. Some local authorities are also looking to cash in by offering "right to rent" checking services. The laws also, of course, create a good black market business opportunity for those willing to take on the risk of housing "illegals" in return for inflated rents.

The civil and criminal structures of the "right to rent" closely mirror the Home Office's procedures for dealing with "illegal working" (see Chapter 6). In that field, it is common practice for Immigration Enforcement to approach bosses and employment agencies for information on "illegals", offering reduced or waived penalties for collaboration such as setting up "arrests by appointment". We may now see similar moves in housing, e.g. involving letting agents in setting up sting operations against prospective tenants on their books.

Implementation and resistance

The "right to rent" has been implemented without any major public setbacks so far. Of course, it is hard to say how far it is actually being respected "on the ground". In June 2018, the JCWI launched a legal challenge against the policy in the High Court.[353]

6. **Homelessness: the rough-sleeper round up**

If the renting ban pushes more undocumented people to sleep on the streets, the Home Office's Immigration Compliance and Enforcement (ICE) teams may be waiting for them. In recent years rough sleepers have become a target group for ICE patrols, which rely on close collaboration from local councils, police, and charity "outreach" teams.

In March 2017, Corporate Watch published a report called "The Round Up" on this topic, working together with campaigners from North East London Migrant Action (NELMA) and Housing Action Southwark and Lambeth (HASL).[354] The report exposed the systematic role played by three charities – St Mungo's, Thames Reach, and Change, Grow, Live (CGL) – in collaborating with London authorities and Immigration Enforcement. Similar developments have also been reported in Bristol, Brighton, and other cities with large numbers of rough sleepers.

In December 2017, after campaigning and a legal challenge led by NELMA, the Home Office was forced by the High Court to end at least a major part of this policy.[355] This was the first conclusive victory against a hostile environment attack. Here we will briefly review what the policy involved, and consider the implications of the court victory.

The round-ups in London

In London, "street outreach" with homeless rough sleepers is carried out by charities, who work under contract to local borough councils and the Greater London Authority (GLA). The biggest player is St Mungo's, which runs outreach teams for Westminster, the borough with by far the highest concentration of rough sleepers, and most other central councils. "Change, Grow, Live" (CGL) runs outreach in Camden and Lambeth. Thames Reach runs a mobile outreach programme for most of outer London, contracted by the GLA.

All of these charities have routinely worked together with Home Office Immigration Enforcement. The collaboration has involved three main routes:

• *Accompanying ICE officers on joint patrols.* Freedom of Information (FOI) responses showed that there were 141 such joint "visits" organised by the GLA and 12 other councils in 2016.[356] Other local authorities, including

Westminster, did not respond to FOI requests, and so the full figure will be considerably higher.

- *Passing location information on foreign rough sleepers through the "CHAIN" database.* This is a London-wide database, commissioned by the GLA and run by St Mungo's, into which outreach teams upload data every night about the homeless people they meet. The GLA then passed CHAIN information onto ICE.

- *Liaising with ICE to target individuals who refuse "voluntary reconnection".* The outreach teams have agreements in place to hand over information on individuals to ICE for "enforcement" if they have refuse to leave voluntarily.

In contrast with some other hostile environment policies, the Home Office's "partners" in this sector have themselves been strong advocates of the tougher regime. Westminster Council has said that it "intensely lobbied" for the move to immediate deportation of EU rough sleepers, pushing the policy through a two month pilot with St Mungo's which involved 127 deportations. Much of the new "partnership" approach was developed by a GLA-led body called the Mayor's Rough Sleepers Group (MRSG), in which managers from borough councils, St Mungo's and Thames Reach were active members.

For the Home Office, the scheme was an easy way to find and arrest vulnerable migrants. For the councils and charities, it was an easy way to meet their own targets of reducing rough sleeper numbers. People were grabbed of the streets of London, and the problem moved elsewhere.

Focus on European migrants

ICE rough sleeper raids have overwhelmingly targeted European nationals. In this they stand out from other ICE operations – e.g. workplace raids, which predominantly hit South Asian people (see Chapter 6). Starting around 2012, there has been a notable rise in the proportion of European Union citizens amongst those detained and deported (see Chapters 7 and 8). There are no precise figures, but we expect that many of these were picked up through the rough sleeper round-ups.

In London, almost half (47%) of all rough sleepers are non-British Europeans, compared to 41% British nationals, with smaller numbers from Africa (5.5%) and Asia (4.9%). Particularly large numbers are from Romania (19.5%), Poland (8.7%), and other East and Central European countries which joined the EU in the 2000s. Elsewhere in England, up to 85% of rough sleepers are British.

European Union and other "European Economic Area" (EEA) citizens normally have a right to remain in the UK for 90 days, and indefinitely after that so long as they "exercise their treaty rights": i.e., are working, looking for work, studying, or are independently wealthy. (See Chapter 3). In the early days of the rough sleeper raids, this meant that ICE and their partners would have to find specific grounds to show individuals were "not exercising their treaty rights" – e.g. that they were not working or actively seeking work over a period of time.

But then, in May 2016, the Home Office streamlined the process with a new policy. This defined sleeping rough as automatically an "abuse" of treaty rights, making people liable for detention the first time they are found sleeping on the street. This policy was written into new legislation (Home Office Rules) in February 2017. ICE officers were now authorised to immediately arrest European rough sleepers and issue a "decision to remove" notice.

Implementation and resistance: December 2017 court victory

Our report in March 2017 brought increased attention to the "round up" policy, which had been kept very quiet by the charities and councils involved. Through 2017, NELMA spearheaded an active campaign against the round-up, supporting migrants under attack, whilst gathering further evidence and publicising the charities' collaboration. Then in November, working with the Public Interest Law Unit at Lambeth Law Centre, NELMA helped three men bring a judicial review of their treatment and the policy in the High Court.

On 14 December, Judge Lang found in their favour.[357] Crucially, she ruled against the Home Office's main justification for the policy: the Home Office "abuse of treaty rights" guidance. With that guidance officially quashed, the Home Office announced that it was ending the round-up policy. The ruling has also opened the way to substantial compensation claims from thousands of people who were detained and/or deported.

This was an important victory for rough sleepers targeted by the round-up. And it was the first major reversal of a hostile environment policy.

Since December 2017, it does appear that raids targeting rough-sleepers have ended – or at least, substantially reduced. However, to sound a note of caution, it is not impossible that they will not resume again once the "heat" dies down. The key piece of the court ruling was against the "abuse of treaty rights" guidance, which the Home Office used to streamline and escalate its raids. However: (i) it was raiding European rough-sleepers before that guidance, and in principle could do so again; (ii) non-European migrant rough sleepers, although their numbers are smaller (and so they do not present as "profitable" a target for ICE squads) remain as vulnerable as ever.

Finally, large numbers of Poles and Romanians are still being deported. For example, in the second quarter of 2017, 424 Romanians and 319 Poles were "removed", according to Home Office statistics. In the same period in 2018, the numbers were 345 and 226. This is reduced, but not dramatically.[358]

7. Work

"Illegal working" has been targeted by the Home Office since long before the current hostile environment approach, and is still a main focus of Immigration Enforcement raids. We looked at workplace raids in detail in Chapter 6. Here we will just recap how recent policy has escalated the attack with new methods of both *criminalisation* and *collaboration*.

Criminalisation

Under the 2006 Immigration Act, it was a criminal offence to knowingly *employ* an "illegal worker". And whether or not the employer could be proved to have knowledge, they could be charged "civil penalties" without any trial. Both criminal and civil sanctions were increased by the 2014 and 2016 Immigration Acts, which also escalated the criminal sanctions. But the biggest change is that now workers, as well as employers, are criminalised. "Illegal working" now carries a maximum penalty of six months prison, plus an unlimited fine. And any earnings from "illegal work" can be seized.

Collaboration

This increased penalty system goes along with an increasing emphasis on employer collaboration by ICE teams. Penalties can be reduced or even waived on a first occasion, if employers agree to collaborate. In 2014, the Home Office ran a London pilot scheme called Operation Skybreaker, which has since been rolled out nationwide. This new approach involves routinely conducting "educational visits" to employers ahead of raids, in which ICE officers seek to persuade them to hand over workers' personal details, or possible arrange "arrests by appointment".

Another trend is the increasing role of multi-agency operations, where ICE teams work alongside other government agencies including Local Authority departments (e.g. alcohol or taxi licensing, environmental health, planning for building sites, street market regulation, neighbourhood "wardens"), HMRC, the Security Industry Authority (SIA) that registers security guards, transport police, etc. These liaisons can involve both intelligence sharing and full-on joint raids.

8. Driving Licences

Many of the hostile environment measures involve the Home Office accessing other organisations' data, particularly to track down current addresses of migrants they are targeting. Another invaluable information partner for Immigration Enforcement is the Driver and Vehicle Licensing Authority (DVLA), which collects detailed personal and location data on drivers and vehicle owners.

This is a long-standing collaboration: according to a report by the Independent Chief Inspector of Borders and Immigration (ICIBI), the Home Office has had an officer "embedded at DVLA" since 2005.[359] But again, it has been ramped up under the "hostile environment".

The 2014 Immigration Act gave the DVLA the power to refuse new driving licence applications to people who are not "normally and lawfully resident" in the UK. This wrote into law what had already been practice since at least 2010, and involves wording similar to the NHS charging rules discussed above. It also introduced a new power to revoke existing licences of people who are not "lawful residents". The 2016 Act added another new criminal offence: "driving unlawfully in the UK", even with a licence, is now punishable by up to five years in prison. This act also gave ICE new powers to search people and buildings for driving licences they are not entitled to.

Again, data sharing is at the heart of the Home Office/DVLA collaboration, formulated through a Memorandum of Understanding (MoU). The arrangement goes two ways. The DVLA asks officers to check the Home Office CID database for the immigration status of licence applicants. And Immigration Enforcement officers are given "read only" access to the DVLA's main database, called the Driver Validation Service (DVS).

Again, there is a double "hostile environment" aim. On the one hand, unwanted migrants are cut off from another right – the right to drive – but also from the use of a driving licence as an ID document that can help access other services. Secondly, the arrangement may help ICE identify and target "illegals" who make the mistake of applying for a licence. This is highlighted by the ICIBI report:

> In some instances, driving licence applications had revealed illegal migrants not previously known to the Home Office, or had provided an up to date address for an individual with whom the Home Office had lost contact. In some cases, the applicant had submitted a valid travel document with their application and this had been retained by ISD as the absence of a valid travel document is a barrier to removal. Some of these migrants received visits from local ICE teams, and some had since either been subject to an enforced removal or had made a voluntary return.[360]

9. Bank Accounts

Before 2014, banks and building societies were legally obliged to verify customers' identities and check for "money laundering or terrorist financing". But they were not required to look at immigration status. This changed with the 2014 and 2016 Immigration Acts.

Under the 2014 Act, banks were obliged to check people applying for new bank accounts; under the 2016 Act, this was then extended to regular checks on existing customers. These were due to start in January 2018.

In May 2018 the Home Office announced it was scrapping the requirement for regular checks. Checks on new accounts are still in force, though.

Stage 1: application checks

The 2014 Immigration Act requires banks to check people applying for a current account against a Home Office list of "disqualified persons" who are known immigration offenders (e.g. illegal entrants, visa overstayers, European citizens with deportation orders). The 2016 Act adds that existing accounts of "disqualified" people can be seized or closed.

The "disqualified persons" list is maintained by a private organisation called Cifas.[361] This is a membership organisation[362] mainly comprised of banks and corporates which runs the UK financial industry's main National Fraud Database. Banks and other creditors (e.g. car dealers, phone companies) already check Cifas databases for fraud alerts when opening customer accounts. Now they can check customers' immigration status at the same time.

Banks must refuse accounts if there is a three point or "best practice match" of name, address, and date of birth against the database; if there is only a "Same Individual At Address" (SIAA) match they have discretion. They can check using the stand-alone "Cifas Immigration Portal" (CIP), or access the database via commercial credit check services run by Callcredit, Equifax, Experian, and Synectics Solutions.[363]

This system was inspected by the Independent Chief Inspector of Borders and Immigration (ICIBI) in 2016. The inspection report tells us:

> The Home Office shares data with Cifas on a weekly basis in the form of updates (additions and deletions) to the list of 'disqualified persons', and the list is updated by Cifas on the same day. At the time of the inspection, the list contained the details of around 200,000 individuals, including permutations of names, dates of birth and addresses, and the weekly updates affected around 2,000 individuals.[364]

The weekly updates are "extracted automatically" from the main Home Office Case Information Database (CID). According to ICIBI "the dataset includes any known aliases used and previous addresses."[365]

But, according to the ICIBI inspection report, 10% of the sample they checked should not have been on the list at all. 5% still had outstanding appeals or applications; and 5% actually had leave to remain.[366]

As with other hostile environment agreements, as well as depriving migrants of a right or service, this system could help ICE track down targets' locations. Every month, CIFAS sends the Home Office a list of all matches, giving details of people on the disqualified list who have tried to open an account, including the addresses and other information they have submitted to banks. However, in its current form this information is less useful for ICE's tracking purposes than other sources. This is largely because any matches are against the same address the Home Office already has.

Stage 2: quarterly checks

The 2016 Immigration Act took the policy a step further. Under this law, banks could be required not only to check new applications, but also to check all existing customers – and re-check them again every three months. Again, checks were to be carried out against the same CIFAS database. The new checks were introduced in January 2018.

Implementation and resistance

The first stage was implemented without any upset. But the second stage, regular quarterly checks., was "temporarily suspended" in May 2018.[367]

The halt came as the Windrush scandal brought widespread attention to the hostile environment policies for the first time. But this halt was clearly announced as a temporary measure, and checks could certainly be restarted in future.

10. Marriages

Another staple of Immigration Enforcement for years has been targeting alleged "sham" marriages. In the past, the ICE approach involved hand-cuff-wielding thugs crashing weddings followed by UK Border Force TV cameras. In the hostile environment era, the Home Office has a less spectacular but more systematic strategy.

The 2014 Immigration Act extended the official notice period couples have to give for a marriage from 15 to 28 days. Registry offices are required to inform the Home Office of all planned marriages involving people of "non-exempt" immigration status that might be suspected "sham marriages". The Home Office then decides whether to investigate further.

If Immigration Enforcement decides to investigate, it can extend the notice period to 70 days. So long as a couple complies with the investigation, by submitting documents and attending interviews, they can marry after the 70 days. If the investigators then decide a marriage is a "sham", the wedding may still go ahead, and in fact couples may not even be informed that the marriage is viewed as a fake. But any later immigration application based on it will be refused.

According to the Independent Chief Inspector of Borders and Immigration (ICIBI):

> The inspection found that the different approach had not been fully understood by all registrars, and the fact that ICE teams no longer routinely attended register offices had created an impression with some registrars that the Home Office was less active in relation to sham marriage.[368]

The Home Office unit set up a specialist team called the "Marriage Referral Assessment Unit" (MRAU), based in Liverpool, to evaluate sham marriages. However, according to the ICIBI report, there have been issues with the unit's performance and the job of judging couples' sincerity may return to local ICE teams.

11. Police liaison: Operation Nexus

Another obvious key partner for Immigration Enforcement is the police. However, despite often working together on joint operations, police and Immigration Enforcement don't always have good relationships. In the eyes of real cops, ICE teams are jumped-up amateurs.

As part of the hostile environment approach, the Home Office has been trying to better integrate police and ICE checks. And there does seem to be a shift taking place towards much more systematic collaboration.

This is reflected in now frequent reports of police handing over not just "criminals" to Immigration Enforcement, but also victims and witnesses of crime. In May 2018, a BBC programme submitted Freedom of Information Act requests to 45 police forces, asking whether they "referred victims and witnesses of crime to the Home Office for immigration enforcement". Over half replied that they did. Only three forces said they did not, while "the rest were unclear, did not reply or said they had no data."[369]

These "illegals" apprehended by police included, for example, victims of rape, domestic violence, or forced trafficking who had gone to the police looking for safety.

Operation Nexus

The main new coordination tool is a collaboration agreement called "Operation Nexus". First started with the Metropolitan Police in 2012, this has since been rolled out to other forces across the country. It has various strands, and operational details differ across regions. Typically it involves:

- Police passing details of all "foreign nationals or suspected foreign nationals" they "encounter or arrest" to the Home Office for immigration checks. Note here the term "encounter" – which can include not only people arrested, but people reporting crimes.

- Police themselves questioning people about their immigration status – including questions designed to determine if European (EEA) nationals are "exercising their treaty rights".

- Serving arrested foreign nationals with notices stating they may be liable to deportation if convicted of an offence.

In London, at least, police are supposed to notify a central Home Office unit called the Command and Control Unit (CCU) when they "encounter" foreign nationals. Staff in this central unit then check their details against the Home Office's databases, primarily the main Case Information Database (CID). If there is a match with a known "immigration offender", the case is then referred to Immigration Enforcement. In addition, ICE immigration officers are embedded as "police liaison officers" in a number of area "hub" police stations for this purpose.

Implementation and resistance

Operation Nexus was first introduced in London in 2012, and the model has been extended to other forces since 2016. Some 3,000 people have been deported so far because of the scheme.[370]

In May 2017, lawyers representing the AIRE (Advice on Individual Rights in Europe) Centre brought a challenge in the High Court against one specific part of the scheme. They argued that it was unlawful for the police to routinely question European citizens to determine whether they are exercising their "treaty rights" – rather than in relation to any criminal investigation.[371] The Court found against them. At the time of writing, the AIRE Centre has an appeal in process.[372]

12. Local Councils: Controlling Migration Fund

Local councils are another group of important partners. These authorities often conduct joint operations with ICE teams and police, e.g. involving departments that manage alcohol or taxi licensing, environmental health, planning for building sites, street market regulation, neighbourhood "wardens", and more. They have also been key in the targeting of rough sleepers, through their charity contractors.

The Home Office is keen to build these relationships further. In November 2016, it announced a fund called the "Controlling Migration Fund" which local authorities in England can bid to for help with projects aimed at "mitigating the impacts of migration on local communities". The amount is in fact small change, £140 million over four years across the whole country. But £40 million of that is specifically earmarked for "enforcement" projects to develop collaborations between councils and ICE teams. The other £100 million for "integration" projects is led by the Department for Communities and Local Government.

The fund's original prospectus highlighted two particular enforcement targets: foreign national rough sleepers, and "rogue landlords" who are breaking the new "right to rent" legislation. But it also invited councils to come up with new ideas in "an entirely different area". The Home Office advertises that £15 million of grants were awarded to 27 councils in July 2017; £18 million more was awarded in November 2017, and £19 million in June 2018.[373]

Many of the grants listed involve enforcement. Above all, a large number are related to housing. These are almost always described as targeting "rogue landlords". The following councils have received money for schemes concentrating on or involving housing enforcement:

Barking and Dagenham, Barnsley, Bolton, Bournemouth, Bury, Bristol, Carlisle, Enfield, Fenland ("Operation Pheasant"), Hammersmith and

Fulham, Hastings ("Operation Discovery"), Hounslow, Hull, Lambeth, Lewisham, Lincoln, Luton, Manchester, Oldham, Oxford, North East Lincolnshire, North Lincolnshire, Nottingham, Redbridge, Rochdale ("Operation Maverick", also targeting "businesses" and "illegal immigration"), Sandwell, St Helens, Thanet, Telford and Wrekin, Wakefield, Westminster, and Worcester.

Others have got money to target migrant rough sleepers, and "anti social behaviour" schemes involving wardens. Numerous projects mention crime, including "counterfeiting", "organised crime" and "modern slavery". Other projects involve research, data gathering and "mapping" to "build a better picture" of migrant communities. Though often framed in terms of inclusion and migrants' needs, these schemes will be of great interest to Immigration Enforcement.

However, there may also be more enforcement collaborations that aren't publicised. The guidance for applicants states that: "Authorities do not need to formally bid for ICE resource. Instead they will need to discuss with the local ICE lead what support can be provided." This could suggest that not all enforcement agreements are "formally" published either.[374]

Many of the Local Authority bids plumb depths of cynicism and double-think. The schemes are framed as helping vulnerable migrants by tackling their "hidden problems" of crime, overcrowding, exploitation by "rogue landlords" and other villains. Of course, what they don't mention is that for every slum landlord arrested in a "joint operation", ICE squads will grab, detain, and perhaps deport many more of their "victims".

Implementation and resistance

We have not yet seen much significant resistance to Council / Home Office schemes. And yet there is great potential here for people to organise and break collaboration in their local areas.

11. **Hostile data**

The UK is already one of the world's most surveillance heavy states, with intensive use of CCTV cameras, routine internet and mobile phone spying, and wide ranging government databases. But in a few years we may look back on this as a time of relative privacy and freedom, the days before all our information and movements became tracked by one Big Datasphere jointly run by the government and corporations.

Immigration Enforcement is one of the main areas where this drive is advancing, and the "hostile environment" approach is built around it. Although, on the plus side, at least the Home Office's notorious IT incompetence is holding things back a bit.

Data-sharing

Many of the hostile environment measures surveyed in Chapter 10 involve boosting Immigration Enforcement's patchy information resources. We can see three stages:

(1) *Tracking existing targets.* Data sharing deals, sometimes in the form of written agreements called Memoranda of Understanding, allow Immigration Enforcement to access information held by other government departments and the private sector. This is used, first of all, to track down existing targets. For example, getting updated addresses of "immigration offenders" or "absconders" from NHS Digital or the Schools Census.

(2) *Identifying new targets.* Immigration Enforcement can also use expanded data to identify new targets – "illegals" who weren't previously on their radar. For example, the information collected by NHS Digital or (until recently) the Schools Census on patients' or pupils' nationality.

(3) *Integrating systems.* But these *ad hoc* sharing agreements are just the beginning. In the next few years, the Home Office and other government departments will work towards integrating separate databases into shared data platforms. When this happens, Memoranda of Understanding to handle trace requests will no

longer be needed – Immigration Enforcement will have our data automatically at their fingertips.

In this chapter we will give a very brief outline of the Home Office's existing data systems, then look at plans to update them – and some other moves on the horizon.

Information bureaucrats have big ambitions to gather, share, and streamline ever more data, not just on migrants but on all of us. But the steps towards a Big Brother state are moving rather slower than they'd like. This is not because of political or legal oversight, but due to deep incompetence and inefficiency. A number of multi-million pound Home Office database "modernisation" schemes have failed, and new systems are typically several years behind schedule.

Existing databases

The Case Information Database (CID)

This is the main immigration records database, used jointly by the three immigration directorates: Border Force, which tracks people entering the country; UK Visas and Immigration (UKVI), which tracks visa applications and grants; and Immigration Enforcement. Collating information from all three departments, the database basically contains "case files" on all migrants in the UK known to the Home Office.

The main data held in an individual's CID file include: name; date of birth; nationality; contact information; photograph; current visa or other immigration status; details of arrival in UK; details of any detention; details of any removal (deportation); reasons for any refusal of visa or asylum applications; and other notes. But on top of these basics, staff in different departments may add hundreds of other pieces of information.[375]

CID was first developed back in 1995, and there are continual complaints about it being out-dated, inaccurate and hard to use. Between 2010 and 2013 the Home Office spent some £347 million on trying to replace CID and improve its casework systems, but ended up staying with the old system. The 'improvements' were criticised by the National Audit Office for "delays and problems" and "delivering significantly less than planned."[376]

In 2014, the Home Office started yet another database relaunch, called **Immigration Platform Technologies (IPT)**. Once again, this has experienced "slippage", and a new contract to lead another overhaul of CID was signed in April 2018, with Accenture. According to a report in The Register, other suppliers involved are 6Point6, Atos, BJSS, Capgemini, Cognizant, Deloitte Digital, IBM and Mastek.[377]

Information and Asylum Biometrics System (IABS)

This is the main immigration biometrics database, also used by all three directorates. It contains fingerprints gathered by UKVI from asylum and visa applicants, which can then be checked by Border Force and Immigration Enforcement officers. It also contains facial images.

Police and immigration officers are able to access (but not, currently, edit) each others' biometrics systems. Police and Immigration systems are now becoming integrated as part of the overall Home Office Biometrics (HOB) platform – discussed below.

There are numerous other databases used by different Home Office units, many of which link to the CID. Here are just some examples.

UKVI databases

- **Central Reference System (CRS):** database of all visa applications, including grants and refusals.

- **Proviso:** a database of visa applications made overseas. The Home Office has awarded a new £91 million contract to Sopra Steria, starting in October 2018, to create a new system for people to re-apply for visas inside the country. This will include people using digital terminals in libraries to upload biometric information.[378]

Border Force databases

- **Semaphore:** the "advanced passenger information" system. This receives and compiles information from airlines, travel agencies, etc., about passengers booked to travel in and out of the country. As of June 2017, the Home Office said it had advance information on the large majority of air travellers; but only a minority of ferry and rail travellers.[379]

- **Warnings Index (WI).** This is the main UK system for flagging up travellers (citizens or migrants) who are "of interest" to the police and security services, as well as to immigration officers. It is managed by Fujitsu.[380]

- **Initial Status Analysis (ISA) database.** This is the main system for checking the immigration status of people arriving into and leaving the country, introduced in 2015. Currently, it is only used for non-EU citizens. It compiles data from other Home Office immigration databases to build up "identities", unique records on people known to the system. At March 2017 there were over 61 million "identities", and the number should be continually growing. It then adds in data on (non-EU) passengers from Semaphore, or when people cross the border (including directly from e-passport reader machines), and checks this against its identity records.[381]

- **General Aviation Risk Assessment Tool (GARAT):** system for flagging up flights "of interest"

- **Maritime Priority Assessment Tool (MPAT):** for flagging ships.

Like the overall casework system, Border Force IT is notorious for inefficiency and costly upgrades which slip years behind schedule or never happen. In 2007 the Home Office launched a project called e-Borders. But in 2010 it terminated the contract with the main supplier, Raytheon, paying them off £150 million plus £35 million in legal fees. By 2016 the scheme – now called Digital Services at the Border (DSAB), with new contractors – was reported to have cost £830 million and was still not complete.[382] As of December 2017, the new systems were expected to be ready some time in 2019.[383]

Immigration Enforcement databases

- **Information Management System (IMS):** intelligence database where tip-offs on "immigration offenders" are logged and analysed (see Chapter 6). This database is also shared by Border Force, although apparently BF prefer using their own internal intelligence system.

- **National Operating Database (NOD):** this is where all ICE operations, from tasking to outcomes, are supposed to be recorded.

- **CPCT** (Civil Penalties collection) databases.

- **National Removals Recording and Tracking Emulator (NARRATE):** the casework database of the National Removals Command (NRC) unit, which is in charge of arranging deportations and authorising detention.[384]

Police and other Home Office systems

As well as these, immigration enforcement staff have access to databases controlled by other Home Office units, for example: Her Majesty's Passport Office (HMPO) applications and passport databases; Her Majesty's Revenue and Customs (HMRC) **Centaur** database of customs seizures and offences; and the General Records Office (GRO) national index of births and other records.[385]

ICE also has considerable access to police databases including the **Police National Computer (PNC)**. This is the main police system which collects records on all individuals who have been arrested, charged or convicted, as well as on vehicles and more. It links to UK criminal records information, and to biometric databases such as the **National DNA Database (NDNADAD)** and the police fingerprint database **IDENT1**. It is also becoming integrated with the **Automatic Number Plate Recognition (ANPR)** system, which has the power to track car journeys across the UK through a massive network of cameras.

Other major police databases include the **Police National Database (PND)** – not to be confused with the Police National *Computer* – which collects "intelligence" (leads, tip-offs, officers' notes etc.) gathered by police forces across the country[386]; the **HOLMES 2** intelligence database for "serious crime" investigations; the National Domestic Extremist Unit (NDEU) databases. Immigration Enforcement probably do not have much access to police intelligence, unless forces choose to share specific information during a joint operation.

Collaboration is more advanced in biometrics. The plan is to integrate police and immigration biometrics databases into one system called the **Home Office Biometrics (HOB)** platform. Individuals will have just one record, linking their "identity" to fingerprint, facial, and DNA data collected by both police and immigration officials. In future this could also hold other types of biometric data: voice and gait (way of walking) patterns. A 2016 Home Office "major projects" document set an end date in 2019 – although delays are standard.[387]

This platform will also be used increasingly for Automatic Facial Recognition (AFR) technology to identify people through computer face scanning. This technology is currently in its infancy with extremely high error rates. According to Big Brother Watch, current police uses have a 95% error ("false positive") rate.[388] For example, in one notorious case, when South Wales police scanned the faces of people attending the 2017 Champions League Final software identified 2,470 "criminals" – but 2,297 (92%) were falsely identified.[389]

In June 2018, after four years of delays, the Home Office published its "biometrics strategy".[390] This was immediately criticised by the Biometrics Commissioner as not setting out a clear legal framework for sharing and using biometric data.[391]

Like the immigration directorates, the police are working on modernising their IT systems. The National Law Enforcement Data Programme (NELDP) is a plan to unite the Police National Computer (PNC), Police National Database (PND), and Automatic Number Plate Recognition (ANPR) systems "onto a single platform". This was announced in March 2016 as part of a new "Modern Crime Prevention Strategy".[392] Integration will also involve handing increasing power to a private sector company called the Police ICT Company, which is being put in charge of managing police IT contracts across the UK. [393] An advertisement for a "systems integration team" went up in January 2018, requesting for work to be finished by March 2020.[394]

International databases

Home Office staff make regular use of the **EURODAC** European fingerprint database. This Luxembourg based system, set up in 2003, collects biometric data on asylum claimants and some categories of "illegal migrants" from all EU countries plus Norway and Iceland. It is the main tool for checking whether asylum claimants will be processed in the UK, or sent back to other European countries under the Dublin agreement (see Chapter 3).

Border Force and other Home Office directorates have access to at least part of the **Schengen Information System (SIS II)**, a massive cross-European database of police and immigration alerts on individuals, which the UK joined in 2015. At the time of writing, the UK can access the database but not post alerts on it.[395] It is managed by a consortium of Sopra Steria and HP (Hewlett Packard).[396]

It is not yet clear what will happen to European data sharing arrangements after Brexit. Politicians on both UK and EU sides have made threats about cutting links. But this is probably one of the areas of cooperation most likely to be kept up.

In May 2018, the website EUobserver cited an "internal EU document" which accused the UK of "multiple violations" of its SIS use agreements. These included shoddy data handling which risked security breaches, and unlawfully copying data and sharing it with further corporate contractors including companies from the US (IBM) and Canada (CGI).[397]

Existing data-sharing arrangements

Government departments

In Chapter 10 we looked at a number of recent Memoranda of Understanding" (MoU) between the Home Office and other departments which have given Immigration Enforcement access to their databases. These were:

- **Personal Demographic Service (PDS).** Department of Health / NHS England.

- **National Pupil Database (NPD).** Department of Education.

- **Driver Validation Service (DVS).** Driver and Vehicle Licensing Authority (DVLA).

- **CHAIN rough sleeper database.** Greater London Assembly (GLA).

In all of these cases except for the DVLA agreement, immigration officers can't directly access the databases themselves. In the health and education memoranda, ICE submit "trace requests" on specific individuals. That means: sending over a form with details from the CID entry on the individual; the partner department then searches their database for a "match", and sends back specified further data. In particular, they are looking for current addresses. The CHAIN arrangement is different: here ICE were not looking for particular named individuals, but getting locations on where homeless foreign nationals are sleeping, in order to carry out round-ups. (NB: the GLA denies that CHAIN data is currently being shared.)

The private sector

In the attack on migrants' bank accounts, the Home Office has partnered with a private sector organisation, Cifas. This is an association whose members include the high street banks, credit card companies, and other creditors, and traditionally has focused on pooling information against fraudsters. The **Cifas Immigration Portal (CIP)** is a privately run database that the Home Office supplies with data on immigration targets from its CID files. I.e., this is a mass transfer of personal information on around 200,000 individuals from a state database to a privately owned commercial system.

Banks can also access the Cifas immigration database through the main commercial credit check systems: **Experian**, **Callcredit**, **Equifax**, and **Synectics Solutions**. So immigration data is integrated with the well-established financial credit data industry.

In general, the private sector credit databases are a useful source for tracking people's locations. Immigration Enforcement subscribes and makes regular use of them.

Experian

One particular company plays an important role in the growing corporate-state data matrix.

In 2015, the Home Office held meetings around the country with local authorities, charities and other "partners" as part of pushing hostile environment schemes. John Grayson attended one of these meetings in Yorkshire. As he pointed out, the presentation from officials was directly copied from the government's counter-terrorism strategy, called Contest – best known for its "4 Ps" of "Pursue, Prevent, Protect, Prepare". It had just been rebranded as "fighting immigration crime" rather than "fighting terrorism".[398]

At the bottom of the main presentation slide are the logos of the eight institutions leading the fight against "immigration crime". Seven are government departments and agencies, from Border Force to the National Crime Agency. The eighth is a private corporation – Experian.

It's not clear, but Experian's inclusion as one of the key strategic partners suggests it may not be simply a contractor, but involved in making decisions and plans at a high level. What we do know is that Experian's data tools support the hostile environment in a range of ways.

Experian's business is gathering information on people, then using its data to run checks on them. Its basic products include: identity checks to "verify" who individuals are; credit checks to assess their finances and so predict their likelihood of paying back debts; and "geodemographic" research which categorises people based not just on personal histories but on factors such as social class, ethnicity and neighbourhood.

Government agencies use Experian's databases to back up or replace their own faulty systems. The Home Office's Security Industry Authority (SIA), which also works closely with Immigration Enforcement, now outsources its identity checks to Experian.[399] At least one police force has hired Experian to organise and "clean" its own databases, merging private and public sector ID data.[400] These are just the publicised examples.

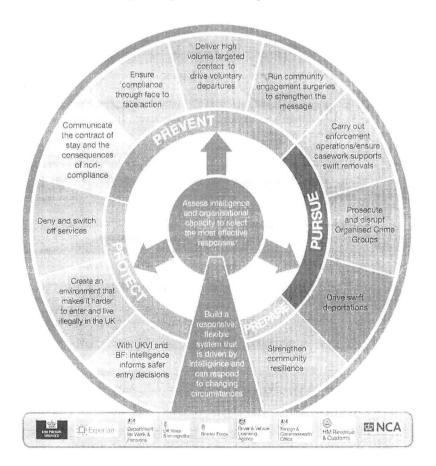

The hostile environment also creates new products for Experian to sell to the private sector. As discussed above, banks are obliged to run immigration checks against the Cifas database. Experian also now sells a "right to work" checking app to businesses.[401] As the middleman between state and private data needs, Experian makes money from both sides.

Another big business line is the Mosaic profiling database. This uses Experian's data to identify households in terms of 67 "geodemographic" categories based on income, location, ethnicity, and "social capital". Initially built for corporate marketing, Mosaic is now used by all major political parties to target voters in election campaigns (see Chapter 16). It is also increasingly used by government agencies, local authorities, and the police. For example, in March 2018 Big Brother Watch revealed how Durham Police use Mosaic data to help assess the risk of re-offending in custody decisions. So decisions about whether to imprison people or grant bail are, in part, being made on how Experian's classifies "consumers" and their postcodes.[402]

The Future: towards the Big Data Platform

The data bureaucrats' ultimate fantasy is One Big Data Platform where all information collected on people by government agencies and private companies is linked together in a unified system.

Step by step, we are moving closer to this vision. But there are still some obstacles along the way. Currently, these are due less to resistance from outside the system than problems within it: institutional, legal, and technical barriers. Here we will just flag some issues.

Institutional barriers

On the institutional level, integration involves retraining staff in new systems, but also overcoming cultural barriers between different teams and departments. For example, even within the Home Office, there is little trust between Immigration Enforcement and the police. Elsewhere we see still greater barriers between the Home Office and other departments, such as education or health. In the next chapter we will look at some ways the Home Office has been trying to overcome this cultural resistance.

Legal barriers

Legal challenges have helped to stop – or at least delay – some hostile environment measures. However, two new pieces of legislation have helped strengthen the Home Office's hand on data sharing: the Digital Economy Act 2017 and the Data Protection Act 2018.

Until 2017, information law was based on the principle that when government departments collect data from people it should be used for a specific purpose. For example, if you give information to the NHS for health treatment, this couldn't be automatically used by another department for a different reason.

Data sharing had to be justified under a specific stated exception. For example, the Home Office / Department of Health Memorandum of Understanding argues in writing that the Health and Social Care Act 2012 allows "disclosure of information" "in connection with the investigation of a criminal offence", and that sharing this information is in "the public interest".[403] Every trace request had to be individually signed by an Immigration Officer confirming that this applies.

In bureaucrat language, the memorandum established an "information sharing gateway" between the two departments, which applies only for a specific purpose. A unified government Big Data system would require a much more open system of general "gateways".

The Digital Economy Act 2017 takes a big step in that direction. Section 35 of the law simply states that organisations sharing data must be "specified persons" pursuing legitimate "specified objectives".[404] The list of "specified persons" includes all major government departments, and also private companies "providing services" to "a public authority".[405]

Before the Digital Economy Act, it was possible to make a legal challenge to a data sharing memorandum such as the NHS agreement, for example by arguing that it is not in the "public interest". The new legal regime has not yet been tested in the courts. But it may make it much easier for the government to routinely swap data between departments and corporations, without needing any argument about the public interest.

On top of this, in May 2018 the Data Protection Act introduced a new "immigration exemption" to data rights. Anyone is entitled to ask government bodies or commercial organisations for data held on them through a "Subject Access Request". Except, that is, for migrants. The Home Office can refuse requests for personal data processed for "the maintenance of effective immigration control".[406]

Technological barriers

Integration has to overcome the historical legacy of hundreds of separate data platforms, using different software architectures, provided by different big suppliers. Government departments have limited budgets, and can't just start everything again from scratch.

However, in 2016 the Home Office launched a project called Technology Platform for Tomorrow (TPT) to simplify its systems. In the past, it had relied on contractors – the biggest ones being Fujitsu and Atos – to build big proprietary IT systems, including databases. These then often ended up being out of date, and incompatible with each other. The new model aimed at one integrated platform, managed by the Home Office, but with multiple development teams brought in on flexible contracts. These are advertised on the government's new Digital Marketplace site.[407]

Tech news website The Register wrote on this project in June 2016, explaining that the TPT project would "lay the foundations for this mega database" using an open source Big Data platform called Hadoop:

> After laying off over a third of its old IT staff, the Home Office has recently been attempting to recruit Hadoop specialists to help it build and maintain this new "single platform", with a presentation and talk seemingly doing the rounds around the user circuit until the Home Office got spooked by The Register. According to one of these presentations, which your correspondent attended, the department will be using HDFS, the Hadoop File System, "for storing all the data" that its various directorates are imbibing, which "could be image, it could be video, it could be anything.[408]

Hadoop was already being used by the US National Security Agency (NSA) and GCHQ, with the National Crime Agency (NCA) and HMRC also looking to adopt it.[409] Tech commentators including Computer Weekly have highlighted issues on the use of the Hadoop "ecosystem" in government projects, and its implications for privacy and data security.[410]

The Home Office hired a company called Hortonworks to help with its transition to the new software.[411] In September 2015 Wayne Horkan, a Home Office "Senior Enterprise Architect", spoke at the opening of Hortonworks' new London office. He discussed his work on "border control and border checking" data, where "that's the piece that's exciting, to repurpose the data, to bring it all together, to reuse it very quickly to make decisions". He explained:

> What I've seen from Hortonworks and enjoyed is the alignment to open source, you are very closely aligned to the open source community. There is a lot of feedback. That's really good for us because it protects us from vendor change and lock-in, which we are not too keen on at the moment.[412]

Here we see the state trying to harness more decentralised methods and cultures for its own purposes of control. There is the move towards open source technologies, rather than closed proprietary systems developed in secret by single suppliers. And adverts on the digital marketplace website describe software development as based on the "Agile" methodology[413], where "requirements and solutions evolve through the collaborative effort of self-organizing cross-functional teams."[414]

It's not so easy to change a regime, though. By October 2016 the Home Office announced it wasn't ready yet to leave its "Single Supplier" IT contracts, and renewed its main deal with Fujitsu for another two years.[415]

Potential for resistance

So far, the biggest factors holding back Home Office Big Data schemes have been its internal failings. But there is also obvious potential for intervention by data workers and the tech communities.

In the US, there have been recent protests by employees of Amazon, Microsoft and other big companies saying that they will refuse to work on technologies sold to US ICE. These do not appear to have yet had significant impact – although larger scale employee action at Google may have made the company back away from renewing a drone contract with the Pentagon.[416] The Tech Workers Coalition is one group trying to grow resistance in this area.[417] And if the Home Office does continue down the route of "open source" technologies largely built by freelancers, could this also increase scope for boycotts, strikes, and other forms of action?

12. The logic of hostility: how collaboration works

The hostile environment approach extends immigration control beyond frontier checks and uniformed raid squads to a range of areas of everyday life. The approach relies on involving hundreds of thousands of people who are not Home Office employees. In this chapter we will look a bit deeper at how this collaboration works. We will think about different roles that people are asked to play in the hostile environment, and about how the Home Office uses different kinds of incentives to encourage them.

As a case study, we will look at one interesting document. This is a report commissioned by the Department of Health from a private consultancy, Ipsos MORI Social Research Institute, about first attempts to get hospitals to ID check and charge "overseas visitors".[418] If you can wallow through the post-Blairite newspeak, this report gives a fascinating glimpse of how the government goes about destroying a culture of care, to create instead a culture of collaboration. In its own words, the aim is:

> ... to support a culture in which all NHS staff are aware of their responsibilities to identify and recover costs from overseas visitors and migrants. It aims for an attitudinal shift to a point where all NHS staff feel a responsibility for recovering money from chargeable visitors and migrants and, where medically possible, do not treat patients until the eligibility for free NHS care has been established. (page 40).

Two forms of collaboration: controlling, informing

By "collaboration" we mean people who are not Home Office employees or contractors acting to support the hostile environment. In the 12 policies profiled in Chapter 10, there are two main kinds of collaborative actions:

(i) *Controlling.* Directly blocking migrants' possibilities of life. Refusing medical care, refusing to employ someone or rent to them, refusing someone a driving licence or bank account.

(ii) *Informing.* Passing on information which can help ICE squads or others carry out enforcement. This could involve reporting a neighbour, employee, prospective tenant as a suspected "illegal". Or it could mean just inputting data that is later shared with the Home Office.

In the first case, collaborating people themselves become part-time "immigration enforcers". In the most obvious sense, enforcement means ICE teams or Mitie guards using or threatening force: arresting, detaining and deporting people. But denying someone medical treatment, or denying someone a home, may also have very damaging consequences.

In the second case, actual enforcement is carried out by other people – but it couldn't happen without the information supplied. There may be various links in the data chain. For example:

1. Pupils give personal information to a teacher filling out a Schools Census form.

2. The teacher gives the form to school admin staff.

3. The admin staff send it to the Department for Education's central data unit (called the National Pupil Database and Transparency Team).

4. Department for Education staff pass it to the Home Office.

Those at the start of the chain may have no idea where the information they pass on will end up.

Collaboration roles

Collaboration of both kinds involves workers in various roles. Here are a few:

- *Front line roles.* Including care roles such as teachers and classroom assistants, nurses, doctors, paramedics, homelessness outreach workers. Or receptionists in hospitals or GP surgeries, or registrars, or bank clerks. Or employers, landlords, or their agents.

- *Admin roles.* People who collect information from front line workers, organise and circulate it. Data workers in schools, universities, hospitals, the DVLA, credit check agencies, NHS Digital, etc.

- *Managerial roles.* People who make the strategies, targets and directives, who arrange collaboration agreements and sign memoranda, who give the orders. From senior bureaucrats or Council leaders down to "middle managers" such as hospital Overseas Visitor Managers (OVMs).

- *Technical roles.* Programmers who build the databases, IT geeks who maintain them. Management consultants who advise on how to achieve "attitudinal shift". And others who lend their expertise to making control and information systems function.

All these roles can be found in public sector institutions like NHS hospitals or state schools. Or in in NGOs and "third sector" organisations, such as homelessness charities or universities. Or in profit-making companies, such as banks or letting agents. In the modern market state, where NHS clinics are contracted to Virgin Care and schools become privately sponsored Academies", these divisions are often fluid or intersecting.

Finally, we can also consider the roles we all play as "members of the public".

Firstly, any citizen, or indeed other migrants, can also collaborate by passing on information on migrants. We saw in Chapter 6 how one of the main sources of Immigration Enforcement intelligence remains tip-offs from colleagues and neighbours. This too can sometimes happen unknowingly. For example, citizens may inform a charity about people sleeping rough, believing this will help them, and never imagine that this information will be passed to Immigration Enforcement.

Secondly, there is a broad sense in which we can collaborate by giving information just about ourselves. The Schools Census or NHS registration data require widespread participation by citizens in this data gathering. If many people stopped answering Schools Census questions, or giving their addresses to GPs, these systems could not be used to track down "illegals".

Collaboration incentives

One motive leading people to collaborate with the hostile environment may be hatred and fear of migrants. Racist xenophobia is a constant and virulent presence in our lives, bombarding us in every politician's speech and TV news broadcast, from newspapers, billboards, social media, talk in the street or the playground (see Part 2 of this book). The norms of stranger-hating shape our environment, and make it much easier to ignore the consequences of our actions and inaction. But for most people this is not enough, on its own, to overpower empathy and guarantee collaboration.

To make the hostile environment happen, government tries to set up a range of incentives that foster collaboration and deter solidarity. We can group these into a few categories:

Punishments: criminal sanctions. The 2014 and 2016 Immigration Acts escalate the criminalisation of migrants with new offences including "illegal working". They also criminalise landlords and employers who don't collaborate in refusing homes or jobs to migrants.

Punishments: financial penalties. Civil penalties are still the mainstay of enforced immigration collaboration. In workplace enforcement, the civil penalties system is used to encourage bosses and employment agencies to inform on or set up workers. This now serves as a model being rolled out to the "right to rent", and perhaps more areas in future. In other sectors, the Home Office doesn't directly fine non-collaborators, but, e.g. removing a licence to teach foreign students will have a massive financial impact on a college. For many contractors or workers, refusing to collaborate could mean losing crucial income, promotion prospects, or your job.

Rewards: money, contracts, and other opportunities. On the other hand, agreeing to collaborate can open up lucrative opportunities for individuals or organisations. Canny bureaucrats in government departments will be quick to latch on to the new big thing. Management consultants, letting agents or councils offering right to rent checks, and many others stand to gain from the hostile environment. For some, like the software engineers working on innovative new Big Data systems, it can even offer opportunities for creativity.

Inertia. For many other workers, it will be more a matter of keeping heads down and "just doing my job". The habit of obedience, and the fear of asking questions or standing out, are some of the most powerful motivations.

Doing good. There are also those who genuinely believe, or at least tell themselves insistently, they are doing the right thing. See the justifications given by charity bosses at St Mungo's and Thames Reach who claim that "reconnecting" non-British rough sleepers with the streets of their home countries is in their own best interests.[419] Or council officials who organise raids against "rogue landlords" – which detain the tenants they claim to be helping.

Case Study: creating a culture of collaboration in the NHS

The Ipsos MORI study on hospital charging shows a government department using all these kinds of motivations in its quest to create a "cultural change within the NHS".

Financial incentives are the base level. In the "Non-EEA incentive scheme", hospitals are allowed to bill non-Europeans 1.5 times the normal "national tariff" set for NHS charges. When a charge is collected, half goes to the local commissioning body that allocates NHS funds. But the other half – so three quarters of the full amount – is now kept directly by the hospital trust. (As opposed to the commissioners who could allocate it to other services outside the hospital.) This is a financial bonus for cash-strapped NHS hospitals.

Then along with the carrot come the sticks. The pilot scheme studied in the Ipsos MORI report used financial penalties: the commissioners "do not have to pay for services provided to chargeable patients if the Trust has failed to take reasonable steps to identify and recover charges from that patient". But now charging has also become a "statutory requirement", meaning the government can use heavier penalties against hospitals and their managers who disobey.

These rewards and penalties will be felt most directly by senior managers. Their career prospects are directly linked to the hospital's financial success and to the approval of their NHS higher-ups. The more incentives bite them, the more they will be encouraged to pass them on to the front line staff who will have to actually ID check patients. To help them, a whole new middle-management profession of Overseas Visitor Managers (OVMs) has been created to oversee charging, and to "educate" hospital staff on the need for it.

So far, hospitals can still operate very different charging systems. Often OVMs do most of the work: "frontline clinical and administrative staff are only engaged to the point of flagging cases to the OVM that need investigation whilst OVMs themselves have retained responsibility for interpreting complex rules, and making decisions on how to proceed." (Page 44). But if ID checks and charging are to become routine, this will require much greater participation from frontline staff.

Furthermore, according to the Ipsos MORI report, financial incentives are not enough to get staff on board with ID checking: they also need to believe that it is right. In the report's wording, the programme's success is linked to "driving cultural change across staff groups". The aim is that staff come to believe they have a "duty to charge", and "understand and support the principles of fairness and entitlement underpinning the Cost Recovery Programme", seeing it as "legitimate and worthwhile at all levels" (Page 35).

The report claims that most hospital staff surveyed did already support the "broad/overarching principles of the Cost Recovery Programme".

> In particular, there was a very strong level of agreement, across all staff groups, that charging overseas visitors and migrants for NHS services is fair. At least two thirds in each group agree, and indeed, almost nine in ten Trust chairs and board members (88%) and OVMs (86%) agree, as do 84% of administrative staff. In addition, at least half, and often much more, of each staff group disagreed that overseas visitors and migrants should have the same access to free healthcare as UK residents. (Page 35).

But broad support in a survey is different from active participation. And the report is concerned that a "significant minority" disagreed. 28% of hospital doctors and 26% of hospital nurses thought that "overseas visitors and migrants should have the same access to free healthcare as UK residents."

Some complained about migrants' "human rights". Some even "refused to be involved in identifying and flagging potentially chargeable patients because they saw their role as being only to treat the patients", not to follow the "'funding-led' attitude driving cost recovery". The report mentions one OVM complaining about senior managers taking down their posters. Few staff actively opposed the policy, but more were half-hearted: "this tended to take the form of ambivalence or a 'reluctance to get involved'". Even those who did participate were unlikely to see ID checking patients as a priority in their busy schedules.

Even more worrying for the programme, the report found that rather than getting stronger, "buy in" for the "duty to charge" actually seemed to be dropping over its two years.

> In particular, the proportion of hospital doctors who agree that charging overseas visitors and migrants for NHS services is fair has fallen from 85% in the baseline survey to 68% at the follow-up survey, while a similar picture is also evident amongst primary care clinicians, CCG Leads and Boards, and Trust Chairs and Boards. [...] The overall decline in support for the principles

underpinning the Cost Recovery Programme among some groups raises the possibility that some Trusts will face ongoing difficulty in making the changes required to improve the recovery of costs. (Pages 36-7).

To counter this, the report suggests that "buy in" of frontline staff was best when OVMs made the most efforts "to engage with them and explain the reasons behind cost recovery and the benefits it could bring to their Trust." Across all staff groups:

> there was a perception that increased communication around the impact of cost recovery would help to encourage staff buy-in at all levels. This particularly related to sharing information on the amount of money recovered and what this might equate to in terms of benefits to the Trust (e.g. being able to purchase a new piece of equipment or employ more nurses).

So the strategy is to counter values based around care with a corporate ethos based around money-saving. But then money-saving must stop being seen as some abstract concern of accountants, and instead appear as a real and concrete imperative, a vital mission for the hospital "team", which all staff need to feel part of.

Sealed compartments

The more you are insulated from the consequences of your actions for other people, the easier it is to carry out hostile environment measures. Front line clinical staff are one of the hardest cases for collaboration: they actually have to see, even touch, the human beings who are targets, directly encountering their pain.

It is heartening that "buy-in" amongst both frontline staff and managers actually seemed to be dropping over the life of the pilot programme. Why would that be? The report doesn't have a clear answer, but makes this suggestion:

> One point to consider in understanding this decrease, supported by anecdotal evidence from the case study visits and interviews with OVMs, is that over time staff have become increasingly aware of the challenges of cost recovery and the difficulties faced by some patients who are not eligible for free NHS care. In particular, OVMs and senior staff stressed the vulnerability of some patients and the sense of empathy they felt for them; although

this did not fundamentally change their views on charging, it did cause them to hold somewhat conflicted feelings and provided a possible explanation for a lack of support among some front line staff. (Pages 35-5).

Empathy: it is one thing to read a poster about cost savings, another to look into a sick and distressed person's eyes. Many doctors and nurses may agree with the "fairness" of charges in the abstract, but this belief is challenged as they see what it actually means in practice.

Hostility flows more easily when flows of information and action are dislocated into isolated compartments. This is the case for many admin workers who process the key data. Inputting a home address could one day mean a death or a broken family, but you see only words and numbers. The GPs who hand over patient data to NHS Digital are also front line doctors – but, crucially, they don't know what use this information is put to. The same goes for teachers filling out Schools Census forms, or outreach workers inputting rough sleeper locations into the CHAIN database.

In the purest form of insulation, these unknowing collaborators may not even realise that Immigration Enforcement can access this data. In other cases, you may know that some of the data you enter is passed to the Home Office, but you won't ever know which files, or what then becomes of them. It's easy enough, then, to put it out of mind. And of course many of these databases have other benign purposes: having that address or next of kin on file could be important in a medical emergency.

Empathy and ethos

Empathy may be broken by distance. But there is also something else that a hostile environment has to fight against: *ethos*. While on the one hand doctors and nurses have to learn a certain clinical detachment, they are also taught a certain ethos of care, an ideal of dignity and compassion. This also comes through in some comments in the Ipsos MORI report: clinicians are not bureaucrats, docs are not cops, they have their own role, to treat patients.

If the hostile environment is to be successful, it will have to fight both empathy and ethos. It will have to create systems that keep us in compartments, links in machine-link chains, where we are not able to see the other's eyes or feel their pain. And it will have to shatter our surviving values and cultures of care and commitment.

13. Does immigration control work? The deterrent dogma

In the previous chapters we have profiled the main structures of the UK's Immigration Control system. We have looked at how it sorts people into categories, and enforces these through measures including border checks, reporting, raids, detention, deportations, and the newer "hostile environment" measures.

To conclude this part of the book, we want to ask the question: what does all this achieve? What is immigration control for?

Immigration control does not control immigration

The official objective, mouthed by politicians and officials, is clear enough. The aim is precisely to "get control" of immigration, to regulate the numbers and type of people entering and leaving the country. Some Home Office bosses may genuinely believe in this. But if this is their aim, it is clearly failing.

In 2010, for the first time the government set itself a clear overall target: to reduce net migration below 100,000 people a year.[420] This was first introduced as a pledge by David Cameron in the 2010 Conservative Party manifesto, and reaffirmed by the Conservatives again in their 2015 and 2017 election campaigns.

The target has never been met. Net migration to the UK has been positive in every year since 1994, and over 100,000 in every year since 1997. It peaked at over 300,000 in 2014 and 2015.[421] The headline figure has since dropped to around 280,000 in 2017 – still well above the target.[422] And the drop had little to do with any government migration policy. The one policy that made a substantial difference was the Brexit referendum – as the vote, and its economic impact, has scared off substantial numbers of European immigrants.[423]

The target's failure is hardly surprising. The reality is that the government does not have the means to control migration in any meaningful way. We can highlight a number of reasons for this:

- *Capitalist demand for labour.* As we will see in Chapter 17, major businesses are strongly against tough controls on people coming to work in the UK. They view immigration as essential for a cheap labour supply. Similarly, the UK's education industry is now entirely dependent on large numbers of foreign students. Big business and its lobbying groups have major influence on immigration policy. In a globalised capitalist economy, governments cannot go against this need.

- *Capitalist demand for movement of goods.* What would it mean to actually shut the borders? As well as controlling people, tighter border controls means slowing trade through the few major ports, where every minute lost costs money.

- *Cost of control.* There are over 50 million entries by "foreigners" into the UK each year. The Home Office's immigration directorates employ around 20,000 people. Border Force and Immigration Enforcement together have an annual budget under £1 billion. Even with the extra 500 border guards promised by Labour, there would be nowhere near the resources needed to question every passenger, raid every business, or chase every "overstayer".

- *Limits of violence.* Even the levels of force seen in Calais, where police often outnumber migrants, have not proved effective at sealing the border there. Actually "controlling" every migrant would involve the kind of violence modern democratic states usually reserve for overseas wars. Other European states are beginning to make the first steps in this direction: notably Hungary, which has recently legislated for automatic detention of all asylum seekers. But Hungary has far fewer migrants than the UK.

To sum up, truly controlling the border would mean crashing the economy by shutting down global trade and labour flows, while waging all out war on migrants. We may one day return to a political climate where these things are possible, but we are not there yet.

Compared with the scale of migration, the Home Office's enforcement actions are small interventions. To take the example of workplace raids: for all the public informing, employer co-operation, and disregard for warrants and other legal niceties, ICE teams only arrest around 5,000 people a year in around 6,000 "visits". Altogether, 27,231 people were detained in 2017. Only half that number (13,173) were actually deported.

At least some Home Office bosses are themselves well aware of this point. It no doubt contributes to the low morale that seems endemic in the organisation (see Chapter 6). The Independent Chief Inspector of Borders and Immigration (ICIBI) writes:

> A senior Home Office manager told us that there was a general awareness within Immigration Enforcement that enforcement visits encountered and removed only a small proportion of offenders and that IE would never have the resources to resolve the overall problem. They described it as 'not a realistic working model'. Another senior manager commented: 'It's a business model that hasn't moved on'.[424]

The hostile environment approach and the deterrent dogma

We could perhaps see Theresa May's hostile environment approach as an attempt to find the new "business model". First, the new measures introduced from 2012 try to substantially increase the resources of Immigration Enforcement – not by hiring more border guards, but by recruiting potentially millions of ordinary citizens as informers and part-time enforcers.

Second, the hostile environment approach has never aimed to actually detain and deport many more migrants. Rather, it is based on a deterrent principle: make people's lives miserable until they leave themselves – so they or don't come in the first place. As Theresa May put it in 2013, to "create a really hostile environment for illegal migrants". "What we don't want is a situation where people think that they can come here and overstay because they're able to access everything they need."[425] Or as the Independent Chief Inspector of Borders and Immigration (ICIBI) explains:

> The government's stated intention was to deny illegal migrants access to public and other services and benefits to which they were not entitled by virtue of their immigration status, in the expectation that this would persuade large numbers to depart the UK voluntarily and would reduce the 'pull factor' for anyone thinking to come to the UK to settle illegally.[426]

This deterrent ideas is not new – although perhaps the government being so open about it in public is. As we saw in Chapter 1, Jack Straw and his officials used very similar arguments in internal documents, as they planned the expansion of detention centres back in 2000. The Home Office permanent secretary Sir David Omand wrote of detaining 4000 people in order to "significantly enhance the deterrent effect for new asylum seekers." Straw himself argued that this would:

> send a strong message to potentially unfounded claimants that we are administering a firm immigration control. The more effective way of tackling the problem of removals is to reduce significantly the number of claimants seeking entry.[427]

Besides increased openness, there is another major difference between the deterrent doctrines of 2000 and 2012. Straw's detention policy was focused just on one small target group, asylum seekers. At the height of asylum arrivals in 2001, these numbered 83,000. The aim was to detain, deport – and so deter – some tens of thousands of people.

Theresa May's policies, on the other hand, have taken aim at a much bigger target. Unlike Labour, the new government promised to address not just asylum, but overall immigration – symbolised by the "net migration" target. And the hostile environment policies took aim at "illegal immigration" as a whole. While there are, of course, no precise figures for "irregular" migrants, the best estimates are somewhere around half a million. So the migrants to be deterred now number hundreds rather than tens of thousands.

Does it work?

For all the rhetoric of "evidence led" policy, the Home Office has not made any published assessment of the deterrent power of any immigration enforcement measure.

It would be extremely hard to measure the effect of policies on the "pull factor" – that is, migrants' decisions to come to the UK in the first place. But it should be easier to see an effect on people deciding to leave. In fact, the Home Office has a basic tool to do this, as it records the numbers of people applying for "voluntary return". Indeed, increasing "voluntary returns" is an explicit goal of the hostile environment approach.

Voluntary returns falling

In 2004, the first year with published figures, there were 3,566 voluntary returns. This climbed every year to reach 27,114 in 2010. Then they hit a peak in 2013, at 32,178. This was just as the new hostile environment deterrent policies were being formulated, and before they were enacted in the 2014 and 2016 Immigration Acts. In 2015, as the first act came into force, there were 29,768 voluntary returns. In 2016, there were 28,655.[428]

In short: there is no sign at all that the new hostile environment policies are having any deterrent impact. In fact, recent voluntary return figures are actually down.

The real effects of hostility

A second piece of evidence here is a study by academic researchers from the University of Oxford's Centre on Migration, Policy and Society (COMPAS), called "Does Immigration Enforcement Matter?"[429] In Chapter 6 we looked at some results of its interviews with civil servants and ICE officers. Another part of the project involved "qualitative interviews" with 175 "irregular immigrants" from five nationalities (Australian, Brazilian, Pakistani, Turkish and Ukrainian). The research aimed to investigate the impact they felt from immigration enforcement measures.

125 of the 175 interviewees were aware of immigration enforcement operations. "18 had experienced workplace raids, 11 raids of private addresses whilst 11 had also been detained at some point and one even removed." Unsurprisingly, Pakistanis were the most likely to have experienced raids – and Australians the least.

It is clear that illegality carries real costs. People spoke of wages as low as £1 an hour, of overcrowded housing, of detention and deportation – although the suffering and danger involved in "removal" differs greatly across nationalities.

What comes across strongest in the research is the psychological impact of enforcement. Most of those who knew about immigration enforcement felt fear. "91 said they feared immigration controls or raids, 29 told us they only feared raids at the beginning of their irregularity and 55 said they did not fear such enforcement". Many individuals talked a lot about the threat of raids. According to the COMPAS researchers:

> This results in two contrasting psychological responses: (a) a little more than half of our interviewees experienced high and constant levels of stress whilst (b) the others were either resilient from the beginning or developed this attitude over time.

As well as psychological responses, people developed everyday strategies for coping with the threat of enforcement. For example, they might avoid "certain locations or neighbourhoods, large companies or construction sites, certain industries like kebab shops, morning shifts, wearing work uniforms" or "addresses that had been raided before, ... houses of immigrants, ... the underground, getting into trouble or otherwise standing out".

They found ways to access the documents they needed, and to get healthcare – although others avoided treatment due to fear of being asked for papers. They used social and community networks to find jobs or housing, and to avoid or resist raids and other controls.

But, for all this, the researchers did not find evidence of a deterrent effect. They write:

> most interviewees still considered life in the UK including employment opportunities and rule of law better than in their country of origin. This explains the low level of deterrence ('being an illegal in this country is still better than being legal in Ukraine').

The explanation for this is straightforward. To deter people from staying in the UK would need to involve making life here more miserable than elsewhere. Until the political climate shifts so far that migrants can be interned in mass labour camps, the main threat the Home Office holds over people is deportation. This threat is greater the more miserable people's prospects are "at home" – but then so is the need to stay.

For some, such as most Ukrainians, deportation is not typically a great threat; while the chance to work in the UK, even given the "illegal discount" on wages, is of great value. For others, such as refugees from countries like Sudan, Afghanistan, or Syria, deportation is indeed life-threatening. How hostile would the hostile environment have to get to scare people away? Can ICE raid teams get as bad as the Taliban or Assad's barrel bombs?

Immigration enforcement does not deter people whose best chance of surviving, living, working, helping their families, or following their own dreams, is to come to the UK. As we saw in Chapter 9, this is true even in Calais, where the hostile environment is taken to an extreme level.

What it does do is cast a shadow of fear over hundreds of thousands of lives. And it also pushes people to resist, to create tools for survival, and networks of solidarity.

So what is the hostile environment really for?

Immigration controls do not effectively control the borders. We assume that politicians and senior civil servants are as aware of this as we are. So what are these attacks on migrants really for?

On the one hand, we don't want to underestimate the inefficiency, incompetence, and short-termism of officials. Probably many politicians and managers cling on to failing policies just because they "need to do something", and they can't think of anything else to do. Others may work hard to believe their own arguments: how else could they justify the misery they've caused?

At the same time, there is also a more rational explanation of recent immigration policies. This is: they are not so much about actually "controlling" the borders as making a show, a spectacle, of control. They strike a pose.

As we saw back in Chapter 1, the history of immigration controls in the UK follows a clear long-running pattern: mass media stir up anti-migrant panics, politicians respond with new laws and clampdowns. We can trace these waves back to the 1880s, or maybe even back to the 13th century. But we can also see how recently they have been mobilised and escalated in new ways. And, in many ways, the story once again starts with the Labour government of Tony Blair, and its intimate relationship with the Murdoch press.

These are the topics we now turn to in Part Three of this book.

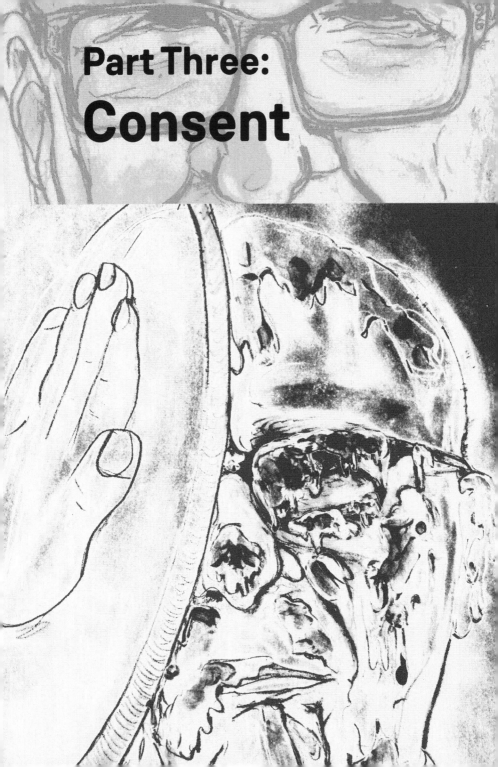

Part Three:
Consent

14. Public opinion: target publics

Politicians and bureaucrats often wheel out the cliché that tough immigration policies respond to the demands of public opinion. But what does "public opinion" mean, exactly? In this chapter we'll try to understand that a bit better. We'll start by looking at the extensive opinion polls about people's attitudes to immigration in the UK.

A note of caution. Opinion polls are skewed towards certain types of people who participate. More fundamentally still, individuals' thoughts, feelings, motivations, can hardly be summed up in multiple choice boxes. But still, polls are really the only tools we have for trying to understand millions of people's attitudes.

Most people say immigration should go down

The polls are consistent on one point: most UK citizens say they want immigration to be reduced.

A recent long-term study of immigration attitudes by major polling firm Ipsos MORI, "Shifting Ground"[430], finds that "Britons are becoming more positive about immigration". In March 2015, 43% people said that immigration had a negative impact on Britain, and 33% said a positive impact. But by October 2016, those proportions had reversed: now 43% though immigration was positive, opposed to 32% negative. Despite that, 60% still said it should be reduced – little different from 62% in 2015. In fact, according to Ipsos MORI:

> this is a common feature of immigration attitudes in the UK over many decades: despite significant ups and downs in actual migration figures and how top of mind a concern it is, our review of historical attitudes to immigration shows that there are always 60%+ who want immigration reduced.

It matters – but how much?

We need to separate two points. First, what people feel – or, rather, say they feel when asked by an interviewer. Second, how much it actually matters to them.

Immigration scares are nothing new to Britain. But the current wave of anxiety over immigration started around the year 2000. Ipsos MORI has carried out its Issues Index every month since the early 1970s. The survey asks people two questions: "what they believe the biggest single issue facing Britain is" and "other big issues they believe are facing the country." Another Ipsos MORI report from 2013, called *Perceptions and Reality: Shifting Public Attitudes to Immigration*, studies the results over almost 40 years.[431]

For most of that time, less than 10% of respondents mentioned immigration as an issue. This changed in the "immigration panic" at the end of the 1970s: over 25% named immigration as important in 1978-9. But that panic didn't last, and the figure fell back below 10% in 1980, where it stayed for 20 years, apart from a brief spike in 1985. Health, defence, crime, and above all "the economy" remained the traditional political concerns.

In 1999, with more people around the world leaving the countries of their birth, the numbers of people concerned about immigration in Britain started to jump, and since 2001 at least 20% of respondents have named immigration as an important issue in almost every monthly survey. So far, the peak of the new panic was in 2006-2008, where over 40% regularly did so. In 16 months in these three years, immigration was the number one issue named. Then in 2009, with the credit crunch and recession, "the economy" retook its traditional position as top issue. But immigration has stayed up there, with a recent peak of 38% in August 2013. As of December 2017[432], the figure had dropped to 21%. One reason is that a new issue, Brexit, has taken over as the top concern.

What causes immigration anxiety?

What has caused rising immigration anxiety? An obvious explanation might be: because immigration has been going up. And that's certainly a factor: the polling data indeed shows a clear positive correlation between immigration levels and the "Issues Index".

But it's not the only factor. For example, the overall immigration level doesn't explain why things started to move around 2000, when immigration numbers were already rising before this. Or why there were previous shorter "panics" in the 1970s and 80s, when immigration was much lower than now. Also, looking at opinion polls across Europe, Ipsos MORI point out that there "is virtually no relationship between levels of net migration and concern across the EU27 countries (and the same is true for every measure of stock or flow of migration or immigration that we examined)." There are clearly other important factors at work.

A few people are very anxious

Another measure of immigration concern is the MPs' Survey, where MPs record the "postbag" of issues brought to them by constituents. This shows an even steeper rise of concerns about immigration. In the mid-80s, less than 10% of issues raised by constituents were about immigration. This began to change in the late 1980s, and in 1992 over 20% of issues were migration related. Since 2002, at least 40% of all constituent contacts with MPs have been about migration. In 2006, at the highest point, just under 80% were about immigration.

We can note two points here. First, constituent concerns started to rise some years before the "general" attitudes surveyed in the Issues Index, and then climbed to much higher levels. Second, while around 20% of the overall population now generally think of immigration as a political issue, a smaller number have become particularly vocal, including making the effort of going to their MPs.

Who's worrying?

Age

Concern about immigration is strongly linked to age. For example, in 2013, 40% of people born pre-1945 saw immigration as an issue, compared to 38% of "baby boomers" (born 1945-65), 30% of "generation Y" (1966-79), and only 22% of "millennials (1980-2000). It is also very relevant that older people are more likely to vote – and to contact their MPs.

Class

Immigration anxiety is also related to social class, but the effect is less strong than with age. In fact, until 2000, Issues Index surveys saw minimal differences between social classes in migration attitudes. Since then, there is a clear trend of "skilled manual workers" (what advertisers and pollsters call

"C2"s) being particularly concerned about migration. An extra 5% or more people in this group are likely to name immigration as an issue. Differences amongst other classes are smaller and less consistent, although concern tends to be lowest at the extremes – "professionals" (A) and "unskilled workers" (E). Very roughly speaking, immigration worry is strongest amongst the lower middle and skilled working classes.

Geography

77% of the total population agreed, when asked by pollsters in 2013, that immigration should be reduced a little or a lot. But the proportions varied a lot by area. The lowest agreement was in areas classed by pollsters as "cosmopolitan London" – where 68% agree. This compares to 85% of white British people living in "new, large freestanding and commuter towns", "migrant worker towns and countryside" and "low migration small towns and rural areas", and 84% in "industrial and manufacturing towns". In "asylum dispersal areas" – which are impoverished areas predominantly in the North and Midlands – 83% agree with reduced migration; and 67%, the highest proportion, think it should be reduced "a lot".

Immigrants can also be anti-immigration

Anti-immigration feeling also exists amongst immigrants. It is closely correlated to how long people have lived in the UK. 70% of immigrants who arrived before 1970 also agreed that immigration should be reduced, whereas only 28% of those who arrived after 2006 did.

Segmentation analysis

To bring together some of these demographic factors, pollsters use a technique called "segmentation" analysis, which involves identifying loose groupings of people who tend to share both similar characteristics and similar views. We will mention two notable studies.

In 2013 the Conservative pollster Lord Ashcroft conducted a detailed study on immigration opinion based on a poll of 20,000 people, called "Small Island: public opinion and the politics of immigration".[433] This broke down interviewees into seven "segments". At one end of the spectrum is a "universal hostility" segment (16% of respondents); at the other a "militantly multicultural" pro-migration segment (10%).

In between, there are two segments who may not be outspokenly pro-migration, but don't see it as an important issue. One is the "urban harmony" (9%) grouping, mainly young and ethnically diverse, who frame their issues in terms of the economy, jobs and public services, rather than immigration. The other are the "comfortable pragmatists" (22%), well-educated and well-off people who don't particularly feel migration to be either a threat or a benefit to them.

The other three segments all have concerns about migration, but for different reasons. The "cultural concerns" group (16%) are usually older people, often owner-occupiers, who talk about immigration in terms of social change and a threat to the British way of life. The "fighting for entitlements" group (12%), also generally older than average and with less education, are concerned about pressures on public services. The "competing for jobs" segment makes up 14%.

Ipsos MORI's analysis in "Shifting Ground" is broadly similar. It identifies four segments:

- A strongly "anti immigration group" (28%), often opposed to migration on numerous grounds, including "immigrants taking away welfare services and jobs", but also because they are "nostalgic for the past". "Older, lower levels of education. Social renters. Highest support for UKIP. Voted heavily to Leave."

- A relatively hostile "Comfortably off and culturally concerned" segment (23%) These "don't feel personally threatened by immigration" but are worried about its impacts on a changing society. "Oldest group, retired, most likely to own house outright. Highest support for Tories. Split on EU referendum vote."

- The "Under Pressure" 25% may say that "other people get priority over them for public services and immigrants get priority over jobs". But immigration isn't the main thing they blame – their biggest concern is "the economy". "Youngest age group, highest number of part time workers." "Politically disparate and highest group of undecided voters. Marginally more Remain than Leave."

- The "Open to Immigration" segment (24%) is "Well educated, highest group of private renters. Highest group of Labour supporters. Mostly voted Remain."

Cultural vs. economic concerns

The segmentation analysis suggests three kinds of ways that people worry about immigration:

- Some people have strong anti-immigration feelings in general. They may cite a range of reasons for concern, including both "cultural" and "practical" or economic issues. But their anti-migrant feeling goes deeper than any of these particular reasons.

- Some people's anti-immigration worry is closely linked to "cultural concerns" – they feel immigration as a threat to an accustomed "way of life". This is particularly true for older white British people. Many people who fear immigration in this way are comfortably off, and don't personally feel economically threatened by immigration.

- Some people may worry about economic or practical impacts, e.g. feel they have to compete with immigrants for jobs, housing or benefits, without fearing cultural change from "diversity". These kinds of concerns may be heard from younger people who live in diverse urban areas, and may come from migrant backgrounds themselves.

One important point, noted by Ipsos MORI, is that "cultural" worries about immigration seem to be stronger than "economic" worries. Inner city workers who feel themselves directly competing with migrants tend to be less anti-immigration than "comfortably off" suburbanites who worry about migration as a threat to a way of life. When asked, they may agree immigration should be reduced. But they are more likely to think of "the economy" as the main problem.

This point is also argued by Scott Blinder of Oxford University's Migration Observatory in a 2011 briefing on "UK Public Opinion toward Migration: Determinants of Attitudes".[434] He writes:

> At least three basic explanations of attitudes toward migration have been researched extensively:
>
> - Contact theory holds that sustained positive contact (i.e. friendships) with members of other ethnic, religious, racial, or national groups produce more positive attitudes toward members of that group.

- Group conflict theory suggests that migrants or minority groups can appear to threaten the interests, identities, or status of the majority (as a group), and that those who feel this sense of threat most acutely will be most likely to oppose migration.

- Economic competition theories suggest that opposition to migration will come from native workers who compete with migrants with similar skill sets, or (conversely) from wealthier natives who feel (or perceive) a financial burden for tax-payers if migrants use public services such as hospitals, schools.

Reviewing the survey evidence and literature at that point, Blinder concludes: "Evidence is quite strong for the first two theories, and mixed for the various economic explanations." In particular:

> Subjective perceptions—of one's own economic security and of migrants' impact on jobs, wages, and the costs of maintaining the welfare state—do seem related to anti-migrant attitudes. But these subjective perceptions are only loosely related to actual individual economic position.[435]

Whose problem?

The Ipsos MORI *Perceptions and Reality* report makes another very important, and related, point. Most people who think immigration is a problem don't think it is a problem for them personally, or for their local area.

Surveying by Eurobarometer, cited in the Ipsos MORI report, asks people for their two top issues "nationally" and "personally". In various surveys over 2008-13, between 18% and 32% of people in the UK named immigration as a national issue; but only between 6% and 10% said it was a personal issue. Similarly, across the EU27 countries, between 7% and 9% named immigration as a national issue, but never more than 4% as a personal issue.

A similar picture emerges from some of Ipsos MORI's own polling between 2006 and 2010. This asked the question:

> Overall how much of a problem, if at all, do you think immigration is in Britain at the moment? And how much of a problem, if at all, do you think immigration is in your local area at the moment?

Consistently across this period, they found a dramatic 50% gap between the two answers. At the highest point of concern, in November 2010, 77% said they thought immigration was a problem in Britain. But only 26% thought it was also a problem in their "local area" as well as nationally. (8% thought it was a problem locally but not nationally, and 22% neither.) As the pollsters say, "these types of gaps exist in other policy areas, such as crime and health services – but they are particularly striking with immigration."

Many people's worries about immigration do not arise from personal experiences, or from what they see in the areas where they live. For many people, we could say, immigration worry is not about concrete problems they experience directly impacting them or those around them. It is something more abstract: a fearful sense of "cultural change", a narrative of loss and threat, felt to be affecting "the country" as a whole.

Summary

There is not one unified "public opinion" about immigration. There are millions of people in the UK with millions of different ideas.

It's true that most British people, when asked by pollsters, say they think immigration should be reduced. But this doesn't mean that most people think immigration is a significant problem.

Some people are really bothered about immigration – and their number has been rising, from less than 10% of the population before 2000, to more like 20% now. Some of these people feel very strongly, and are very vocal. Importantly, they are often people who are likely to vote, to contact their MPs – and also to buy newspapers. As we will see in the next chapters, they will have a particularly strong influence on politicians.

We can think of two main groupings of people who are most likely to worry about immigration – two anxious anti-migrant minorities. Both are typically older and white. But their social circumstances may be quite different:

· Typically older, white, working class people hit hard by poverty and social tension, often living in run-down neighbourhoods in the North or Midlands with large migrant populations, including "asylum dispersal areas". Excluded from the economic consumer dream, they may feel directly impacted by immigrants, identifying them as a threat to jobs, services, benefits. But they also feel immigration as a "cultural concern" – a feeling reinforced by personal experience of seeing their neighbourhoods changed by new arrivals. Economic and cultural concerns may build together into a deeply felt "universal hostility" towards immigrants.

- Typically older, white, middle class people, often living in suburban or rural areas. They may be more or less comfortably off, and do not perceive immigration as a personal threat – maybe they rarely meet migrants except those serving them a curry. But they feel anxiety about immigration as a cultural concern, a threat to their values and identity.

Some of those who worry about migrants are excluded from mainstream society and blame migrants for their troubles. Others are comfortably included. The common factor across these two groupings is not economics, or personal experience, but a more generalised anxiety about migration as a cultural threat. Where does this anxiety come from?

15. **Media: communication power**

How much power do media have to shape our views on immigration, or indeed on any issue? There is a lot of academic research on this question, from different perspectives.[436] Still, as Scott Blinder at the Migration Observatory writes, it is hard to pin down a final answer.[437] This is because:

> it is virtually impossible to discern whether people learn their political viewpoints from the media sources they rely upon, or if conversely they choose to rely on media sources that reflect their pre-determined political viewpoint. It would seem likely that both processes occur, but research to disentangle one from the other faces formidable challenges and is likely to remain inconclusive.

We can't hope to untangle it all here either. But our starting point is that people do not form their attitudes in isolation. Our views are shaped throughout our lives in continuing communication with many others.

For example, I may have personally experienced being turned down for a job, being on a housing waiting list, or seeing my neighbourhood change. But also, I have talked about these experiences with friends, family, neighbours, work colleagues, and these conversations shape how I understand what has happened. They give me new information, and they help me grasp contexts or "frames" that fit events into patterns, making them part of shared narratives. All of us are continually receiving ideas from many others. At the same time, we transmit our ideas to others, and influence their views.

However, some people and institutions have much greater influence than others. We use the term "the media" as a shorthand to mean: organisations with particular access to major communication channels. To be clear, big media are certainly not the only sources of ideas. But in a landscape where a few big players still dominate mass communication channels, they have concentrated power to spread and shape people's views. In this chapter we will look at these questions:

· Just what reach do big media have?

· What ideas do big media spread about migration, and how have these been changing?

· And why? What agendas or projects drive them?

Media reach

We'll start with one more Ipsos MORI survey. This 2011 poll, also cited in the "Perceptions and Reality"[438] report we looked at in the last chapter, asked: "which two sources would you say provides you personally with most of your information about immigration and asylum in Britain?" These were the answers people gave:

· News programmes on TV or radio: 55%
· National newspapers: 44% (tabloids 20%, broadsheets 18%)
· TV documentaries: 23%
· Personal Experience: 16%
· Internet: 10%
· Radio programmes: 9%
· Word of mouth: 9%
· Local newspapers: 8%
· Friend's and/or relative's experience: 7%

Without putting too much weight on these figures, at least they indicate the importance many people themselves give the media in their thinking about immigration. Again, we need to be clear that there is no one "public" – there are many different people, reached by different media outlets in different ways.

Audience segments

As that survey indicates, television is still extremely powerful. Although if the poll were carried out now, we could expect a stronger role for online media. According to more recent Yougov / Oxford University sampling, UK use of online news sites overtook TV for the first time in 2016.[439]

Both TV and internet are more widely accessed than newspapers. On the other hand, newspapers are often considered to have particular influence in the self-referential media "debate" – what some academics call "intermedia agenda setting".[440] There are TV programmes dedicated to "what the papers say", and broadcast news often takes the lead from the morning papers. The most influential newspaper commentators, in particular, may play an agenda-setting role for the media overall.

There are strong generational differences in media reception. E.g. 84% of people aged 24 and under said online news and social media is their main source, with only 9% saying TV. But 54% of people over 55 put TV first, and 15% of this age group relied most on newspapers. Of course, this is particularly relevant for the key demographics with most immigration anxiety – older white people.

Indeed, to go back to the main Ipsos MORI attitudes study we discussed in the last chapter, here is another interesting fact: people who said they saw immigration as a problem "nationally but not locally" were particularly likely to be newspaper readers. 51% of this group said they read newspapers – as opposed to 41% of those who saw a "national and local" problem, and 43% of those who didn't see immigration as a problem at all. And 16% of them read "mid-market" newspapers – i.e., the Daily Mail and the Daily Express – as opposed to 9% and 6% in the other two groups.

Media content

There is considerable research on how UK media cover immigration. We will review a few highlights from four notable studies:

- "What's The Story?", Article 19's study of the original asylum scare in 1999-2001 which led to the closing of the Red Cross refugee centre in Sangatte, near Calais.

- *Bad News for Refugees* by researchers from the Glasgow Media Group, which includes case studies of coverage during May 2006 and June 2011.

- "Press Coverage of the Refugee and Migrant Crisis in the EU" a UNHCR commissioned study by Cardiff School of Journalism, which analyses reports from 2014-15 in five countries: UK, Germany, Italy, Spain, and Sweden.

- "A Decade of Immigration in the British Press" by David Allen from Oxford University's Migration Observatory, which studies press coverage over 2006-15.[441]

All of these are "content analyses". That is, they categorise and analyse the use of language, key words, different sources, narrative patterns, "frames"[442] and other elements. Most focus on newspaper reports, but *Bad News* and

UNHCR also look at TV reporting. To start with the obvious point, the UNHCR study notes that:

> coverage in the United Kingdom was the most negative, and the most polarised [of the countries they looked at]. Amongst those countries surveyed, Britain's right-wing media was uniquely aggressive in its campaigns against refugees and migrants.

All countries' media gave space to anti-migrant views, but the UK stands out for the way major newspapers actively campaign in their own voices.

Volume

The volume of media coverage of immigration roughly mirrors the public attitudes surveys we discussed in the last chapter. The Migration Observatory study charts the overall volume of stories mentioning "immigration" or "immigrants" over ten years, looking at all national newspapers for which there are full records. In 2006 there were just under 600 articles per month on average; coverage declined to under 400 stories per month in 2008-2012, with the exception of a jump around the 2010 general election; but then rose again to new highs of over 800 stories per month as the "refugee crisis" began in 2014-15.

So the more media talk about migration, the more people surveyed by pollsters say it is important. Again, it is hard to separate cause and effect: it could also be that media talk more about migration because "the public" is already doing so.

Threat stories

Media overwhelmingly frame migration as a problem and a threat. Migration Observatory write: "About 7 in 10 articles (69%) mentioning EU immigration, and about three-quarters (76%) of articles [mentioning] illegal immigration […] contained only mentions of problems."

Migration Observatory identify eight main problem themes. The most frequent, by far, is the sheer quantity of immigrants, followed by "rules too weak or abused", and "poor quality of debate". It's also interesting that the much smaller number of "pro-migrant" stories are also typically framed in terms of problems: the "rules are too tough", "racism/xenophobia", "suffering of migrants".

215

The problem themes change over time, as do the terms used to describe migrants. We could broadly identify three periods:

- In the early 2000s, the big focus was on "asylum seekers". As Roy Greenslade writes, editors succeeded in "having demonised the concept and practice of asylum-seeking, and turning the very phrase into a term of abuse".[443]

- By 2005-6, "illegal immigrants" replaced "asylum seekers" as the main bogeyman, while EU migration became a major issue.

- In the next ten years, references to "illegality" died down a bit. The main focus shifted to the overall number of migrants.

Migration Observatory track the use of "modifiers" describing immigrants. Across 2006-2015, in 30% of all times migrants are described, they are described as "illegal". In 2006, illegal was in fact over half of all descriptions in tabloid and "mid market" papers. By 2015 this had fallen to around 30%, while broadsheet descriptions of illegality had dropped from over 30% to 14%.

But the main kind of description, and increasingly so, is about scale. Common words include 'mass', 'uncontrolled', 'high', 'more', 'unlimited', 'unrestricted', 'excessive', 'unfettered', etc. By 2015, 63% of all descriptions of "migration" or "immigration" were in terms of scale.

And along with scale comes the need for "limits". 20% of all verbs used in migration articles in 2006, rising to almost 40% by 2015, concerned actions to do with limiting: 'control', 'manage', 'tackle', 'regulate', 'reduce', 'cut', 'curb', 'limit', 'restrict', 'stop', 'cap', 'slash', 'prevent', 'discourage', 'stem', 'halt'.

As asylum-seekers lose centre stage in the mid-2000s, new concerns arise with "European migrants", and later with "refugees". But the essential narrative remains: immigrants, in masses and/or illegally, asylum-seekers or Europeans, threaten peace and order, and the problem must be controlled. There are two central villains in this story: first of all, migrants themselves; secondly, politicians who are failing to exert control.

Voices

The Migration Observatory and *Bad News* studies analyse the "messengers" or "voices" telling the stories in reports. Most often, the "messengers" are journalists themselves, asserting a fact or interpretation often without giving any other source. "In nearly half of [articles about EU or illegal immigration] the author of the article is the person who is communicating the main issue—asserting whether it is problem or success."

18% of articles give the "messenger" role to a politician. The UNHCR study breaks down the parties of politicians featured: "68.6% of political sourcing [in 2014-15] came from the coalition government whilst the main voice explicitly opposing government policy came from UKIP (9.3%)."

Much smaller numbers of articles centred civil servants, or spokespeople from NGOs or think tanks. Only a tiny handful gave the "messenger" role to migrants themselves.

Media roles: campaigners and debaters

Of course, there is considerable difference in how media outlets treat migration. We divide the big UK media into two broad categories on migration. First, there are a number of outlets that brazenly campaign on anti-migrant agendas. Second, other media frame migration as a "debate" in which different voices – within a more or less narrow range – are given space.

Anti-migrant campaigning media

The two "mid-market" papers, the Daily Mail and the Express, are the notorious leaders of anti-migrant campaigning. Murdoch's tabloid The Sun follows just a few steps behind. Its owner is known to support the benefits of economic migration (see below), but does not interfere with rabid commentators or infamous articles such as the July 2003 "Swan Bake" front page (which accused asylum seekers of "barbecuing the Queen's swans").[444] In the broadsheet sector, the right-wing Telegraph also takes a consistently hard line.

These four papers between them have around 60% of all UK national newspaper sales. The Sun and the Daily Mail are the two biggest selling newspapers by some margin.[445] The Sun still sells over 1.5 million copies a day, or 25% of all national daily newspaper sales (as of January 2018); the Daily Mail around 1.3 million. The next biggest-selling daily is the Mirror, with around 580,000. Newspaper sales are declining across the board, and these figures are well below their historic peaks. Two obvious reasons are free papers and internet use. The Metro gives out almost 1.5 million copies, the London Evening Standard nearly 900,000. Newspaper websites are still some of the biggest news sites, and the Daily Mail remains the notable success with over 13 million "unique browsers" per day.

The Sangatte study gives in-depth analysis of these papers' all-out campaign against asylum seekers at the end of 2002. As Roy Greenslade writes, "at one point in 2003 the Daily Express ran 22 'splashes' (front page lead stories) about asylum-seekers and refugees in a 31-day period." Headlines included the likes of "ASYLUM: Tidal wave of crime". The constant connection of asylum and crime was also the Mail's signature. "As early as 1998, the Mail ran a story headlined, 'Brutal crimes of the asylum seekers', which claimed that asylum-seekers were having a 'devastating impact' on crime in London".

Outlets which present a "debate"

Other print media, and TV channels, tend not to take openly partisan anti-migrant lines. This does not mean their reporting is pro-migration. Just that there is an appearance of "balancing" different views.

Of course, the range of views they report is another question. In most cases it is heavily skewed against migrants. For example, the main TV channels BBC and ITV will often invite comments from UKIP or the anti-migrant think-tank Migration Watch (see Chapter 18) to provide an oppositional voice to government, which is presented as "soft" on migration. As the Huffington Post reported, UKIP spokespeople appeared on a quarter of all BBC Question Time shows in 2010-2017.[446] Liberal pro-migrant voices are also given some space on main news and commentary programmes – but less of it.

Of all big media outlets, the Guardian newspaper stands out in two main respects. First, it gives greater space to quotes and opinion pieces from pro-migrant NGOs, academics, or activists. Second, it has a higher proportion of stories using "humanitarian" rather than "threat" frames – e.g. reporting on the suffering of migrants and their experiences along routes. That said, Guardian articles still often use the indiscriminate language common across the media, e.g. referring widely to "illegal immigrants". And pro-migrant voices and humanitarian narratives feature alongside anti-migration narratives from official figures and other commentators.

That is, the Guardian is not a migrant "friendly" paper in the same way the Mail is a "hostile" paper. It appears as *relatively* friendly because, more than other outlets, it attempts to balance hostile with friendly messages in a two-sided debate.

Media agendas

Why do media push anti-migrant messages? First, we need to note that "the media" are made up of multiple actors: not just different competing outlets, but different people within each organisation, each with their own goals. Yet media organisations tend to be extremely hierarchical, with political lines set from the top down. We will look first at why media owners and editors might want to campaign against migrants; and then, at why their reporters play along.

Media owners

UK media ownership is highly concentrated. According to the Media Reform Coalition's 2015 report[447]:

> three companies dominate 71% of the national newspaper market [...] When online readers are included, just five companies dominate some 80% of market share. In the area of local news, six giant conglomerates account for 80% of all titles.

In broadcasting, there is even less variety. The BBC still dominates with around one third of all viewing, followed by ITV with 22%, Channel 4 with 11%, Sky with 8%, and Channel 5 with 6%.

Not only are there few competing companies, but their ownership is concentrated in few hands. Nearly 60% of national newspaper sales are effectively controlled by two family businesses: Rupert Murdoch's News Corporation owns The Sun and The Times; Lord Rothermere's Daily Mail and General Trust owns the Metro free sheet as well as the Daily Mail. The next biggest circulation free paper, the Evening Standard, as well as the Independent, is owned by ex-KGB oligarch Alexander Lebedev and his son Evgeny.

We might think about two kinds of agendas for the media barons:

- *Profit motive*. To maintain their position, they first of all need to make profit, which means sales and audience share – but also, finding and monetising new media forms online.

· *Specific policy agendas.* Their highly centralised control gives scope to pursue more particular political, campaigning or personal agendas.

There is a long tradition of media owners pursuing "hobby horse" campaigns – but there are also limits to how far they can go. Essentially, they can't rub too hard against the grain of existing audience attitudes. For example, in the book *Mail Men*, Adrian Addison explains how a dash of antisemitism pleased Daily Mail readers in the 1930s – but Lord Rothermere went too far when he started to openly support Hitler. Using the paper to parade his fascist views helped push the paper into a decades-long decline against its rival the Express.[448]

Owners and editors

Many media owners still take strong command of editorial lines, determine campaigns, and write editorials under their names or unsigned. For example, Murdoch has declared himself a "traditional proprietor" setting the editorial line on major issues at The Sun – but is supposedly less hands-on at the Times.[449]

Elsewhere, editors are given a free rein. At the Daily Mail, the current (fourth) Lord Rothermere reputedly left editor Paul Dacre in full charge – so long as the paper maintained its sales position. Dacre ran the Mail from 1992 to October 2018, on a personal crusade to voice the hateful anxiety of the pure white Middle England he remembers from a 1950s suburban childhood. It proved popular with the paper's ageing readership. Dacre, who barely leaves the office and then only in a chauffeur driven car, was also a particularly vicious boss known for his abusive ranting at staff (the so-called "vagina monologues") – though he is not the only editor to keep up the good old ways of Fleet Street bullying.[450]

As we write, Dacre has just been succeeded by former Mail on Sunday editor Geordie Greig, known as a softer pro-European, and there is much speculation about how this will change the Mail's tone. Dacre in his last months issued warnings against shifting the paper's direction, saying "support for Brexit is in the DNA of both the Daily Mail and, more pertinently, its readers."[451]

So why does The Sun hate migrants?

While Dacre's views are clear, Rupert Murdoch makes an interesting case study. On the whole, Murdoch has used his global empire to push standard neoliberal policies favouring global business elites: privatisation, deregulation, free trade, the occasional profitable war. As we will see in Chapter 17, big business is generally pro-immigration – in the limited sense of free movement of labour.

And in fact, Murdoch appears himself to have largely pro-immigration views in that sense. In the US, he has publicly called for "sweeping, generous immigration reforms"[452], and mocked Trump's[453] xenophobic rhetoric on twitter. In the UK, too, he has more occasionally taken pro-migrant stances, such as speaking against Michael Howard's immigration cap policy in 2005.[454]

At the same time, Murdoch allows his editors and columnists to launch full-on anti-migrant campaigns. How to explain this? Here are maybe some parts of an answer.

First, the Sun's anti-migrant populism is, indeed, popular. Its target audiences lap it up. By now, the feeding of anti-migrant fear and hate at the Sun has been going on for decades, and stopping the machine might be costly. This is a winning model, and selling papers is the top priority.

Second, Murdoch relishes the power of the Sun to make politicians jump. He is known for making, and breaking, political careers – and for switching allegiances. The power to whip up controversies around immigration is a handy stick to hold over politicians. The interests and power of media in helping "manufacture consent" for political systems have been well analysed.[455] But media power agendas may also involve manufacturing dissent – at least in controllable doses.[456]

Third, to pick up our key argument from Chapter 13, it's not as if The Sun's anti-migrant rhetoric actually leads to effective general immigration controls. In fact The Sun has played an instrumental role in directing anti-migrant rage onto more limited, and business-friendly scapegoats such as asylum-seekers.

We should also note that The Sun's "populism" has clear limits. For example, after some dallying, Murdoch swung the paper behind Brexit.[457] An hour after the referendum result, Sun editor Tony Gallagher gloated in a text message to the Guardian "so much for the waning power of the print media."[458] But then the Sun rallied behind the mainstream Conservative party against UKIP.

So far, the UK right wing press has played this game successfully. It gleefully wields language and narratives that in other European countries are associated with neo-fascist or "outsider" politicians. But then it swings behind the establishment parties – in effect, using far-right rhetoric to mobilise for the centre-right mainstream. The game might not play the same way in other countries where a more "radical nationalist" right looms stronger.

Journalists

We might think of three main classes of journalists at the coalface of anti-migrant propaganda.

First, there are prized commentators, columnists and presenters, who have xenophobia as part of their shtick. They are famous, highly paid, seen as assets by their employers, and may be head-hunted across outlets. Do they sincerely believe in their diatribes? Do they crave the attention and controversy? Are they in it for the money and power? All of the above? Does it matter?

At the other end of the spectrum, junior reporters starting their careers are often ordered to write "monstering" attack articles. *Bad News for Refugees* quotes from confidential interviews with a number of journalists:

> Invariably it's the younger reporters who are sent out to do these sorts of monstering jobs because they want to get on. The newsroom is an authoritarian place [ ] the imbalance between news editor and young inexperienced reporter is enough to get the person to put their conscience aside and go and monster an asylum seeker.

> In general the approach used to be to use young reporters of Asian background to 'do their own'. [A reporter] was used to do a lot of these stitch-up jobs on asylum seekers. The paper wants to cover itself by using a reporter of an ethnic background to do these sort of jobs.

Those who refuse, if not simply fired, may be bullied into quitting:

> [One journalist] very openly spoke out and said 'I don't want to write these kinds of stories, you know, I don't want to do this.' As a result, she got absolutely, sort of, screamed off the news room floor and for the next couple of weeks she was given every anti-Muslim, anti-asylum seeker story to do, every single one until she just resigned.

Roy Greenslade notes that many stories come from even lower down the food chain, from local freelance agencies and individual "stringers" who sell stories to the nationals.

> they also understand that certain papers are more likely than others to publish specific stories – due to their political prejudice, possibly, or their penchant for human interest or humorous tales – and therefore, in order to secure an income, try to satisfy that appetite.

In between the big-name commentators and the muckraking grunts come the middle ranks of ordinary hard-working journalists clocking their copy. The profession is well paid (apart from the lowest ranks), 94% white (in 2016), 86% university educated, and over 50% privately educated.[459] Although older generations of tabloid journalists were often from working class backgrounds, this is less and less the case. Many may have no particular axe to grind with migrants. But few have experienced migration themselves, or interact closely with those who have. Their attitudes, in general, are unlikely to differ greatly from the "public opinion" they may feel themselves to represent.

If they do have different views, they will find it tough to get these past editorial lines – even on "left-leaning" media, pro-migration stories are known as a hard sell. The fact is that media don't typically see migrants as their "target publics". And it may be simply that big media themselves absorb the worldview they help create. To quote another *Bad News* interview:

> There's an assumption in the news desk that the readers will believe that there are not enough jobs, that there are simply too many people coming in, there are too many problems in our own country and it's difficult to put in sympathetic stories on asylum or refugees.

Conclusion: propaganda spirals

Let's now revisit the big question about media influence. One thoughtful publication is veteran journalist Roy Greenslade's 2005 essay "Seeking Scapegoats: the coverage of asylum in the UK press".[460] Greenslade starts by reviewing the history of anti-migration reporting in the British media since the birth of the late nineteenth century "popular press" (see Chapter 1). Throughout this timeline, "popular" media have argued that they are simply speaking the established views of their mass audiences: "a xenophobic press for a xenophobic people". Greenslade argues that this is partially correct:

> Popular papers rarely, if ever, publish material that is diametrically opposed to the views of their readers. There is a reciprocal relationship between newspaper and audience. In general, papers reflect what people think or, to be more specific, they reflect what they think people think.

But, he continues:

> the press is not a simple mirror when it seeks to reflect existing public attitudes. Publication endorses and reinforces those attitudes, lending them credibility. [...] The reflecting mirror is therefore distorted [...]

Greenslade presents a "spiralling" dynamic, a dance between media and audience involving two "vicious circles":

> the press both reflects and enhances public attitudes and thereby sets off a chain reaction in which the reflection and enhancement go on escalating until reality is buried under layers of myth and prejudice.

We could fit Greenslade's observations within a rough framework informed by classic theorists of propaganda such as Edward Bernays[461] and Jacques Ellul[462]. We need to distinguish two kinds of propaganda:

- *Short-term activating propaganda:* messages or actions that "activate" or trigger existing deep-seated attitudes.

Newspaper campaigns are classic examples, alongside election stunts or other political spectacles. As Bernays, the great twentieth century PR guru, writes: "The public has its own standards and demands and habits. You may modify them, but you dare not run counter to them." "There has to be fertile ground for the leader and the idea to fall on." So when The Sun launches an attacking "asylum week", it is stirring a well of existing hatred. But, consciously or otherwise, it is doing something else too: helping form future attitudes.

· *Long-term accumulating propaganda:* actions and messages that help form attitudes, customs and "fixed ideas", through a slow drip of repeated messages.

This is what Ellul calls "strategic propaganda". It may involve deliberate long-term campaigns by states and other powerful actors, or more diffuse "sociological propaganda" in which many actors contribute, often without any coordinated plan. The deep-seated attitudes of a "xenophobic people" have been built up over years and generations.

The media is certainly not alone in repeating and reinforcing xeno-racism: politicians, teachers, academics, advertisers, and all of us in our everyday communication can play our part. But the populist media's endlessly repeated threat stories and hate speech makes a major contribution. So, too, does the more liberal media's accepting presentation of this hate speech as a valid part of "the public debate".

Pie-ing of Rupert Murdoch by Jonnie Marbles, 19 July 2011

16. **Politicians**

Politicians live off the approval of others. They hunger for votes, media attention, funding, and support from colleagues as they build their careers. In this chapter we look at three ways in which their quest for approval shapes immigration policies.

- First, when they run for election, political parties need the support of key "target publics". We will see how policies are made to please the anxious anti-migrant minorities discussed in Chapter 14, who are crucial voters.

- Second, politicians are extremely ambitious. They make policies to build their personal reputations as they climb the greasy ladder of power. In particular, Home Secretaries court approval by posturing with tough anti-migrant policies.

- Third, most politicians are intensely focused on the media. Policies are made not just responding to media campaigns, but anticipating how they will "play" in future headlines. And politicians and journalists work, and socialise, close together. Policies are formed in the close bubble or "ecology of ideas" they share.

Just one thought before we go on: politicians are also human beings with the full run of human failings. In this chapter we will look at more "rational" motives behind political decisions, but we don't want to suggest that policies are all crafted with cold calculation. We are sure that ignorance, inefficiency, short-sightedness, and sheer panic, play big roles as well.

Election strategies: target voters

No policy is going to please everyone. But politicians don't need to please all the people – just those whose support matters for their success. At the most basic level, this means the people they need to vote for them.

How aware are politicians of who they are targeting? Perhaps much of the time effective politicians work with an intuitive idea of who they need to reach. But in modern election campaigns, intuition and prejudice are supplemented by more sophisticated techniques. Understanding election targeting can give us a start to understanding policy targeting in general.

Who are the decision-makers?

Here there is no better guide than the infamous "Wizard of Oz" Lynton Crosby, known in the UK for the 2005 and 2015 Conservative election campaigns, as well as Boris Johnson's mayoral victory. However, Crosby's techniques are by no means exceptional, and similar approaches are now the norm across the political spectrum. As Crosby explains in a "campaign masterclass" the core of any successful campaign is identifying the crucial decision-makers.[463] "Who is the target, who matters? What matters to them? Where are they? How do you get to them?" Most basically, this means identifying three types of voters:

- *The base:* those you can rely on to support you

- *The antis:* the opposition's base

- *The swingers:* people who could be persuaded either way

Campaigning is about the best use of limited resources: money, activists, and time. None of these should be wasted trying to persuade committed antis – the best you can hope for is to discourage them. So the campaign consists of, first, "locking in" the base; second, targeting those voters identified as most likely "swingers". In the UK, those swingers are particularly important in "marginal" constituencies where there are only a few votes between the main parties.

For example, in the 2015 UK general election the Conservative "40/40" strategy identified 40 defence seats, the Tory marginals where they needed to lock in existing voters, and another 40 attack seats identified as potential swings to the party.[464] The bulk of the party's "ground" campaign – including thousands of bussed-in canvassers, local advertising and targeted direct mail-outs – was directed at just these 80 seats.

A massive data gathering operation was planned two years before the actual election. This involved door-knocking not just to classify every voter as pro or anti, but to make a detailed profile of each individual using a ten-point questionnaire.[465] Throughout the campaign, unpublished opinion polling in the 80 seats was supplemented with information from commercial databases. This included detailed demographic profiling from the Mosaic database: run by the big credit rating and consumer profiling corporation Experian, all major parties now consider this an essential tool. (See Chapter 11 on Mosaic and Experian). According to one account:

> Behind closed doors, [chief campaign pollster Jim] Messina boasts that he has 1,000 pieces of data on every voter in the U.K., one admiring Tory official revealed. [ ] Messina knows where every target voter shops, what they buy, how they travel to work and much more besides.[466]

All of this data was crunched to provide a highly detailed picture of the key voter "segments" to be targeted. These targets were then hit with precise messages, differentiated both in terms of issues and of delivery (e.g. email, phone, text, hand-signed letter, doorstep visit).[467]

As many noted after the 2015 result, this local propaganda effort went largely unnoticed by London-based media pundits – and by many opinion polls. They saw only the nationwide "public campaign", or "air war": the impact of big politicians' speeches and television appearances, the famous Saatchi billboards and national advertising campaigns. They missed the "ground war" taking place "below the line". While the public "broadcasting" campaign set the main campaign messages, an equally crucial role was played by "narrowcasting" which didn't talk to one great general public, but to highly targeted segments in specific marginal constituencies.

Another increasingly important form of "narrowcasting", recently in the news due to the Cambridge Analytica scandal[468], involves the use of Facebook and other social media data. But we shouldn't forget that this is just one aspect of the political use of Big Data.

Differentiating issues

Crosby is famous for insisting that parties focus on just a small number of key issues – "scrape the barnacles off the boat."[469] Although this stripped-down messaging can misfire – as in the 2017 election where Theresa May looked like a vacuous robot endlessly repeating her "strong and stable" mantra. Crosby gives a four point test for identifying issues to campaign on:

Salience: "Is it out there and people are talking about it"?

Relevance: "Is it personally relevant, [does] it relate to people and their lives"?

Differentiation: Can you use it to "set yourself apart from your opponent"?

Actionable: Does it lead people to want to vote a certain way.

Connecting this to the points above, the issues must be ones that matter to your specific target publics. So the campaign strategy asks: what issues are these target voters talking about, and what issues do they feel emotionally connected to? And it's important to remember here that "there are lots of things people disagree or agree with but have no influence on people's vote." E.g. people may agree immigration is too high, but is this something that will bring them out to vote?

But an issue will only work if you can use it to differentiate from the opposition, to say you're the ones who are on the targets' side on this – unlike the other lot. The aim is to downplay or "minimise points of differentiation on issues where you are weak", and "establish differentiation on your terms", highlighting the issues that make your story stand out.

Of course, a campaign may have a number of different target groups, each with different issues. But "these days you will get caught out", says Crosby, if you try to tell completely different stories to different groups. The trick is to use the public "broadcast" campaign to "set up your overall position" with "messages designed to appeal to everybody". And then use the targeted "narrowcast" campaign to direct more "fine tuned and relevant messages to particular groups".

Finally, besides manifestos and campaign literature, there are also more subtle ways parties can flag up their issues and stories. For example, Crosby advises focusing on "positive" campaigning in official propaganda. Negative attacks on opponents are best done by using "proxies", e.g. let friendly media outlets fling mud on the opponents, while your own hands stay looking clean.

Immigration as an election issue 1997-2017

Now let's look at some of how these campaigning basics have played out in recent immigration politics.

Blairism

When Blair came to power in 1997, immigration was not an issue on either of the main party's agendas, nor did it feature in "public opinion" lists of political issues. The climate began to shift from 1998 with the fevered media reporting of the "asylum crisis". As we have seen, polling on immigration as an issue for "public opinion" now began to rise. Yet in 2001, Labour still effectively ignored immigration as an election issue, focusing on its list of five big topics such as education and healthcare. Only in 2005 was immigration explicitly added as a sixth election pledge, under the slogan "Your country's borders protected."

At first sight, this may seem odd. But strategically, it made good sense for Labour not to flag up immigration when electioneering. It was one of the few policy areas where opinion polls saw the Tories firmly ahead of Blair. The election strategy was thus clearly to "neutralise" on immigration and shift attention onto stronger ground.

However, outside election time, it was another matter. Then Labour home secretaries made clear efforts to respond to anti-immigration public opinion with an unprecedented succession of tough new laws. The most obvious feature of these was that they focused on a just one small group of migrants: asylum-seekers.

Conservative opposition: "Are you thinking what we're thinking?"

Despite the attacks on refugees, Labour's overall immigration policy was still seen as too "soft" by some voters. In the 2001 and 2005 general elections, Conservative challengers William Hague and Michael Howard attempted to capitalise on this. In 2001, Hague made immigration – and the asylum scare in particular – one of his top three issues, alongside tax cuts and Europe ("saving the pound"). But the attempt was notably unsuccessful in making inroads against the Blair machine.

In 2005, Howard again played the immigration card, alongside crime and hospitals. The campaign was run by Lynton Crosby, hired after a notable run of successes for the Australian right-wing Liberals, which had centralised anti-migration anxiety. The slogans "Are you thinking what we're thinking?", and "It's not racist to impose limits on immigration", epitomised the "dog whistle" tactic: framing messages in a way to chime with certain target publics, whilst avoiding open hostility that might offend others.

Polling suggested that the Tories had a strong lead over Labour on immigration. But Labour still beat them on all the other main issues: by a long way on health and education, and even slightly at that point on traditional Tory issues of tax and crime. It may well have made sense for the Tories to flag immigration: it was one of very few issues where they clearly stood out from, and beat, Labour at that point. However, immigration was only fourth on the list of "salient" issues: it played to some of the Conservatives' own base, but didn't sway many swing voters.

Conservatives under Cameron: detoxifying

After 2005 the new leader, David Cameron, tacked back to the centre ground. The plan was to target "small l liberal" swing voters, which required "detoxifying" the "nasty party" by rolling back on the right-wing messages. The 2010 election campaign was fought on the economy, again a winnable issue for the Tories after the 2008 crash. The 2015 campaign continued the economy story, but became largely a full-on assault on Ed Miliband's weakness, from his bacon sandwich issues to his potential dependence on a coalition with the SNP.

Yet, as Tim Bale and co-authors write, Cameron managed to "have his cake and eat it" on immigration in the run-up to 2010.[470] Leaving immigration out of the broadcast campaign package helped reassure the "small l liberals". But the party could still gain from the immigration issue, largely thanks to "proxies" who would flag it up for them.

In the "long campaign" before official electioneering, backbench Tory MPs did the job of making more outspoken anti-migrant comments. In the 2010 campaign itself, the notable example was Bigotgate, when Gordon Brown was unwittingly recorded calling a pensioner who had complained to him about immigration numbers a "bigoted woman".[471] With the media frenziedly running the issue, there was no need for party leaders to introduce it themselves. Thus the Tories managed to attract anti-migrant voters, whilst at the same time not alienating "liberals".

Labour in opposition: apologies

Labour did not have to worry too much about its immigration weak point so long as it led the Tories on other more salient policy issues, including the economy. After 2010, with its economic reputation smashed, it no longer felt this luxury. Under Miliband, the party took a new approach, symbolised by its infamous "controls on immigration" branded mugs.[472] It now embraced a "tough" stance on overall immigration, which included apologising for its previous "mistakes".

In the wake of defeat, Labour strategists were finally waking up to the idea that the party needed to reconnect with working class voters taken for granted by Blairism. Groupings such as Prospect[473], the Fabian Society[474], and the Blue Labour[475] tendency, were influential in arguing that the way to do this was to cleave to "socially conservative" and nationalistic values.

This attitude was galvanised by the threat from UKIP, growing in the build-up to the 2015 election. Although so far UKIP had done more damage to the Conservatives, a 2014 Fabian Society report identified five Labour seats as under direct threat from UKIP victories – and, more importantly, a greater number where losing votes to UKIP would let in Conservatives.

The battle for UKIP voters

Throughout recent decades, the mainstream parties have worried about losing votes on immigration to smaller parties emerging from the far right. In the 1970s, it was the National Front; in the 1990s, the British National Party; and recently, UKIP. Although UKIP's official main issue was independence from the EU, their growth in support in 2010-16 largely came from positioning themselves as an anti-immigration protest vote. In the run-up to the June 2016 Brexit referendum, immigration was the number one reason people gave for deciding to vote Leave.[476]

Ahead of the 2015 election, losing votes to UKIP was a crucial threat for both Conservatives and Labour. It was now they, rather than the Conservatives, who "owned" immigration among many target publics. Not only because UKIP would always use tougher rhetoric, but also simply because the Conservatives were now in government, and so faced the fact of their failure to meet targets and keep migration "under control".

Labour's strategy guidance on "Campaigning against UKIP", leaked and published by The Telegraph, makes clear that "Immigration is the issue people most often cite when explaining support for UKIP."[477] Like the Conservatives, Labour based its "ground war" on the Experian Mosaic database, alongside in-house research. The leaked report analyses UKIP's support using Experian's categories.

According to this analysis, UKIP's main target public was "older traditionalist" voters, who make up approximately 23% of the population. This category is broken down into four Mosaic groups: D "small town diversity", E "active retirement", L "elderly needs" and M "industrial heritage". D and E are more affluent segments of older people who usually tend to vote Conservative. That is, they are the key "comfortable but culturally concerned" demographic of anti-migrant "public opinion" we looked at in Chapter 14.

L and M are older, white working class people, classic Labour targets – that is, the other key anti-migrant demographic we looked at. The absolute model of a UKIP switcher was "White, Male, Aged 47–66, Further education – not university educated, Mosaic Type 42 – 'Worn Out Workers', Lives in Yorkshire." In addition, Labour identified two other Mosaic categories – called J "claimant cultures" and I "ex-council communities" – of younger traditionally Labour voters who were also in danger of UKIP's lure.

These four Mosaic categories became Labour's main target publics in seats identified as UKIP threats. Campaigners were instructed to "listen to their concerns" and explain Labour's new hardline policies on immigration, then steer conversation onto "our key policies". In order not to alienate pro-migrant base voters, a tough line on immigration was not a major part of the "broadcast" message, but only flagged to specific target publics as part of the "ground war".

To sum up: Labour's campaigning effort in 2015 was largely directed at the particular demographics we discussed above in Chapter 14. The "public campaign" was not explicitly fought over immigration, but a large part of the "ground war" was fought over the hearts and minds of those target publics seen as most anti-migrant.

Labour's 2015 campaign was a notable failure – although, as it turned out, the main problem was not UKIP but the Tories hoovering up Lib Dem seats and the SNP decimating Labour in Scotland. And by the 2017 election, the UKIP bubble had burst, while Corbyn's Labour managed to make an unexpected comeback. The new tougher line on immigration stayed in the manifesto, which promised to outdo the Tories in hiring 500 extra border guards[478].

Summary

In fact we can see clear parallels between Conservative immigration policy in 2010-18 and Labour policy in 1997-2010. In both cases, it makes sense for the governing party not to explicitly flag immigration as an electoral campaign issue. There are obvious reasons:

- Whatever its rhetoric, no modern government is actually able to get immigration "under control" – certainly not to the satisfaction of anti-migrant media and "public opinion".

- Both governments are vulnerable to attacks from the right on immigration – recently, from UKIP in particular. This is because both parties have important target publics who fall into the key anti-migrant minorities. For the Tories, these are the "comfortable but culturally concerned". For Labour, excluded older white working class voters – those who the party rushed to try and win back with its "Blue Labour" turn.

- At the same time, neither party wishes to alienate its more "liberal" target publics by overplaying toughness against vulnerable migrants.

But governments can help to neutralise their perceived "failing" by taking action between elections. Although the government can't actually "control" immigration, it can use policy to make spectacular attacks on easy scape-goats. Under Labour, this meant a spiral of ever tougher asylum laws. Under the Conservatives, it came in the form of the hostile environment policy against "illegals". Attacks on these marginal groups won't scare off too many "liberal with a small l" voters, but can – the logic goes – be displayed as signs of toughness to help assuage anti-migrant defectors.

So to sum up: these policies are directed not at "the public" as a whole, but at particular "target publics" identified as key electoral demographics. Governments launch vicious attacks on scapegoat groups as a way of trying to appease these anxious minorities.

Looking tough: Home Office agendas

The more immigration is a salient election issue, the more immigration policies will be directed by the overriding logic of electioneering. But there are also other dimensions of immigration policy-making to consider. So long as they fit within the broader electoral baseline, Home Secretaries and their juniors also have scope to pursue their own agendas.

The Home Office is one of the senior ministries where politicians who distinguish themselves may go on to challenge for the prime minister's job. Theresa May is the latest example of this. Other recent party leaders who made their names as home secretaries or shadow home secretaries include Tony Blair and Michael Howard. None of them have done so by being "nice". Rather, the way to make your mark as home secretary is to introduce new policies showing you are tougher than the last.

In the last Labour period, there were six home secretaries: Jack Straw (1997-2001), David Blunkett (2001-4), Charles Clarke (2004-6), John Reid (2006-7), Jacqui Smith (2007-9) and Alan Johnson (2009-10). Four out of six (Straw, Blunkett, Clarke and Smith) introduced new "tough" immigration acts.

Blunkett, who particularly relished his "hard man" image, managed two. After Straw had presided over the rapid expansion of the detention and deportation machine, and other measures such as restricting trial by jury, Blunkett boasted of making his predecessor look like a "liberal". Both revelled in provoking outrage from those they labelled "woolly-minded Hampstead liberals"[479] or "airy fairy libertarians".[480] Legislation was just one part of the posturing. As Frances Webber writes, in the summer of 2002:

> Blunkett announced his plan for TV crews to film removals to deter asylum seekers, slammed a Lottery Fund grant to anti-deportation campaigners and had the Ahmadi family's sanctuary in a mosque destroyed by a battering ram. The Blunkett template of ruthlessness in the removal of asylum seekers has been followed by home secretaries ever since.[481]

Blunkett's successor Clarke didn't manage to play tough enough: his resignation was caused by the "foreign prisoners scandal" of people still being released after serving their sentences rather than deported. The authors of the book *Go Home* trace aspects of the current media-focused climate in the Home Office back to a communications strategy developed under the next home secretary, John Reid. They write:

> a rebranding of the UK borders was undertaken in 2006, so as to amplify the sense of a national border, via flags, insignia, uniforms and other symbols. Meanwhile, a communications strategy

aimed at getting more images of immigration raids into the media was launched [...] this included inviting journalists along to witness raids, so as to divert media attention to the physical 'toughness' of the border, and away from the rhetoric and perceived elitism of politicians.[482]

The best known fruit of this strategy was "UK Border Force", a Sky TV series sponsored by the Home Office, which ran in eighteen episodes from 2008.[483] It featured star narrators Timothy Spall and Bill Nighy over footage of stowaways being caught in lorries and raid squads breaking up weddings. The series ended in 2009, but the Home Office continues to sporadically run stunts "embedding" TV crews and other journalists in operations.

One useful research project on Home Office policy at the top is a 2014 PhD thesis by Lisa Thomas, which involved interviews with four Labour Home Secretaries about their policy-making and their relations with media.[484] Although the research focuses on terror rather than immigration policy, there is clear crossover. At the same time as the new asylum laws, these Home Secretaries also pushed through five major terrorism laws in 2000-2008.

In fact, we can see both sets of legislation as part of the same overall "security" agenda. Blunkett himself makes this clear in his interview, where he discusses the asylum scare and the Oldham race riots of summer 2001 as building a heightened sense of insecurity in the UK ahead of the 9/11 attacks later that year:

> Immigration, subliminal fear of rapid change, threat to the 'normal' way of living, the instability that that causes, obviously has implications as to how people receive messages about other aspects of security and of what's happening in the world. Coupled with the fact that we had just moved into an era of seven days a week, 24-hour news. We were also beginning to see people using the internet and mobile technology. All of those things came together at the same time.

Blunkett says he believed the Home Office had actually "got on top" of the asylum issue. However, a major concern was the "massive upsurge of the right across Europe". He says:

> Some of us had been arguing that we needed to be aware of this, and not panic or pander, but actually get a grip to the point where

people were secure in their minds that we knew that there was an issue to be addressed. Providing them with that reassurance was as much a part of the security, because it affected their psyche and the way that they saw things, as was the physical security.

In short, the big motivation of Home Office policy, on both asylum and terror, was to provide a show of reassurance through toughness, thus warding off threats from the right.

In fact this pattern goes back at least to Blair's own time as shadow home secretary in 1994-7. Blair made his reputation politicising the murder of two-year old Jamie Bulger, as part of positioning himself as a tough guy responding to public anxieties about crime. As he wrote later:

Very effectively I made it into a symbol of a Tory Britain in which, for all the efficiency that Thatcherism had achieved, the bonds of social and community well-being had been loosed, dangerously so.[485]

In short, home secretaries became a succession of tough guys taking up the cudgel against shadowy ranks of national bogeymen, where asylum-seekers, then terrorists, joined criminals and paedophiles. Theresa May followed the pattern set by Blair's boys. Thus Home Office positioning, as well as party electioneering, leads politicians towards "spectacular" anti-migrant policies.

Media and politicians: a dense ecosystem

The third crucial factor is the politicians' relationship with the media. If immigration policy is a spectacle, "big media" provides the stage where politicians can strut their stuff. But it also gives them the prompts – and sometimes even writes the whole script for them.

Probably the most blatant case of media-political collaboration in recent immigration policy is the 2003 "asylum week" case, exposed by political journalists Peter Oborne and Simon Walters. The Blair government knew in advance that the Sun was planning a week of attack stories against asylum-seekers in August 2003. An interview with David Blunkett was already scheduled ahead of the week, where he would announce "tough measures to crack down on asylum cheats".[486] It is not clear if Blair's and Murdoch's aids planned the whole campaign together as equal partners, or if The Sun presented it as a done deal. In either case, the government went along with the scheme – so guaranteeing stories for the journalists, and coverage for the politicians.

This example is just a tiny glimpse of how media and politicians work together to shape policy. To look further, we will draw on research by Aeron Davis in a 2007 book, *The Mediation of Power*.[487] This was based on interviews with 40 sitting MPs, plus also other ex-ministers and some political journalists.

Heavy exposure

Most politicians are "news junkies". According to Davis: "on average, MPs consumed four to five different news sources, including three newspapers, each day. Just over two-thirds listened to radio news and the same amount watched television news. A third used online news services." Many have 24 hour news constantly playing in their offices.

Aeron Davis asked politicians: "What are your main sources of information when it comes to informing yourself about, and deciding where you stand on, political issues?" He found: "news media was the second most mentioned source by all interviewees with four out of every seven listing it." It was most common source given by back-benchers, who don't have a staff of civil servants to brief them. To quote one interview, with Sadiq Khan, now mayor of London:

> Obviously the newspapers are very important to me. I read habitually […] and I try to keep up with what the latest thinking is. And then, if something's referred to, I'll go look up the original source […] So those daily and weekly newspapers and magazines signpost me where to go.

Media campaigns

Davis critiques a popular "stimulus-response" model of media influence – the idea that media raise an issue, then politicians jump. But this is not to say that it never happens. The most obvious cases of media influence are where several journalists, perhaps across several outlets, mount a concerted steam-rolling "campaign" to highlight an issue or call for a policy. Most MPs interviewed could "think of examples of when the weight of a media campaign had been responsible for initiating or altering new legislation and budgetary decisions". Immigration was one of the issues named here – alongside casinos, dangerous dogs, or funding for schools and hospitals.

But perhaps even more than issues, media campaigns are often directed at individual politicians themselves. "Several [of Davis' interviewees] also talked about media campaigns being the main driving force behind a ministerial resignation or sacking." On the other hand, ambitious politicians can get a considerable career boost if they can become favourites of journalists and outlets who highlight their actions, champion their policies, and laud them with gushing profiles. Blair's pact with the Murdoch press is the classic recent example, alongside the Daily Mail's promotion of Thatcher – and, less successfully, Theresa May.

Anticipation effect

A more subtle mechanism is what Davis calls an "anticipatory news media effect". That is, politicians take account of the likely reactions of media while shaping policies in the first place.

> Former government ministers and shadow ministers explained that discussions of policy were frequently linked to the issue of how the policy would play in the media. For many, in fact, this had bordered on media 'obsession'. Almost every interviewee who had served in a cabinet or shadow cabinet since the late 1980s, talked in such terms.

Ann Widdecombe, the 1999-2001 Conservative shadow home secretary who led on the asylum scare, says: "We never discussed a policy without discussing the media impact ever." Labour's Frank Field describes the Blair government as "obsessed" by media, saying: "The number one priority [in 1998–99] was the media coverage because at all costs we had to win a second time . . . Never mind about getting reforms." Former Conservative minister John Whittingdale similarly describes Tory leaders John Major and William Hague as media "obsessed". He explains:

> the concern was always how can we get coverage. And the only way you get coverage is by saying something new. And by saying something new you were having to announce something.

Former Labour minister Chris Smith similarly talks about a media-driven "'something must be done' syndrome". And Ann Widdecombe specifically talks about Conservative immigration policy in this way:

> Asylum was huge during our time [...] I don't think the media actually dictated policy but it did create an atmosphere in which it was felt something had to be addressed. Something had to be done about it.

Political go-betweens

Politicians exist in a viciously competitive micro-world, always wary of attacks from rivals – and keen to find ways to strike first. These rivals may be in their own party, as well as on "the other side". Big media provide the bulletin board, as it were, where politicians read about each other's actions and announcements – and get a sense of each other's plans and positionings. "A quarter of MPs also stated that news was a way of gauging what others, either in one's own party or in rival parties, were thinking on issues."

In addition, as Peter Van Aelst and Stefaan Walgrave argue, the media is not just an information source for politicians to keep track of "the debate", but also itself a primary arena where the game takes place.[488] Politicians use media to make both public announcements and more subtle signals – off the record comments, leaks, etc. Some of these are targeted at "the public", but much at the other players.

On the team

We might think of politicians and media as two separate "teams" of independent actors. But Davis' interviews show how the lines are much more blurred. First of all, politicians are in very regular contact with journalists.

> In all, just over two-thirds talked to journalists, on average, at least once a day, and usually several times a day. At busy periods some said they could have between 10 and 20 conversations with journalists in a single day.

Some MPs present the relationship as a close functional symbiosis: journalists need stories every day, politicians need to get their messages out. So politicians need to keep journalists close because, as Iain Duncan Smith puts it, "you want to be able to feed them with your information." Some of the MPs Davis interviewed go further.

> Many used terms like 'friend' or 'colleague' and would meet for social as well as professional reasons. Others referred to relationships as part of 'alliances' or 'coalitions'. In all these cases it seemed clear that journalists were very much part of the policy networks that evolved within parliament.

The political journalists interviewed were still more explicit on the nature of this relationship. For example, Guardian columnist Polly Toynbee says: "people are very keen to talk [to me] about policy when they're sitting there all day wondering how to make their particular department work better." The Telegraph and Daily Mail commentator Simon Heffer says: "People in the last Conservative administration [consulted me] all the time", adding "I had friends who were well known to be sympathetic to the Labour party, who were often consulted by Conservative ministers."

Politicians and political journalists occupy a shared micro-world based around Westminster. They work on the same issues, share information, share social environments. There is continual crossover between the two professions, and through the in-between category of "special advisors", press officers, PR gurus, etc.

Quid pro quo

Another possible form of media influence is not mentioned by Davis or his interviewees, and it would be hard to gauge its extent. As in other workplaces, gossip swirls in and around the Westminster bubble, and much information is widely known that doesn't get into print. Sometimes this may be for legal reasons, e.g. in the case of the numerous public figures with "super injunctions". Other times, it is due to editors upholding "gentlemen's agreements" – or purposefully holding back information in order to build and maintain the relationships on which Westminster thrives.

For example, in 2016 Davis' interviewee John Whittingdale was sacked as culture minister after his relationship with a sex-worker was exposed.[489] The story had previously been investigated by four newspapers, from The Sun to The Independent, but all held off publishing. The Hacked Off campaign group has alleged the newspapers withheld the story whilst Whittingdale was making media-friendly moves on press regulation.[490]

Conclusion: the media-political ecosystem

We have looked at three forces that shape politicians' moves on immigration.

- First, parties seek to win or keep "key voters" – and many of these are precisely the people who are most anxious about migration.

- Second, ambitious politicians, above all home secretaries, use tough anti-migrant posturing to build their reputations and careers.

- Third, politicians respond to – or anticipate, or indeed share – the anti-migrant lines pushed by popular media.

How do these three forces work together? One easy answer might be: politicians are so focused on media because they see it as representing their main concern, "public opinion". But this is unlikely to be the case. If politicians want to judge voter attitudes, they are more likely to turn to polls or focus groups. And in fact:

> Only three [of Davis' 40 interviewed MPs] believed news was an actual reflection of public opinion and looked to it for that purpose. Just under half, without prompting, described political coverage as overly 'trivial' and dominated by 'personalities' and the 'dramatic'.

And yet, despite that, media is a major driver of immigration policy. Here are some likely reasons why:

- First, politicians know that, while media don't "reflect" current public opinion, they do have power to shape people's future views. Most of all, they know that media have particular power over key target voters.

- But above all, media have power to mobilise their audiences' feelings around specific campaigns. These include attack campaigns that can destroy a politician's career – and positive campaigns that can raise a politician's profile. The media is the stage home secretaries play on when they pose as "tough guys".

- And it goes beyond strategy. Politicians are "news junkies" living in a media hothouse where all their thinking and feeling is framed by 24/7 media exposure. They work and socialise alongside editors and journalists, they speak the same language, share the same values. In short, politicians and media share a dense media-political ecosystem, where they feed off each other in spinning and weaving their stories.

However, there is still one other crucial form of political approval we need to look at. Politicians can't get anywhere without money, and this means the support of business.

A street in Calais

17. Corporate power

In the last two chapters we have looked at two important types of actors who shape the Border Regime: media and politicians. Now we need to look at another powerful group: capitalists. Corporations and other business interests have massive power to shape immigration policies through their control of wealth.

We often don't see this power directly, as it is typically wielded behind the scenes by influencing other actors. In particular, we can think about a number of routes through which business influences the media and politicians.

Business influence on media

(1) *Ownership and finance.* Most media outlets are directly owned by profit-making businesses – whether families, or institutional investment funds managed by the big finance houses. And even non-profit making trusts like the one that owns the Guardian still rely on financial markets for commercial deals, or loans and other forms of credit.[491]

(2) *Advertising.* All media are dependent on advertising sales. Explicit or implicit threats or offers over advertising have tremendous power to shape media coverage.

(3) *Making stories.* Businesses, their PR departments and agencies, and the think tanks, institutes, universities, associations and other bodies they set up or sponsor, are themselves major sources of news and ideas pumped into the media.

(4) *"Flak".* Businesses closely monitor coverage and can respond with legal and other threats to reporting they see as harming their interests. In this way business can have an "anticipatory" influence on media, similar to that of media on politicians discussed above.

(5) *Shared culture.* Media owners, editors and senior journalists are part of the same elite circles as business and political bosses, and will be likely to share the same world-views. More junior journalists may aspire to get there.

The seminal reference on how capital shapes media coverage, which studies these points and more, remains Edward S. Herman and Noam Chomsky's book *Manufacturing Consent*.[492] The points we have just noted correspond to what they call the "five filters" of editorial bias.

Business influence on politicians

(1) **Funding.** Politicians depend on business for donations and loans, without which they cannot run election campaigns.

(2) **Kickbacks and revolving doors.** Most politicians supplement their incomes with extra jobs as "consultants", etc.; or go on to well-paying corporate jobs after their political careers end. This is without taking into account personal gifts, zero interest loans, and other legal or less legal payments that standardly flow from business elites to ambitious politicians.

(3) **Lobbying.** In return, business is given continual access to politicians, at the least being "consulted" on proposed policies. This involves both official recorded "lobbying" meetings and more informal wining and dining. Lobbying may be carried out directly by business leaders, or through specialist proxies such as think-tanks they fund. (For much more on how this works see *A Quiet Word* by Tamasin Cave and Andy Rowell; and a summary in "Your guide to corporate lobbying" by Spinwatch.[493])

(4) **Shared culture.** From the "old boys networks" of the British establishment past, to today's global gangster capitalism, business leaders and politicians share alliances and friendships, ambitions and values, as they mingle in the same elite circles.

Much of capital's influence on our attitudes goes through the two channels of politics and media. But business elites also make other interventions into our "ecologies of ideas": for example, through the advertising that immerses us everywhere; by sponsoring large parts of education systems; and by funding think tanks, charities, and many other organisations that we interact with every day.

Do capitalists use these channels of influence to promote ideas about immigration? If so, what ideas – do business interests align or conflict here? And how are they using different channels? In this chapter we'll just outline a few introductory thoughts.

Supporting the status quo

Wealthy elites are also human beings with a range of values and attitudes. A few are outright fascists or psychopaths. A few consider themselves progressives and donate portions of their money to good causes, including helping migrants. A few want to overturn governments or economies because they see profit in it, or because they enjoy the thrill of great power. But probably most wealthy people, and perhaps even more so most large corporations and financial institutions, have a more "middle of the road" conservative position. Their main political interest is stability: a reasonably well-functioning state and legal system propping up a growing economy.

By far the bulk of political donations in the UK go to the two main parties, and within them to "centrist" politicians more than "extremists" of either left or right. For example, in 2015 UKIP found a few notable rich backers such as Arron Banks – but still only managed to raise £5.8 million, compared to the Conservatives' £41.9 million, or Labour's (largely union-funded) £51.2 million.[494] *(NB: you can search through all official donations and loans to parties and candidates registered on the Electoral Commission website.[495])*

On the whole, business leaders are happy with things as they are, the free market capitalist status quo. Very few would question the basic pillars of the current system, which include the nation-state, national identity, and the state's claim to control borders and "manage migration".

Business demand for labour

But within those limits, big business in the UK is broadly "pro-immigration". That is, unlike the majority of the "British public", they favour reduced immigration controls. They want to be able to hire workers with minimal cost or bureaucratic meddling, and they believe significant numbers of these workers need to come from abroad. At the same time, they have no problem with attacks on "low value" migrant scapegoats such as asylum seekers or "illegals"

This is clear to see in recent government consultation on a post-Brexit immigration system. The UK business establishment has a number of main lobbying alliances which help represent it to politicians. All of these submitted position papers to the consultation, and all take effectively the same line.

The Institute of Directors (IoD) proposes a 12 point plan which includes scrapping the "ill-advised net migration target" altogether, significantly loosening work visa controls, and completely unrestricted access for foreign students.[496] Public hostility should be appeased with increased state support for integration measures such as the "Migration Impact Fund". The Institute agrees with the hostile environment approach, so long as this targets "illegals" rather than useful workers. However, they complain about business being expected to do police work for free, and instead call for increased funding of Immigration Enforcement.

The Confederation of British Industry (CBI)'s submission[497] includes setting out four "Business priorities for a new migration system".[498]

> Clear priorities emerged when we asked businesses what they wanted to see from a future migration system. Access to labour to fill labour shortages, a system that is responsive to economic need and access to skilled workers topped the list [...] both labour and skills migration is required by business.

And the CBI makes clear this is "not just a skills issue". With the unemployment rate in the UK at an 11 year low, many industries are struggling to recruit low wage "unskilled" workers too:

> some areas of the labour market, such as the care sector, horticulture and construction are struggling to find and retain the volume of workers to fill current vacancies. The care sector is facing a shortfall of 200,000 workers by the end of this Parliament, while a survey conducted by the National Farmers Union indicated that employers in the horticulture sector were already facing a labour shortage that employers anticipate worsening by 2018.

The other key area is foreign students, with the CBI also complaining about government moves in recent years to limit numbers. "The UK university sector is a critical sector for national prosperity. The value of international students to the UK is estimated to be £7bn, supporting over 130,000 jobs."

The CBI recognises public hostility to immigration, but suggests politicians can help overcoming this by dropping the headline emphasis on net migration levels.

Perhaps the clearest statement of all comes from London First, a lobby group representing big City banks and other London-centred businesses. Its "Immigration Proposal" advocates a number of liberalising measures including: seasonal and short-term work visas for unskilled labour; lower salary thresholds for "skilled" migrant visas; students counted as "visitors" rather than migrants; and "unrestricted entry" for "exceptional talent". But the same document also calls for "robust enforcement to clampdown on illegal activity, overstaying and low value migration".[499]

To sum up, the main business lobbies have a clear and united message on migration. They disapprove of post-Blair moves to cut overall numbers, and want the net migration target to go. They want easier entry for economically valuable migrants. But they have no problems with a "clampdown" on "low value" migrants – although they don't want to pay for it themselves.

Profiting from illegality?

Those business lobby statements all present Immigration Enforcement as a necessary tool to appease "public opinion". But is there also a business case for chasing illegals?

First of all, there are some businesses who directly gain from the existence of a two tier workforce in which some workers' wages are pushed down by what Shahram Khosravi calls the "illegal discount".[500] However, these are not the big corporations who wield media-political power. Big corporations do widely use "illegal" labour, but only through chains of contracts and sub-contracts that keep their hands "clean". As we saw in Chapter 6 looking at workplace raids, undocumented office cleaners or factory hands will be directly employed by gangmasters or fly-by-night agencies well down the chain – and these have little political clout.

Do the much more powerful ultimate employers gain from the existence of a second-tier illegal workforce? No doubt. But we expect such gains are not significant in the scale of these corporates' accounts, and probably do not play a major role in decisions about immigration lobbying.

In short, what these bosses are aware of is that their need for relatively open labour marks runs against public hostility. For them, again, Immigration Enforcement is a necessary spectacle. So long as it only bothers "low value" migrants, it makes no real business difference either way.

Goods flows

There are some more specific business segments whose profits are directly bound up with border control. One is the transport industry. For example, as we saw in Chapter 9, Eurotunnel[501], the Boulogne-Calais Port company[502], and freight industry[503] alliances have all pushed the recent escalation of security at the UK-France border.

For transport business, immigration control presents a certain dilemma. On the one hand, their whole business is based on goods containers flowing fast and with minimal interruption. They are not interested in free movement of humans, only of goods – but it isn't easy to keep the two separate. Every security check holds up traffic and so costs money. The ideal solution would be fully open borders, or at least minimum controls.

On the other hand, companies of course know that they don't exist in a borderless world. If humans are being blocked, this blockage should be as effective as possible – while interfering as little as possible with the flow of transport. In Calais, transport businesses lobbied for ever tougher measures to build fences, station police, and clear migrant camps, and for government funding of private security.

Border profiteers

Another group of businesses directly profit by winning contracts to provide security guards, run the detention centres, sell the drones, tear gas and x-ray scanners, maintain ID databases, etc. There is no doubt that these "border profiteers" have gained substantially from the escalation of anti-migrant policies. But have they actually influenced these policies?

Firstly, this interest group is considerably smaller than the general business interest in labour migration. While the industry is growing, it doesn't compare with the use of migrant labour by finance, agriculture, construction, education and other major industries.

However, as we have been arguing, immigration control isn't about "controlling" the overall flows of immigrants at all, but at making spectacles of control directed at small scapegoat groups. In this context, the two interests are not at odds. There is no reason why corporations can't profit both ways: from a cheap migrant labour supply overall; and from helping target a few scapegoats in particular. In fact, this is exactly what we see where companies like G4S, Mitie or Serco win contracts to lock up "illegal" migrants in detention – then hire other migrants to work as their guards.

One clear example of – unsuccessful – pro-detention contractor lobbying involves the charity Barnardo's. In 2016, the government closed down Cedars, its small detention centre for families with children, as the family units were "under-used". Barnardo's lobbied MPs for Cedar's to be kept open, including issuing a report arguing that Cedars was "an example of good practice" which "should not be lost".[504]

There are more signs of contractor influence in EU border policy – particularly around the militarised responses to the "refugee crisis". The 2016 report "Border Wars" by Mark Akkerman documented the scale of the industry being built to securitise "Fortress Europe", including the role of major arms companies who see this as a valuable new market.[505] Akkerman argues that these corporations are also pro-active in shaping the EU-wide political agenda:

> The arms and security industry helps shape European border security policy through lobbying, through its regular interactions with EU's border institutions and through its shaping of research policy. The European Organisation for Security (EOS), which includes Thales, Finmecannica and Airbus has been most active in lobbying for increased border security. Many of its proposals, such as its push to set up a cross European border security agency have eventually ended up as policy   see for example the transformation of Frontex into the European Border and Coastguard Agency (EBCG).

It would certainly be worth further research on how companies try to shape profit opportunities in UK border control. And on how this may increase as the hostile environment escalates, creating lucrative openings for newer profiteers such as data and technology corporations.

Media barons

As we noted in the last section, some of the UK's most influential media outlets actively campaign for anti-migrant policies. Why do the media barons push these positions against other business interests – and perhaps even against their own personal views, as may be the case for Murdoch himself? In the last section, we argued that media barons may gain not only in audience, but also in political leverage, by adopting sensationalist and populist positions. And again, if the resulting policies are limited to affect just "low value" scapegoats, there is not too much threat to broader business interests.

Agitators

While many Big Business leaders are "pro-immigration", this is certainly not true of all. Although some rely on migrant labour, others have very different business models. And business leaders are not driven only by the profit motive: some may be strongly anti-migrant out of personal conviction. Just as there are multi-millionaires who give their money to liberal causes, there are others who use their wealth and power to back the right. Notable recent examples include the so-called "bad boys of Brexit", such as high-profile businessman and referendum funder Arron Banks, or UKIP-backing hedge fund manager Crispin Odey.[506] We will look at the role of the "populist" voices they back in the next section.

Summary

Overall, Big Business is "pro immigration" – in the limited sense of desiring minimal bureaucratic interference with their ability to import labour. This is clearly evident in lobbying reports from major business associations such as the CBI, IoD, or London First. Some business sectors clearly profit from immigration controls – including those using discounted "illegal" labour, as well as Border Profiteers who provide the staff and infrastructure to harass migrants. But these are minority interests.

At the same time, Big Business is well aware of "public hostility" to free movement. It thus happily encourages politicians to launch spectacular attacks on "low value" scapegoat groups. These attacks are profitable for some corporations, and don't hurt the major labour flows relied on by many others.

18. **Agitators**

> Nearly all western thought since the last war, certainly all 'progressive' thought, has assumed tacitly that human beings desire nothing beyond ease, security and avoidance of pain. [ ] Hitler, because in his own joyless mind he feels it with exceptional strength, knows that human beings don't only want comfort, safety, short working-hours, hygiene, birth-control and, in general, common sense; they also, at least intermittently, want struggle and self-sacrifice, not to mention drums, flags and loyalty-parades.

George Orwell, introduction to Hitler's *Mein Kampf*, 1940

In the last three chapters we looked at important "mainstream" actors – big parties, big press, big business behind them. But we've also kept bumping into a cast of smaller players with more extreme anti-migrant views. Sometimes these punch above their weight in terms of power to influence immigration politics.

We will look at two main kinds of "agitators" who promote and spread more extreme views. The first are political parties, from the National Front to UKIP. The second are propaganda outlets which don't compete for votes themselves, but produce and spread ideas. Under this category we include right-wing think tanks such as Migration Watch, and "new media" platforms such as Breitbart. In the UK, however, the loudest demagogues are housed in the bosom of the "mainstream" press.

Far-right parties and mainstreaming

Over decades of UK politics, anti-migrant policies have often begun as fringe positions, before becoming widely adopted by centrist politicians.

We saw one famous case back in Chapter 1. In 1968, after Conservative minister Enoch Powell made his infamous "rivers of blood speech", he was condemned by the party leadership and thrown out of the shadow cabinet. Ten years on in 1978, Conservative leader Margaret Thatcher's "swamping" interview brought similar rhetoric into the centre of political debate.

Here we have a classic example of what writers such as Aristotle Kallis[507] and Paul Stocker[508] call the "mainstreaming" of ideas initially pushed by the far-right. Or as Steve Cohen put it, in his book of that title, the British government *"Standing on the Shoulders of Fascism"*.[509]

What had happened between 1968 and 1978 was the rise of the fascist National Front, with growing electoral successes in the early 1970s as well as a notable street presence. After Thatcher's Conservative leadership victory in 1975, the party adopted much more open anti-migrant policies. Soon after the "swamping" interview, the Conservatives jumped to a poll lead over Labour, and won the 1979 election with a landslide. The NF vote share collapsed to 1.3% (from 3.4% in 1974), and the party became an irrelevance.[510]

In 2002, Labour home secretary David Blunkett was the one talking of "swamping" – this time by asylum-seekers.[511] As we've seen, Labour's asylum clampdown was tied closely to media campaigns. But the growth of the NF's successor, the far-right British National Party, was another intertwined factor. Daniel Trilling documents how all main parties, including the Labour government, adopted BNP language and positioning in the early 2000s, after the BNP capitalised on the 2001 race riots with local election successes.[512]

Labour's line of response was set at a meeting a month after the May 2002 local elections, according to Nigel Copsey and David Renton, where senior strategists including pollster Philip Gould warned Blair that thousands of "angry young working-class men" could switch to the BNP.[513] Further warning signs came from the success of Jörg Haider's Freedom Party in Austria, and the continuing rise of the Front National in France. Trilling writes:

> New Labour was in thrall to triangulation, the strategy which had helped the party defeat the Conservatives by occupying the political space normally held by the right, pushing them further away from the centre. What would it mean to "occupy" the space held by fascists? [ ] This time, Gould advised, the party should embrace voters' concerns on immigration and asylum.

The BNP's electoral challenge peaked in 2009, when it won nearly one million votes in European elections. That same year, Gordon Brown was campaigning on "British jobs for British workers"[514] – a slogan that can be traced back to Oswald Moseley in 1937.[515]

However, BNP support collapsed shortly after, until within a few years it was no longer even registered as a political party. Major infighting certainly played a part – notably after the leak of its membership list in 2008.[516] But perhaps he main reason for its decline was mass switching of support to UKIP: in 2014, Nigel Farage proclaimed proudly that his party had taken a third of BNP votes.[517] Less partisan research confirms substantial overlap between UKIP and BNP support bases.[518] UKIP managed to pick up much of the BNP's anxious "white working class" demographic, whilst also adding a more middle class Daily Mail-reader segment the BNP couldn't reach.

Maybe the ultimate example of "mainstreaming" is the Brexit referendum itself. In 1997, multi-millionaire James Goldsmith's Referendum Party[519] was a laughing stock; in 2015, UKIP picked up 3.9 million votes. More significantly, it had pushed the Conservative Party into adopting its landmark policy as an election pledge, leading to the referendum vote. Meanwhile, as internet commenters have pointed out, much of Teresa May's 2017 Conservative manifesto seems to have been lifted point-by-point from the BNP's in 2005.[520]

Of course, not all far-right policies become "mainstreamed". What explains why some are? Here are three factors to consider:

Electoral strategy

When centrist parties start to feel that extremists represent a threat at the polls, they may adopt versions of their policies in order to "neutralise" the threat – reducing the challenger's "differentiation". We looked at how this works in Chapter 16. For example, Labour's line on immigration in the 2015 election had much to do with trying to neutralise the UKIP threat. This doesn't have to mean the challenger threatens to actually win seats – just that they could "split the vote". So even a small party threatening to win, say, 10% of the vote in certain key marginal seats, can be a significant danger and require neutralisation.

Threat of unrest

Another possible factor pushing mainstream parties, particularly those in government, is fear of unrest on the streets. The National Front in the 1970s combined an electoral programme and street mobilisation, with a strategy involving mass demonstrations often held in inner city areas then at the frontline of demographic change. These demonstrations deliberately provoked clashes and riots, which helped create media hysteria. Similarly in the early 2000s, BNP organisers both politically positioned themselves around, and sought to instigate, street unrest in areas such as Oldham and Burnley. In the 2010s, far-right street mobilisation was roused again by the English Defence League.

Throughout history, riot and insurrection – or the threat of them – have been paramount causes of political and social change. Although the UK is one of the world's least unruly places, even now politicians can still panic at the thought of unrest – as, e.g. Gordon Brown when considered "troops on the streets" following the 2008 financial collapse.[521] Have governments reacted not only to the threat of losing votes, but also to the possibility of riots escalating into "race war"? We haven't seen evidence of this, but wouldn't write off the idea out of hand.

Media amplification

Finally, there is a long tradition in the UK of mainstream media picking up ideas from the far-right. We will look more at this below.

Culture shift: hate preachers and think-tanks

Far-right political parties are not the only actors pushing extreme anti-migrant views. They also come from propagandists unattached to electoral or "street" parties. A few notable types are listed below.

Think tanks

In the US, there is a legion of well-funded think tanks and "institutes" dedicated to developing and spreading anti-migration arguments. In the UK, while a number of generalist right-wing think tanks occasionally work on migration, there is one pre-eminent player: Migration Watch.[522] This is a small research outfit founded in 2001 by Lord (Andrew) Green of Deddington, a former ambassador to Saudi Arabia, and eugenicist professor David Coleman.[523] It has strong parliamentary connections, managing an outfit called the "Cross Party Group on Balanced Migration", which unites mainly Tory and DUP right-wing MPs with a few "blue Labour" fellow travellers.[524] It also regularly has one-on-one meetings to discuss migration with Home Office ministers.[525] It presents itself as "independent", and publishes regular reports about the damaging effects of migration, which are widely quoted and used by media and politicians.

Right-wing media platforms

Fascist magazines and websites come and go. More recently, a new generation of "alt right" and "alt light" platforms is spreading from across the Atlantic. Breitbart UK is one of the most notable.

Individual commentators

An assortment of rabid right shock jocks and scribblers have made their name ranting against migrants and other hate figures. Many of these have homes within the mainstream right-wing media, rather than "alt" outlets – until they go too far and may have to relocate, as with the sackings of Katie Hopkins.[526]

How do these agitators disseminate their ideas? We can think about a number of channels.

Local distribution

The traditional methods of distributing local leaflets and news-sheets, as well as posters, graffiti, or actually talking to people, have not altogether died. These communication methods reach only reach small audiences: but they may be dense "ecologies of ideas", and ones which are particularly susceptible. For example, targeted far-right local propaganda in towns like Oldham was important in building anti-migrant attitudes there in the early 2000s, before national media paid attention.

Web networks

Dedicated "keyboard warriors" may reach well beyond their local areas on internet forums, social media, blogs, etc. More sophisticated outfits can spread ideas widely through internet channels. Often the challenge is to break out of segregated "bubbles" of web users who are already largely on side. Money certainly helps, e.g. by buying social media rankings. Internet propaganda may reach different, often younger, audiences than printed speech. The internet is increasingly the primary channel for the new waves of "alt right"-style propaganda.

Mass media

But for the moment, the main channel remains mainstream media. In the UK, to a greater degree than some other European countries, there is a close symbiosis between far-right agitators and major media outfits.

As discussed in Chapter 15, Big Media generally support "centre right" establishment parties, and the bulk of their political outlooks do not stray from mainstream neoliberalism. None of them, yet, openly embraces fascism. But, particularly on immigration, they help broadcast extreme right views and hate speech. They do this in a number of different ways, depending on the types of sources:

- **Identified fascists:** condemned but given a platform.

These days recognised fascists are condemned in the UK, even by the right wing press. For example, one well-known Sun headline called the BNP "Bloody Nasty People". But this doesn't stop them being given extensive coverage, their views quoted and discussed. Right wing campaigning media will typically argue that, while fascism is a historical throwback, not all their views on immigration are so wrong.

More liberal media may abhor their views: but still, they need to be "listened to" because they express "genuine" popular feeling. The BBC first invited[527] Nick Griffin on the Today programme in 2001 to talk about the Oldham riots, and in 2009 he made a highly controversial Question Time appearance.[528] After 2010, UKIP became a regular feature on the show.[529] Although UKIP share many policies and much rhetoric with the BNP, they do not have the baggage of a fascist past, and so are treated as a small mainstream party.

- **"Unaligned" hate preachers:** given free rein.

People like Hopkins and Littlejohn are given leading column space and air time in right wing media. Their views are more extreme than their media outlets' general lines, but are printed unredacted. While their statements on migration are often indistinguishable from those made by recognised fascist groups, they can be presented as "unaligned" voices of "common sense", or as part of "mainstream conservatism".

- **Think tanks and academics:** treated as independent sources.

Think tanks are usually presented as respectable information sources, without discussion of their political agendas or financial backers. Migration Watch's self-description as "independent and non-political" is taken at face value. After all, it is headed by a Lord with numerous well-connected establishment patrons – and is also known for threatening law suits against anyone linking it to fascism. The Mirror apologised and paid damages[530] in 2007 for comparing Lord Green to the Nazi Party and the Ku Klux Klan.[531]

Research compiled on the "powerbase" website shows that by December 2017 Migration Watch had been directly cited in 2365 newspaper articles.[532] In some cases, articles are simple cut and paste jobs from Migration Watch press releases.[533]

More than half of citations were in the Mail and Sunday Mail, the Express group papers, or the Murdoch press. But the think tank is also a regular go-to source for the BBC, with Lord Green making numerous appearances on Newsnight and other programmes.[534] BBC reports equally tend to present the group simply as "the think tank Migration Watch". As Ian Dunt writes:

> The relationship between Migration Watch and the press is basically that of a conveyor belt. They release an alarming report about how many migrants are coming to the UK, or how much they cost UK taxpayers, and the press treats it like some respectable piece of academic research.[535]

Conclusion: shifting the window

In the UK, there is currently not too much risk of far-right forces taking state power. This does not mean they don't present other dangers. Above all, right-wing agitators play a key role in pushing other more "mainstream" actors towards ever more hostile positions.

Andrew Breitbart, founder of the Breitbart News Network, is credited with a key slogan of today's alt-right: "politics is downstream of culture".[536] Culture comes first: ideas, stories, values, beliefs and ways of life, developed and spread through textbooks, movies, songs, rumours, trends, internet "memes", and every other kind of human communication. Politics, in the narrower sense of politicians competing for state power through elections or other means, always follows behind. The implication is that if you can shift culture, you shift politics.

This point chimes particularly well in the world of newsfeeds and social media. Previously, culture was something slow moving and intangible. Now culture wars unfold in speeded-up real time, as hashtags trend, memes evolve, and users are herded to rally and attack on social media platforms.

But of course there is nothing new in the basic idea. For example, we can see a similar pattern in the think tanks and research institutes that championed neoliberal economics. "Alt right" propagandists such as Breitbart's successor

Steve Bannon boast of having prepared the cultural ground for Trump's political victory. Similarly, the likes of Milton Friedman or the UK's Institute for Economic Affairs (IEA) cleared the way for the ultra-free market policies of Reagan and Thatcher. As Richard Cockett documents in the book *Thinking the Unthinkable*, that "anti-collectivist counter-revolution" involved almost fifty years of committed propaganda and lobbying before it paid off in government.[537] In the internet age, today's right wing propagandists probably expect faster returns.

One popular formulation of this idea is the Overton Window, named after Joseph Overton of US free market think tank the Mackinac Center.[538] There are many possible policies – for example, everything from "no borders" to "shoot all migrants on sight". But only a certain "window" of these are "politically acceptable options". As Mackinac's Joseph Lehman explains, the window "is primarily defined [...] by what [politicians] believe they can support and still win re-election."[539] And this is not defined by politicians themselves, but by what Breitbart would call culture.

> Many believe that politicians move the window, but that's actually rare. In our understanding, politicians typically don't determine what is politically acceptable; more often they react to it and validate it. Generally speaking, policy change follows political change, which itself follows social change.

The role of a think tank, then, is to "shift the window":

> Since commonly held ideas, attitudes and presumptions frame what is politically possible and create the "window," a change in the opinions held by politicians and the people in general will shift it. Move the window of what is politically possible and those policies previously impractical can become the next great popular and legislative rage.

Or as Friedman himself wrote back in 1982:

> That, I believe, is our basic function: to develop alternatives to existing policies, to keep them alive and available until the politically impossible becomes politically inevitable.[540]

But just how do you shift the window? Here it may be worth making some comparisons between yesterday's think tank neoliberals and today's online alt-right.

- **Commitment.** They may start out small, but they have passion and dedication, they keep at it. Unlike many mainstream politicians, people like Friedman or Breitbart may actually believe in the ideas they preach.

- **Beyond organisation.** Neither neoliberals nor the alt-right have much loyalty to particular parties or other organisations. It is about power – but in terms of often unseen influence rather than winning formal positions.

- **Resonance.** There are audiences, if only small at first, with whom their ideas will resonate. They chime with people's existing hopes, fears, needs, identities.

- **Funding.** They have rich backers: both think tanks and big websites need funds.

- **Connections.** They may present themselves as outsiders going up against "liberal elites", but in fact are well connected to establishment figures.

- **Amplification.** They thrive when mainstream media "amplifies" their messages, giving them coverage and attention – even if this coverage is negatively labelled.

- **Channels.** Here we may see a bigger difference between old and new models. The think tanks' target audience was largely mainstream media and political elites. The alt-right, at least in part, takes a different tack, because the internet gives it new communication channels.

Alt-right propaganda has found ways to bypass big media and spread ideas directly into different ecosystems. This does not mean that it can't also thrive off mainstream media attention. But it has succeeded in reaching whole new audiences beyond the older white people who form the traditional "target publics" – including young people, and others largely turned off mainstream media and politics.

This threatens to transform the landscape of immigration media-politics. Looking at recent developments in other European countries such as Hungary or Italy, we can see how charismatic right-wing agitators have pushed immigration to the top of the political agenda. In the UK, currently only around 20% of the population see immigration as an important issue. But this could certainly get worse if anti-migrant propaganda manages to connect with whole new audiences.

19. **Anxiety engine**

In the last few chapters we looked at some of the main actors involved in spreading anti-migrant propaganda. In this chapter we want to look a bit at the nature of this propaganda itself. There is a basic pattern to much of the hate speech pushed by media, politicians, and far-right agitators. Perhaps it has always been there, but it has accelerated in the last twenty years or so: politics based on *anxiety*.

The nature of anxiety

In the UK and other rich post-industrial countries, anxiety is a disease of our time. In NHS England's mental health surveys, "generalised anxiety disorder" is now the most common mental health diagnosis.[541] Anxiety is where the "fight or flight" mechanism, our basic mind-body response to danger, gets stuck in "on" mode. Muscles are tensed to hit or run, blood pumps fast, senses and thoughts scan the environment for threats – but there is no action, no clash, and the tension is not released. Fear becomes a constant background.

Trying to explain this sense of peril, the anxious mind seeks out and invents threats. But as each worry is disproved, another one replaces it. Addressing particular imaginary worries doesn't remove the anxiety, and may even feed it.

The world we live in thrives off and feeds our anxiety. Consumer capitalism fuels anxiety as the motor of economic growth: keep working, keep buying, keep distracting, because you are ugly, empty, unsuccessful, never good enough. Twenty-first century city and internet life plugs us into a 24/7 drip-feed of social pressure and surveillance.

Anxiety media-politics

The economic power of anxiety was well recognised by advertisers at the start of the 20th century.[542] At the end of the 20th century, its political power came to the fore. In the UK, Tony Blair was the modern master of anxiety politics: learning lessons from Thatcher and other predecessors, and in a close dance with the media, above all Rupert Murdoch. The asylum scare was one strand in this approach, alongside manipulating panic over the Jamie Bulger case or creating fictions of "weapons of mass destruction" and the "war on terror".

This is the basic pattern:

- First, media outlets broadcast threat-stories: tales of terrorist cells, hooded youth gangs, rampaging asylum seekers, virus pandemics, etc. These stories both arouse anxiety and direct it onto particular targets.

- Second, politicians promote measures to regain "control". Clampdowns, wars, tough new laws, police or soldiers on the street, extended surveillance, etc. These may be in direct response to demands from media campaigns.

The control measures rarely achieve their goals. It is not actually possible for governments to stop immigration. CCTV cameras don't stop assaults and murders. "Anti-terror" repression of local communities, or bombing campaigns abroad, only sow more anger.

The clampdown measures are not real solutions, but spectacles, displays of control. The issue returns, and the next Home Secretary will introduce a new even tougher clampdown. If one issue goes away – e.g. we haven't had a virus pandemic scare for a while – others will take their place. Control measures don't resolve but escalate the sense of threat.

Anxious target publics

Anxiety politics targets many different people, playing on our different recurring areas of anxiety. There are threat stories for old people scared of youth crimes, parents scared for their children, workers scared for their jobs, families anxious about getting a house, everyone scared about their health.

Immigration anxiety is particularly intense in the two broad demographic groupings we identified in Chapter 14 as media-politicians' main anti-migrant *target publics*. In terms of economic position, these two demographics are very different. People in one group have much more material "reason" to be anxious, while those in the other are "comfortably off".

But what unites many people in these two groups is more a sense of cultural identity, of a world made meaningful in terms of tradition, nation, language, race. And a sense that this identity and meaning is under threat.

Shows and stories

Anxiety media politics feeds and directs anxiety. This is not "evidence based" policy-making, it is story-telling.

Effective right-wing propagandists, whether working from the radical fringes or the mainstream, understand this. As conservative campaign guru Lynton Crosby puts it, effective politics involves telling "a story about yourself, a simple story that defines what you're trying to achieve":

> I don't think people vote for policies [...] but they do vote for what policies say about a candidate or a party and their values and their beliefs, and whether they are in touch with what matters to you and relate to the life you lead or the hopes you have for your life.[543]

Your hopes – or your fears. In any case, the point is "making an emotional connection with people". Crosby often quotes the US political strategist Drew Weston: "in politics when reason and emotion collide, emotion invariably wins". As he expands in an interview at the Oxford Union: "ultimately it's what your policies say about your values and your beliefs, because it's emotion that makes the motivating connection with people."[544]

In anxiety politics, two key kinds of stories come to the fore: first, stories about threats; second, stories about tough measures to re-establish control. Again, it is not important that either the threats or the responses are "real", just that there is some *show* of response to display toughness.

And the two kinds of stories can combine, so forming the "populist" right-wing narratives getting so much attention. For example, as Sun editor Tony Gallagher puts it in a New York Times interview, Brexit "was about a combination of migration, sovereignty under the broad umbrella of taking back control, and a sense that, as a country, we were no longer able to control our destiny." Migrants and trans-national forces threaten "our country", "our destiny", our home and place of meaning.[545] Absent a strong leader to take back control, even buffoonish ones like Farage, Johnson or Trump will have to do.

How can we counter anxiety stories?

We can sum up a few key points from the last five chapters.

- Tough immigration policies are not really about controlling immigration. They are just poses, spectacles of control.

- Tough immigration policies are not aimed at "public opinion" as a whole. There is no such thing as one "general public", or as one "public debate" on migration. Anti-migrant policies aim to appease quite specific target publics who have high anxiety about migration. As we saw in Chapter 14, currently these only make up about 20% of the population. Although we have no reason for complacency here: the numbers of people worrying about migration could certainly rise, as it is doing rapidly in other European countries.

- Immigration media-politics doesn't work with facts and arguments. It is about arousing anxiety and telling stories.

This is not a debate, it is a propaganda war. So what does that mean for people who want to fight the propaganda of the border regime?

Sharing a jacket in the rain

NO ONE IS ILLEGAL

Part Four:
How can we fight it?

NO ONE IS ILLEGAL

20. Fighting the border regime

Every moment of every day, people are fighting the border regime: crossing borders, resisting raids, organising inside detention centres, stopping deportations, supporting each other with networks of mutual aid. As we have seen, despite decades of escalating attacks on migrants, including the recent hostile environment measures, the state is far from being able to actually stop people moving.

Yet there's no denying we're up against a strong tide. The fear and hatred is rising, in the UK as across Europe. The scapegoating of migrants by media and politicians is only likely to increase, as capitalist elites seek to direct anger away from the root causes of economic, social and ecological crises.

Throughout this book we have looked at examples of different ways people fight back. In this concluding part, we pull these examples together, and ask why some have been more successful than others. We're not trying to dictate what anyone should do. But we think it's vital to open conversations and share ideas. The following thoughts are just a small contribution to that.

Who's fighting?

First, who do we mean when we talk about "people fighting the border regime"? Most obviously, the thousands of people trying to evade it. For many people migrating, the basic aim is: get across, get "status", or survive under the radar. That is: win basic freedoms from the border regime's control, for myself and my loved ones.

You could call this an individual-centred goal. But, very often, the best way to pursue our individual goals is to join with others. The examples through this book show how solidarity is everywhere vital to fighting the border regime. This includes joining together for large-scale collective actions such as mass border crossings or detention revolts. And also creating networks, meeting points, and other shared resources that are essential for supporting individual struggles.

Very often, undocumented migrants have to fight alone. But many powerful examples involve people with and without papers acting together.

We don't want to downplay the tremendous courage and resourcefulness of so many undocumented people, but we think really pushing back the border regime must involve getting many more citizens to stand alongside migrants. We will return to this point below.

Many ways to fight

That struggle takes many different forms. These are just a few:

Evasion. Bypassing or avoiding controls. Crossing borders without being noticed, avoiding being fingerprinted and registered on databases, managing to live "under the radar". Sometimes escapes, quiet sabotage. These activities are, for obvious reasons, often little known outside of close communities and networks. But it is important to remember that so much of the struggle is largely unseen.

Getting through with dignity. The border regime traps hundreds of thousands of people in a maze of bureaucracy and uncertainty, including the "limbo" of reporting and asylum dispersal. Just getting through the labyrinth is itself an achievement. Is this also "fighting the border regime"? In one sense, the system actually relies on a proportion of people winning "status". But on another level: the system also works by isolating and grinding people down. Just maintaining dignity and solidarity can itself be a victory against the border regime.

Confrontation. Other times, struggle breaks into the open, as people stand up and refuse to be controlled. For example, the mass crossings at Calais, neighbourhoods chasing off raids, resistance in detention from protests and hunger strikes to full-on revolts. Often, people find strength in numbers. But people also confront the system alone – for example, the countless successful cases of individuals resisting being dragged onto deportation flights.

Support networks. For all forms of struggle, solidarity is a vital force. Individual and collective actions are made a thousand times easier by networks of mutual aid. These may involve resource centres, alarm systems, "underground railroads", detainee support groups, meeting places and ways to share information and contacts, safe houses and refuges, however formally or informally organised. Organising these resources is crucial to all aspects of the fight.

Legal action. Court cases are a common part of life for individuals caught in the immigration system. For example, as we saw in Chapter 3, the Home Office's basic attitude to asylum claims is to refuse people then "let a tribunal sort it out." Court challenges also set precedents that collectively affect thousands. Some important recent rulings have stopped: charter flights to Sri Lanka and Afghanistan (see Chapter 8), the Detained Fast Track system that automatically detained people from certain nationalities before processing their asylum claims (in 2015), and the round-up of East European rough sleepers (in 2017).[546]

Targeting partners. Some campaigns have focused on breaking relationships between the Home Office and its partners, including contractors or foreign governments. For example, the International Federation of Iraqi Refugees succeeded in getting the Iraqi government to end its charter flight agreement. There have also been some successes getting airlines to stop flying deportees: Virgin Airways was a recent case in 2018.

Spreading ideas. In Part 3 of the book, we looked at how the border regime is maintained by consent from large parts of the population – and at how this consent is maintained through propaganda. Another crucial form of struggle is fighting anti-migrant propaganda, and spreading different visions of solidarity and resistance.

Finally, we note that struggles against the border regime may involve both "direct" and "indirect" action:

- Direct action is where people act directly for themselves to break controls. For example, crossing a border without asking anyone's permission, or standing together with neighbours to chase off raids.

- Indirect action involves asking other more powerful actors to intervene on your behalf. Legal action is probably the most common form of "indirect" struggle against the border regime: here the powerful actors are judges, and the legal system in general. Other examples include trying to persuade companies to pull out of contracts, or politicians to change Home Office policies.

However, the lines are often blurred, and the two very often go together. For example, in the Calais collective crossings in 2015-16, people marched to the fences calling on the authorities to "Open the Borders" – and also cut the wires to open the borders themselves.

The problem of migration politics

We left out one other common form of action from the list above, because we want to discuss it in more detail now. This is political campaigning – that is, action directed at politicians, to try to get them to change their policies.

Political campaigning may involve lobbying politicians directly: writing to or visiting them, sending petitions, organising demos or publicity stunts to get their attention. It can also work through media campaigning. As we saw in Chapter 15, many politicians are very focused on media coverage, and so one way to move politicians may be to raise the profile of an issue in the media.

Political campaigning can work at multiple levels. At an individual level, there are many successful cases of people getting local MPs or councillors to support their immigration cases, help get bail from detention, or stop their deportations. At a local or regional level, a good example is the recent campaign which blocked the opening of a new Short Term Holding Facility in Scotland, discussed in Chapter 7. (Although, an unintended consequence was that the government kept Dungavel detention centre open instead.) Also in Scotland, at the time of writing political campaigning has helped hold off the eviction of 300 people being evicted from Serco housing (see Chapter 5).

At the national level, perhaps the most significant recent example is the government pausing several hostile environment policies following the Windrush media scandal (see Chapter 10). But here's the thing: this is actually a very rare example of UK politicians backing down on national immigration policy. And, so far, all we have seen are small retreats. The rhetoric has been softened, but the main thrust of the hostile environment approach very much continues.

On the whole, we would argue, the most effective struggles against the border regime have worked on a grassroots level, far from the political stage of elections, lobbying, and big media. Politicians and media have an obvious interest in persuading us that political campaigning is the main way to get change – after all, their power and jobs depend on it. But we think it is important to question this attitude.

Political leverage

To think about this point further, we should ask: what makes politicians change their policies? Looking through the examples in this book, we can't see any where politicians dropped tough immigration policies because they woke up one morning and decided to be nice. To quote the anti-slavery campaigner Frederick Douglass: "Power concedes nothing without a demand. It never has and it never will." Any concessions are "born of earnest struggle".[547]

In Chapter 16, we looked in depth at what does influence politicians' thinking. Most commonly, politicians shift when they feel: (a) an issue could win or lose them important voters; or (b) media coverage could damage or boost their personal reputations and careers.

On both points, pro-migrant political campaigning in the UK faces serious problems. First, migrant issues are rarely important with voters. Think of different groups that might matter to politicians:

- *Undocumented migrants:* as they can't themselves vote, their views count for little.

- *Pro-migrant voters:* are few in number, and are rarely election "targets". Although, as discussed in Chapter 16, the need to keep "small l liberal" voters has so far served to stop main parties lurching even further to the right.

- *Anti-migrant voters:* the anxious anti-migrant minority, somewhere around 20% of the population, have proved important as target voters, and carry disproportionate weight.

- *The majority in between:* for most voters, migrants' welfare is rarely a main political issue affecting how they vote.

Second, the major media outlets, which significantly shape politicians' attitudes and responses, themselves pursue anti-migrant agendas (see Chapter 17). Pro-migrant campaigns typically only win coverage in liberal or left-wing media, which generally have less sway on politicians.

These two reasons largely explain why standard approaches based on raising issues with media and politicians have not had so much impact on UK migration politics. The situation can be different locally, if areas have their own political and media dynamics – as perhaps in Scotland. But at the UK level, for 50 years and more, politicians have moved relentlessly towards increasing xenophobia and control.

We are not saying this political slide is unstoppable. Just that lobbying politicians may not be the best place to focus energy if we want to stop it.

The limits of the border regime

So what does work? Let's start with a general observation. Very often, victories come when people's actions find *weak points* in the border regime – points where it is pushed against its limits. To give an obvious example, people crossing borders may find spots where fences are weaker, where there are no lights or cameras, where the guards aren't looking. But we can also think about less visible kinds of limits, including political and cultural factors.

Operational limits. The resources regime actors currently have for their work: officials and contract staff, vehicles, fences, weapons, surveillance equipment and other kit, computer systems for managing information, etc. Often, the border regime is beaten because it doesn't have its people and equipment in the right place at the right time. It can't search every lorry, it can't send out police back-up on every raid. Understanding the limits of its forces, and how it allocates them, is a basic first step for many forms of resistance.

Institutional limits. Control also depends on the ability of Home Office and private units to organise, plan, communicate, and carry out orders. For example, we have seen how the Home Office and its contractors are plagued by rivalry, bullying, and low morale.

This can be a crucial point for understanding many struggles: the wages, skills and training levels of ICE raid squads, G4S detention guards, or Mitie deportation escorts, are far lower than, for example, police officers or experienced state prison guards. This is a major reason why, for example, ICE raid squads often "tactically retreat" when people stand up to them (see Chapter 6), or why so many people are able to resist deportation attempts (Chapter 8). These enforcers often rely on calling in police back-up if they experience serious resistance, and police only have limited resources and will to help them.

Financial limits. Operational limits are closely tied to financial limits. On its current squeezed budgets, the Home Office can't afford to hire and train more staff, build more detention centres, or get decent computer systems up and running. Institutional limits, too, can be money related: e.g., low wages and overtime bans aren't great for morale.

Relationship limits. Regime actors are often reliant on other partners: for example, foreign governments, contractors, other government agencies who share information or coordinate operations, or "community leaders" who give information or help calm tensions. The need to maintain these relationships will impose limits on what they can do.

Legal limits. Officials and contractors continually flout the law – but there are limits. For example, raid squads are happy smashing in doors without warrants, but are cautious about using physical force when there are citizen witnesses around.

The law is never fixed in stone. As barrister Frances Webber writes in *Border-line Justice*:

> The law is intensely dynamic and as far from the Mosaic stone tablets as it is possible to be – constantly fought over, in flux, pulled this way and that by conservatives and progressives in the courts and in the increasingly vocal struggle between the executive and judicial branches of government, and sometimes the legislature too.[548]

Operational units generally follow internal Home Office guidelines written with government lawyers. But these are just their interpretation of the law: for example, almost all the rules around raids have never been tested in courts. Legal challenges can successfully end abuses of law and force the Home Office to back down on its interpretations. Webber's book recounts numerous examples of this.

That said, legal action certainly isn't always the solution. Many challenges fail. Many drag on for years before winning rulings that are ignored, draining people's money and their spirits. Very many immigration lawyers are crooks preying on the unfortunate. And, of course, the law itself can always be changed. Indeed, quite a few anti-migrant laws have been brought in by politicians responding to court judgements they see as undermining their power.

Political limits. Home Office orders ultimately come from politicians. Politicians' agendas shape the operational, institutional, financial, relational, and legal limits on the border regime in many ways.

- Politicians introduce new policies where they see a chance to score votes or boost their careers, or in response to media campaigns.

- Most of the time, politicians leave operational control to managers. But these managers will always have an eye on avoiding media scandals which could get the politicians involved. This vigilance effectively sets limits to both "right" and "left". On the one hand, bosses try to minimise the regular tabloid scandals about foreign criminals, asylum cheats, etc. On the other, they will watch out for the danger of more occasional "humanitarian" scandals like Windrush or Brook House.

- Political agendas set budgets. The current squeeze comes, first, from the overall "austerity" drive that has dominated UK politics since the 2008 crash. Secondly, from competition between government departments and within the Home Office. For example, police funding is politically more important than immigration budgets.

- Politicians make laws. In the long run, legal limits are set and changed by politics.

Culture limits. But, as we suggested above, politicians are not the ultimate decision-makers. Political agendas are themselves limited by the views of the millions of people whose support politicians need.

In Chapter 18 we looked at the idea of the "Overton window": "the window of what is politically possible", which "is primarily defined [...] by what [politicians] believe they can support and still win re-election." Politicians themselves only play a small part in creating this window. It is made of "commonly held ideas, attitudes and presumptions" shaped by millions of people. As Breitbart put it, "politics is downstream of culture".

In a nutshell: politicians change their views to chase voters and media coverage. Ultimately, if you want to shift politics, you need to shift the bigger "window" of people's views that underlies it.

Finally, we should note that cultural limits don't only shape the world of politics. For example, the judges who decide tribunal cases, the managers who make daily operational decisions, right down to the guards on the ground, are also acting within cultural "windows" too.

Growing the struggle: from weak points to openings

Rather than relying on politicians, we could look to grow and spread resistance from the "bottom up". This means communicating, sharing examples, stories and ideas, and so learning from each other. But perhaps most of all, it involves encouraging and inspiring each other through action.

Here's just one idea that may help think about this. We have talked about identifying *weak points* in the border regime. The next step is to take action against those weak points, to turn them into *openings*. An opening means: an immediate victory where people manage to break through the regime's control; but which also has the potential to grow and spread.

For example, here are three kinds of openings you can often see in border struggles – and struggles against other systems of control too:

- *Lines of freedom*. Crossing routes, "underground railroads", networks of solidarity and safe passage helping people move freely across and within the territory.

- *Spaces of freedom*. Areas where the regime's control has broken down – at least, to some degree – allowing self-organisation to flourish. A safe house or place of sanctuary, self-organised jungles and squats in Calais, a school or hospital that refuses to enact hostile environment measures, a neighbourhood where raids are not welcome. Meeting places, hubs where people get to know each other, share ideas and make new plans.

- *Moments of freedom*. Temporary collapses and power cuts of the system, strikes, prison rebellions, bursts of revolt.

An opening is a place or time where the regime's control is overcome, or at least substantially weakened. It is still only a limited victory, relatively small or local. But it can become the start of something bigger.

Think of a tear in a fabric. Every tear starts as a small hole. It may get quickly patched up and closed. Or it may widen, linking up with other tears, until the whole fabric comes apart.

Any action can have many effects and repercussions, both immediate and long-term, both positive and negative. The question is: overall, does this help to weaken the border regime and empower people resisting it?

What determines whether an opening spreads or gets closed down? Basically, this depends on how three types of people respond. First, friends and allies, meaning people who already support the struggle: are they inspired to join in, or to take action in their own ways? Second, how do enemies react? Third, what about the many "bystanders" who are not committed to either side? Will this action push them against us, or encourage them to join the struggle?

Friends and allies: inspiring each other

One way that an opening can grow is when people rally to join in or support it. We saw many examples of this in the border struggles of the last few years. A new crossing route or resource centre opens, word spreads, and people come. In 2015-16, migrants came to Calais and other border flashpoints forming a critical mass to cross, while hundreds of citizens joined the call for solidarity (See Chapter 9).

Another way is when people copy and adapt the opening, making a new one elsewhere. In 2015-16, new occupations and crossings proliferated along the European refugee routes. (It is also significant that a fair number of people involved had earlier taken part in the uprisings of the Arab Spring, and brought that revolutionary energy and experience with them). In various periods, protests, hunger strikes, and revolts have rolled across detention centres (see Chapter 8). Resistance to raids appeared to "go viral" across London in 2016 (Chapter 6).

What factors make an opening more likely to grow and spread? Here are three:

- *Success:* people see it as a victory, it helps them advance their needs and visions.

- *Accessible, replicable:* it is easy to join or repeat.

For example, probably one reason raid resistance spread so rapidly is that it is very easy for people to get involved. Raids happen right where we live and work, and you can take effective action without any special training, equipment or planning.

- *Communication:* however successful and replicable, an action won't spread if no one knows about it.

Sharing news of an action may be just as important as the action itself. But who are we talking to, and using what channels? For example, the most important channels in migration struggles are often not mainstream media, but low profile networks working through word of mouth or social media, and through different languages and communities.

A final point: although we talk about spreading and growing, it isn't all about numbers. The more general aim must be: to increase our power as people fighting the regime. This can also mean growing the confidence, courage, and initiative of individuals and groups already involved.

A struggle that makes its participants exhausted and bitter will not thrive. A key question is: do our actions empower us – help us feel stronger, able to carry on and push further? Do they spark new ideas, bring us together with friends and comrades, feed our passion?

This is another reason why it may help to think about actions that are accessible. For example, legal battles can play important roles in winning ground and breathing space, as well as helping individuals' cases. But it can be disempowering if we come to depend on them too much, and get used to seeing ourselves as passive "clients" reliant on trained professionals to act for us. Similarly, relying on elected politicians, rather than taking direct action for ourselves, can be a recipe for long-term disillusion.

Know the enemy: reaction patterns

Any successful action may provoke a reaction from the border regime's actors. One important part of understanding the enemy is identifying its capacities and limits. Another is understanding how it thinks – particularly, how it is likely to respond to our victories.

We can see a few basic patterns playing out time and again. Here are three big ones: retreat, repression, and reform. We will illustrate them with the example of the 2002 Yarl's Wood revolt and its aftermath (see Chapter 8).

Retreat. The fire of 14 February 2002 destroyed one half of the new Yarl's Wood complex, over 400 detention places. The destroyed wings were never rebuilt, and Yarl's Wood remains at less than half its original intended capacity. One obvious factor was simply cost: the damage was estimated at over £40 million, and rebuilding would have been a heavy bite out of Home Office budgets. But also, the political agenda had shifted and Jack Straw's rush to expand detention places no longer seemed urgent. Here, perhaps, two common motives for retreat combined: on the one hand, lack of capacity; on the other, recovering the lost ground was just not a priority.

Repression. Yet, like any gang boss, state authorities hate to think someone can beat them and get away with it. Even while retreating they may make a symbolic show of authority, for example punishing scapegoated "ring leaders". In Yarl's Wood, and in fact most detention or raids resistance trials we know of, the legal repression was bungled and most of the defendants were eventually acquitted – although after spending months on remand. We should also highlight the solidarity campaign that sustained them. The danger of repression, from the state's perspective, is that if it doesn't succeed in terrifying people, it may fire them up even more.

Reform. The authorities give up some ground, but also use this concession as an opportunity to divide resistance. Those who accept the concession are good, cooperative subjects. Those who carry on fighting for more are troublemakers. As the troublemakers are now fewer in number, it is easier to isolate and target them.

This is a core strategy of state authorities throughout history. Stephen Shaw's official report after the Yarl's Wood revolt gives a very clear account of the thinking. Shaw argued that detention centres needed to make various reforms, learning from the main prison system. In particular, he praised the "dynamic security" theory promoted by a reforming prison governor called Ian Dunbar. As Shaw summarises, this is based on three principles: "individualism, relationship and activity". In essence:

- 1) *Individualism.* Prisoners should be encouraged to engage with the system as individuals, including through incentives rewarding good behaviour, rather than being left to form a collective identity.

- 2) *Relationship.* Prison guards should form "friendly" relationships with prisoners, winning their trust. They can then encourage them to separate from troublemakers and pursue personal improvement. "Sensible" prisoners with privileges can also play a similar mentoring function.

- 3) *Activity.* Prisoners should be kept motivated and busy with work. Writing in 2004, Shaw complained that immigration detention centres didn't use work as a way of keeping detainees busy and rewarding them because the minimum wage still applied to them – unlike in other prisons. The law on this was later changed, and detainee labour (usually paid at £1 per hour) is now common.

We could list many more cases of such divide-and-rule reformism. For example, in the Calais Jungle in 2016, the French government sought to persuade people to disperse from the camp without using extreme force while the cameras were rolling. Again, it started with individual incentives: promising people that their asylum cases would be treated quickly if they agreed to register and be scattered on buses to "welcome centres" around France. (These promises were then widely broken.)

Because people didn't trust the state's promises, two kinds of proxies were used to spread the message: "community leaders", who were migrants (often business owners) offered privileges inside the camp; and workers from state-funded NGOs. These could also help to identify and spread slanders against people deemed "trouble makers" – rebellious migrants, or citizens in the camp who refused to register as official NGO volunteers. Racial and religious divisions were also mobilised: e.g., Syrians vs. others, "white" Middle Easterners vs. black Africans, Christians vs. Muslims, where one group were seen as "genuine" refugees and the other as "bogus" claimants causing trouble. Pretty much identical techniques were used at other border flashpoints such as Lesbos, Idomeni, and Piraeus in Greece.

We can also see similar patterns at work, for example, in the asylum dispersal system (see Chapter 5), or when Immigration Enforcement works with religious and community leaders (Chapter 8). Or, indeed, in the basic structure of the immigration categories that sort people into citizens vs. migrants (Chapter 3).

To sum up, this is perhaps the number one strategy of the border regime wherever it sees rising resistance:

- push hope in individual incentives against collective action;

- promote "good" leaders to support this message;

- isolate, slander and punish those who continue to rebel.

Breaking open the window

As we have seen throughout this book, the border regime relies on the tacit consent of millions of "bystanders". Grassroots action against the border regime is crucial, and has to be the basis for any movement that can grow the power to really push back the border regime. But we won't really turn the tide until we can connect with many more people whose passive support allows the system to function.

Migrants cannot win this struggle alone. Standing alone, migrants – and particularly people without papers – are easily isolated. First, they are made invisible as non-voters, non-citizens, non-people. Next, they are targeted with levels of violence the state cannot regularly use against citizens.

To move forward the fight against the border regime, people with and without papers need to create new relations of solidarity. The border regime works by dividing us into identity categories: citizen vs. migrant, legal vs. illegal, resident vs. new arrival, etc. The citizen is meant to stand by quietly while the migrant is targeted. When we refuse to be defined as citizens vs. migrants, and become instead friends, neighbours, workers, *people*, the fight is on.

This can't just mean citizens acting *in sympathy* with migrants. In 2015-16, the European "refugee crisis" prompted a response from many thousands of citizens, ranging from donating old clothes to joining in clashes at the frontiers. But it was short lived. As the images left the news screens, the aid faded too. Compassion is soon fatigued and can sour into resentment. The repression left hundreds of migrants forgotten in European prisons, and thousands more in the new Libyan concentration camps, while attention moved on to the next cause.

Sympathy cannot sustain an ongoing movement of struggle. Solidarity has to mean not just a desire to help someone else, but the sense that our lives, our needs and battles, are bound together. That we share "one common struggle."[549] This means seeing the border regime not just as a threat to other people. Rather, it is part of an interconnected system of control, domination and exploitation that attacks all our lives.

Here we run up against a ceaseless propaganda machine. For well over a century, the "popular press", and its newer media descendants, have done their work attacking and undermining solidarity movements by spreading racism, nationalism, and other forms of fear and division. We are up against enemies with far greater resources, including state institutions, mass media corporations, or newer "alt-right" platforms bankrolled by multi-millionaires.

How can we take them on? This is a big question not just for migrants' struggles, but for all the battles we face today. We'll end with just a few last discussion points.

1. The most powerful propaganda is lived experience.

Of all the success stories we have seen, some of the most powerful involve people with and without papers joining together in our streets, workplaces, and neighbourhoods. For example, refugees and unemployed young locals creating and defending social spaces together in Calais (see Chapter 9). Market traders and passers-by of all backgrounds fighting off raids together on the streets of London (Chapter 6). Tower block residents together stopping dawn raids in Glasgow (Chapter 5).

In these examples, people are united across identities by a shared need or project. Often, this means the experience of facing a common enemy. Migrants and white kids living in certain neighbourhoods of Calais are both continually hassled by the police. In London areas like Elephant & Castle, Whitechapel, or Deptford, anti-migrant raids are closely tied to gentrification and the "social cleansing" of all working class people. Though of course people also come together through more positive projects, building shared spaces and communities.

In these examples, the direct experience of fighting together beats the abstract categories of identity. I get to know my neighbour as a living person, with needs and dreams that may overlap with mine, not as just a label. The experience of practical solidarity in Calais or London can beat a thousand news stories or Youtube videos.

2. Finding new channels.

But you can't connect with everyone face to face, and there's also a need to spread ideas through mass communication channels. One question here is: exactly who are you trying to reach, and how can you reach them?

Most pro-migrant propaganda reaches small, and already friendly, audiences. Some reaches migrant communities themselves. Some tries to get positive messages into the liberal media and social media spheres. Little ever reaches the anxious "target publics" that the politicians are talking to (see Chapters 14 and 15), let alone the more excluded populations the "alt-right" are starting to reach through newer internet channels (Chapter 18).

Not long ago, many people were optimistic that the internet could help break the dominance of state and corporate media, bypassing their control to make information freer, more "democratised". It is indeed worrying that the "alt-right" has, in the last few years, proved so successful in colonising internet channels, spreading hate and fear instead. The truth is, of course, money and power still matter in cyberspace too.

But the internet infowars are not over – they're only just beginning. We have to keep learning and developing ways to reach people.

3. Finding new stories.

Supposing we can reach people, what do we say? One common approach in pro-migrant propaganda is to make factual arguments: for example, debunking dodgy statistics, or showing that migrants actually benefit the economy and welfare state. This is often ineffective. For one thing, because, to quote Lynton Crosby one last time, "in politics when reason and emotion collide, emotion invariably wins" (see Chapter 19). Anxiety isn't beaten with facts.

Another common strand in pro-migration rhetoric does use emotion, making appeals to sympathy. As we argued above, this isn't enough either.

We need to find visions, stories, that show clearly how our struggles are bound together, whether we're migrants or citizens. To break the grip of bad ideas, such as the myths of racial and national identity, we need to put forward others that are more powerful, more vivid. They can't just be abstractions and hollow slogans, but must relate clearly to our own lives today.

Perhaps this could involve giving old ideas of class struggle and internationalism new life and meaning – but then that has go beyond just mouthing the same old slogans. Or perhaps we need to find new stories altogether.

Where will powerful ideas come from? Not from theorising in an ivory tower or chatting in a social media bubble. But in the midst of life and struggle. The only way is to get active, talk to each other, and listen too, make connections, keep an open mind, and develop our ideas as we do it.

Annex 1.
Border profiteers:
list of major Home Office immigration contracts

This is far from a complete list of larger (generally, over £1 million in value) contracts.

One easy way to find basic contract information is to check the UK government's ContractsFinder website, or the EU's TED database.[550] Searching either for "Home Office" will give numerous results. The Home Office is legally obliged to publish contract tender and award notices on these sites. But note that award notices are often published only long after the contracts were signed.

The actual contracts are sometimes published in a heavily redacted form. Contract information can also be requested by Freedom Of Information requests. However, the Home Office will generally try to withhold as much as possible using the argument of "commercial confidentiality".

1. Detention Centres

Management contracts[551]

Heathrow IRC: Harmondsworth and Colnbrook

Contracted to **Mitie**, September 2014-22. Total value at award: £240m.

Previous contractors (Harmondsworth): Securicor (now G4S), 1970-1988; Group 4 / GSL (now G4S), 1988-1999; Burns International, 1999-2001; Sodexo (under name "UK Detention Services UKDS", later rebranded "Kalyx"), 2001–2009; GEO, 2009-14.

Previous contractors (Colnbrook): Serco
(originally under name "Premier Detention Services PDS"), 2004-14.

Campsfield

Contracted to **Mitie**, May 2011-19. Total value at award: £42 million.
Value per year: £5.25 million.

Previous contractors: Group 4 / GSL (now G4S), 1993–2006; GEO, 2006–2011.

Gatwick: Brook House

Contracted to **G4S**, 2009-18; now extended to 2020.
Total value at award: £90.4 million. Value per year: £10m.

Previous contracts: this is still the original contract.

Gatwick: Tinsley House

Contracted to **G4S**, May 2009-18; now extended to 2020.
Total value at award: £43.6 million. Value per year: £4.8 million.

Previous contractors: Wackenhut / GSL / G4S: 1996 – 2009.

Yarl's Wood

Contracted to **Serco**, 2015-23. Total value at award: £69.9 million. Value per year: £8.7 million.

Previous contractors: Group 4 / GSL (G4S) 2001-2008; Serco 2007-2015.

Dungavel

Contracted to **GEO**, 2011-19. Total value at award: £45.2 million.
Value per year: £5.65 million.

Previous contractors: PDS (Serco) 2001 – 2006; G4S 2006 – 2011.

Morton Hall

Run by Her Majesty's Prison Service (HMPS).

Short Term Holding Facilities

Mitie – as part of Deportation Escorting contract, see below.

Other services in detention

Yarl's Wood

Healthcare: contracted to **G4S** by NHS England in 2013, "provisional expiry date" August 2019. Annual contract fee is £1.2 million per year.[552]

2. Deportations

Deportation escorts (security guards)

Mitie. 2018-2028. Value at award: £514 million.[553]

Previous contractors: G4S, 2005-11; Reliance (renamed Tascor when bought by Capita in 2012), 2011-2018.

Travel Services

Carlson Wagonlit. 2018-25 (including 2 years extension period). Value at award: £5.7 million. (NB. Estimated cost of tickets, plane charters, etc., administered under the contract is £200 million over 7 years.)[554]

Previous contractors: Carlson Wagonlit, 2004-2010; Carlson Wagonlit, 2010-2018.

Charter Airlines

NB. Airlines are sub-contracted by the Travel Services contractor and their names are not published officially. The following are well evidenced in eye-witness accounts:

Titan Airways

Coaches

NB. Like airlines these are sub-contracted by the Travel Services contractor and their names are not published officially. The following are well evidenced in eyewitness accounts:

WH Tours

Hallmark Coaches

Medical services

IPRS Aeromed. Contract paramedics service for charter flights.[555]

Previous contractors: Armatus, 2011-16.[556]

3. Housing and support

A new round of Asylum Housing contracts are currently being tendered. These will start in September 2019, lasting 7 years until 2026, and have an estimated total value of £600 million.[557] At the time of writing the contract winners had not yet been announced.

The current contracts for 2012-2019, called COMPASS (Commercial and Operational Managers Procuring Asylum Support Services), are held by three companies:

- **G4S:** North East England, Yorkshire and the Humber (£391 million); Midlands and East of England (£374 million).

- **Serco:** Scotland and Northern Ireland (£221 million); North West England (£425 million).

- **Clearsprings Group:** Wales and South West England (£170 million); London and South East England (£119 million).

Redacted versions of the contracts, with the estimated values at award, are available at the Government's "Contracts Finder archive" website.[558] These main COMPASS contractors also employ numerous sub-contractors. These include:

G4S: **Live Management Group Ltd, Target Housing Association, UHS Ltd, Mantel Estates Ltd, Jomast, Cascade.**[559]

Serco: **Orchard and Shipman** (manages contracts with multiple private landlords).[560]

4. Border Force

Calais port security

Eamus Cork Solutions (ECS). Provides 40 "authorised search officers", three of whom are also trained as "detainee custody officers", to assist with Border Force controls and detention in the ports of Calais, Dunkerque and Coquelles. 2017-2020, with two one-year extension clauses. Value at award: £26.8 million. [561]

Calais search dog services

Wagtail. 2014-20. Value at award: £9.3 million.[562]

NB: for other Calais security, fencing, etc., contracts see Chapter 9.

Healthcare in Border Force custody suite

Castlerock Recruitment Group Ltd. 2017-20. Value not disclosed.[563]

5. **Data gathering and IT**

Home Office Biometrics (HOB)

Currently being tendered: major 10 year £308 million contract for new biometrics systems integrating police and immigration enforcement fingerprint, DNA, and other databases. The contract will run March 2019-29.[564]

Some parts of the system development have already been contracted:

Identity E2E Ltd (Sevenoaks, Kent). "Technical architecture services for the Home Office Biometrics programme". January 2017-19. £4.9 million.[565]

Immigration Enforcement fingerprint scanners – software/support

Airwave Solutions Ltd. January 2018 – 2020. Value £1.3 million.[566]

Digital Services at the Border (DSAB): developing new border control software systems

Capgemini. £2.3 million "DevOps" development contract, initially six months February-July 2018 but with option for further 6 months extension until February 2019 (valued at another £2.3 million.)[567]

"Border Crossing": development of new border watch-list systems

Capgemini. A one year £350,000 March 2018-19 contract awarded to Capgemini as "solution architect".[568]

Records management

Iron Mountain (UK) Ltd. Document storage and archiving services. 2012-27. Value £63 million.[569]

General Home Office IT contracts

Accenture. Metis: new "back office" system for Enterprise Resource Planning (ERP), "Business Intelligence", payroll, and more. August 2017 – July 2019. £10.2 million.[570]

Alpine Resourcing Limited (London EC1). "Technical and functional cloud services". July 2017-November 2018. £1.9 million.[571]

6. Other

Tagging and satellite tracking of "foreign national offenders" (FNOs)

Currently being tendered. October 2019-24. £50-70 million.[572]

Recruitment

Previous contractor: **Manpower**. "To provide recruitment services for the Home Office." June 2016-18. Value £1.7 million.[573]

UKVI new visa application system

Sopra Steria. Development of a new "digital visa and immigration service" for people to re-apply for visas within the UK, with ability to apply at 60 locations across the UK including 56 local libraries. October 2018 – ?. £91 million.[574]

Annex 2.
Border profiteers:
company mini-profiles

G4S

G4S is one of the world's biggest security companies, active in over 90 countries. And it's one of the world's biggest employers of any kind, with around 570,000 staff. Most of its business is in providing guards and security tech to corporate clients. It has a nearly endless list of scandals.[575]

Business basics

The head office is in Crawley, not far from Gatwick Airport. There are three main divisions:

- "Secure Solutions": human security guards, security technology, war zone mercenaries, and "facilities management" which integrates security with other management and maintenance contracting.

- "Cash Solutions": cash transport vans and related technology. It is active in 42 countries and makes up 14% of the company's core revenue.

- "Care and Justice": a sub-division of Secure Solutions operating just in the UK, Australia, New Zealand and South Africa. It runs prisons, immigration detention centres, police stations, and some other government services including UK asylum housing.

Globally, the company has 150,000 customers and 55,000 suppliers. 80% of customers are in the private sector, particularly big corporations and banks. The biggest customer is Bank of America. Only around 5% of G4S's business now comes from the UK government. In 2017 G4S exited from some unprofitable and controversial business lines, including UK children's homes and youth detention.

Finances. Total revenue in 2017 was £7.4 billion. Profit after tax was £236 million, showing a reasonable profit rate for a major company. Most sales come from the "developed markets" of the US and Europe. However, the "emerging markets" employ the majority of G4S's staff: 31% of workers are in the Middle East and India alone.

History. G4S's roots are in Scandinavia, going back to 1901. It has expanded by buying up businesses in the UK, US, and elsewhere. The current name was adopted in 2006 after the merger of Group 4 and Securicor.

Investors. G4S is a Public Limited Company (PLC) with its shares listed on the London Stock Exchange. Like most other big PLCs, the bulk of its shares are owned by big global "institutional investors" including pension funds.

Bosses. G4S's current directors are a grey bunch. There are no ex-politicians on the board, and members are mainly from the world of European corporates and finance. Chief Executive Ashley Almanza (appointed 2013) is a South African accountant connected to the oil and gas industry. He was paid £3.85 million in 2017, down on £4.79 million the year before.

Outlook and strategies. Global security is a boom industry. As the world becomes a more hostile and dangerous place, and with growing inequality and ecological collapse, corporations, states and the rich have a growing demand for security guards. G4S sees growth everywhere, but notes "Asia-Pacific" as particularly promising. It sees the best prospects in "sophisticated security technology", and "integrated products" which combine tech with "manned security".

Detention and prison profiteer: G4S Care and Justice

The "Care and Justice" division locks people up in UK, Australia, New Zealand and South Africa. It makes up 7% of G4S' total revenues. Care and Justice also takes on other government contracts related to managing imprisoned and vulnerable people, e.g. asylum housing and electronic tagging.

In August 2018, the UK government ended G4S's contract to run Birmingham Prison, after a succession of scandals, deaths, and riots. This had been the only example of a formerly public sector prison transferred into private management.

Following that loss, the current UK contracts include: four HMP prisons; Gatwick detention centres (Brook House and Tinsley House); a separate contract to run the Tinsley House family unit where children are detained; detention healthcare contracts; the two COMPASS asylum housing contracts (Yorkshire, Humberside and the North East; Midlands and East of England); electronic tagging contracts; police support and police station management contracts.

G4S Care and Justice (South Africa) has a 25 year deal to run Mangaung maximum security prison. Opened in 2001, G4S describes Mangaung as "the second largest private prison in the world", with nearly 3000 inmates. Others call it "a private hell".

G4S Care and Justice (Australia and New Zealand) runs three Australian prisons, plus tagging and police support services in the two countries. It previously ran Australia's notorious Manus Island offshore immigration detention centre – but exited this contract swiftly in 2014 after horrific mistreatment was exposed, including one G4S guard being convicted of murder.

The detention and prisons part of the business is extremely profitable. According to the Financial Times, these "contracts earn margins of more than 15 per cent, higher than for more mundane guarding." Our analysis shows profit rates in detention centre contracts are often over 20% (See Chapter 7). On the other hand, G4S has been losing substantial money on the COMPASS contracts (See Chapter 5).

Conflict zones

In 2017, G4S sold its main Israeli business, which had been heavily involved in prisons and the occupied territories, for £88 million. However it still retains a 25% stake in the central Israel police training facility, called Policity. In fact its most recent Annual Report stills list three Israel subsidiaries: G4S Israel PPP Ltd; G4S international Logistics (Israel); and Policity Ltd (25%).

G4S bought the Armorgroup mercenary company in 2008, which was a major private military contractor in Iraq and Afghanistan and involved in numerous scandals. G4S continues to win major security contracts in both countries.

G4S has subsidiaries in tyrannical regimes including Sudan (Armorgroup Sudanese Co Ltd) and Syria (Group 4 Syria, a 29% share). Its Sudanese business has included working closely with the Sudan People's Liberation Army – now the army of South Sudan, accused by the UN of war crimes involving "appalling instances of cruelty".

Mitie

Mitie is a "facilities management" company providing a mixed bag of contract services to both corporations and government, from cleaning to consultancy. It is predominantly active in the UK. With a recent run of contract wins, it is now the UK's biggest migrant detention profiteer.[576]

Business Basics

Mitie has some 53,000 employees. It has an annual turnover of around £2.1 billion. Around three quarters of its sales are to business customers; the other quarter to national and local government. It has over 3,000 "major customers", and says the biggest client represents 7.5% of sales.

Its head office is in Bristol, and 95% of its turnover comes from the UK. It has small operations in other European countries, Africa (Nigeria, Kenya, Ghana) and the United Arab Emirates. Mitie's services are grouped into several divisions with quite different business models.

Engineering is the biggest division, with £834m revenue in 2017/8, and mainly involves heating and property maintenance. Big customers include Heathrow and Manchester airports, arms dealer Thales, and the Scottish Parliament.

Security. Mitie is the UK's second largest security firm after G4S, and the market leader in the transport and aviation and retail sectors. This division, which also includes the Procius employee vetting business, made £432m revenue last year.

Cleaning and property management. Mitie is perhaps best known as a corporate cleaning contractor. This brought in £406m last year. However cleaning work has been making losses, and Mitie is looking for new ideas including increasing use of robots to cut wage costs.

Catering. This division has two subsidiaries: "Gather & Gather" does in-house catering for corporates, e.g. Vodafone and Nuffield Health, and also runs restaurants and bars, including two bars at the top of the Shard. "Creativevents" caters outdoor events such as Royal Ascot and the Chelsea Flower Show.

Finances. Mitie is having tough times: after a series of profit warnings the company made losses in the last two years. Since 2016 it has gone through a major management reshuffle, large scale restructuring, and the sale of the failing MiHomecare business. However, the Security division has always remained profitable, as has Care and Custody.

A number of official investigations have been launched into aspects of Mitie's recent financial reporting by the Financial Conduct Authority (FCA) and the Financial Reporting Committee (FRC).

History. Mitie was started in 1987 in Bristol by two businessmen called David Telling and Ian Stewart. It grew fast in the 2000s under CEO Ruby MacGregor-Smith, the first Asian woman to run a FTSE 250 company and now a Conservative Baroness. But then austerity ended the days of easy government outsourcing profits, and fears around Brexit also started to spook corporate clients.

Bosses. Mitie reshuffled its management team in 2016-17 after losses hit. New CEO Phil Bentley, a trained accountant from Bradford, was formerly Managing Director of British Gas.

Shareholders. Like other PLCs, Mitie is mainly owned by international institutional investment funds. But it is noticeable how shareholders have changed since financial trouble struck. Five funds with shares of 5% and more currently seem to be betting on the company.

Detention profiteer: "Mitie Care and Custody"

Mitie is currently the UK's biggest detention profiteer. It runs the two Heathrow detention centres, and Campsfield in Oxfordshire. It recently won the £525 million ten year deportation "escorting" contract, taking over from Capita subsidiary Tascor in May 2018.

Imprisonment is still only a small part of Mitie's business – contributing just around 2% of total sales. But it has a higher profit margin than other Mitie divisions. (See our discussion of detention profits in Chapter 7).

Mitie does not have any full management contracts in prisons. But it provides "facilities management" services "including planned and reactive maintenance, cleaning, project management, and catering" in HMP Brixton and HMP Youth Offender Institute Isis.

Another growth area within this business is prisoner health care. In 2017, Mitie bought Tascor Medical Services, now renamed Care & Custody (Health) Ltd. It is also expanding in "Forensic Medical Services", winning new police contracts. These businesses were not sold off with the rest of Mitie Healthcare, but have been incorporated into the Care and Custody division. It seems that healthcare is more profitable when patients are imprisoned.

Serco

Serco is a specialist public sector outsourcer. It runs services in five areas of defence, "justice and immigration", health, transport, and "citizen services". It works for 20 governments worldwide, but 40% of all its business remains in the UK, another 19% in Australia.[577]

Serco has been hit by numerous scandals, most famously in 2013 when it was exposed along with G4S for overcharging the government by millions on its electronic tagging contract.

Serco was also the first of the big-name outsourcers to hit financial trouble recently, with a run of profit warnings starting in 2013. Damage was done by numerous loss-making contracts taken on as the company raced to expand. Serco is struggling to get back on track, but hopes that its outsourcing model will prove profitable again long term: prisons and wars still seem a winning bet.

Business basics

Serco has an annual revenue of around £3 billion. It employs over 50,000 people.

Serco specialises in running services outsourced by governments and other "public" institutions. It has five business areas. **Defence** (29% of revenue) involves support services to the military, such as running bases, or "maritime services". **Citizen Services** (26%) includes call centres and case management, back-office admin and IT, employment and "skills" services. **Justice and Immigration** (17%) is prisons, detention centres, and prisoner transport. **Transport** (17%) includes rail and ferries, road traffic management, and air traffic control. **Health** (11%) sees it outsourcing non-clinical and admin services.

Serco operates in four regions: UK and Europe, USA, "Asia Pacific" (mainly Australia and New Zealand), and the Middle East. Middle East is the smallest region, with just over 10% of revenue, but the only place where sales grew last year.

Finances. Serco is just keeping afloat financially. It made a small loss in 2016, and broke even in 2017. So far its creditors and investors are keeping it alive as it hopes to return to profit. Losses are largely due to the hangover of a number of big unsuccessful acquisitions and contracts Serco took on in the early 2010s, when an ambitious management sought rapid expansion. But also, Serco is finding it hard to build up profitable work again in tougher conditions for outsourcing.

The 2017 Annual Report named these as the "principal" "loss-making operations": "COMPASS UK asylum seeker support services, the Caledonian Sleeper, Future Provision of Marine Services (FPMS), Lincolnshire County Council, and the Prisoner Escort & Custody Services (PECS) contracts".

Investors. Serco is a Public Listed Company (PLC) listed on the London Stock Exchange. Its investors are mainly large global investment funds.

History. Serco started out in 1929 as a company called RCA Services Ltd, the British "electronic services" subsidiary of Radio Corporation of America (RCA). It first ventured into outsourcing by running military radar installations. Later, it grew rapidly through the privatisation programmes of Thatcher and Blair.

Bosses. CEO Rupert Soames, grandson of Winston Churchill, and brother of Conservative MP Nicholas Soames, took over in 2014 after the previous management hit losses and an investigation loomed from the Serious Fraud Office. He was paid £3,804,924 in 2017. Board Chairman Gardner was CEO of Centrica – but best known as former chairman of football clubs Manchester United (2002-5) and then Plymouth Argyle in 2009-10. The board includes a number of other corporate high-flyers and a former top civil servant, Rachel Lomax.

Outlook and strategies. After recent bad experiences with corporate outsourcing, Serco says it is sticking to its "core" model of chasing government contracts. There are challenges in this. Margins are tighter as governments are under financial and political pressure to toughen contracts. In particular, prisons and immigration control look like a long-term growth business. While other jobs are being hit by automation, Serco reckon, "a prison custody officer can sleep soundly in the knowledge that his or her skills will be required for years to come."

Detention and prisons profiteer: "Justice and Immigration"

Serco Justice and Immigration runs six adult prisons in the UK, with a total capacity of 5400. They are HMPs Ashfield, Doncaster, Dovegate, Lowdham Grange and Thameside in England, and Kilmarnock in Scotland.

Serco has long been a player in the UK immigration detention business. However it currently only has one detention centre: Yarl's Wood. It continues to bid for new ones. It bid unsuccessfully for the major deportation "escorting" contract won by Mitie.

In Australia, Serco won the 2009 contract to run all detention centres on the Australian mainland and an offshore processing centre on Christmas Island. The contract was renewed for another five years in 2014, valued then at $1 billion. However, its value has been dropping as Serco is paid "per immigrant", and refugee arrival numbers are down due to interceptions at sea.

In 2016, Serco tried to enter the US market with extensive lobbying at federal and local level to open a family detention centre near the Mexican border. The proposal was eventually rejected by officials in Texas.

GEO Group

GEO is the second largest US private prisons company (after rival CoreCivic). It boasted of locking up 265,000 people in 2017. It is the main contractor of ICE immigration enforcement in the US, locking up 32% of all their migrant detainees.[578]

Business Basics

The large majority of its business is in the US, where its clients include many state authorities as well as federal government agencies. But the number one client, ICE, represents around 19% of all its business. It boasts 75,365 "correctional and detention beds" in the US. This is more than the entire prison population of any western European country except the UK – though in fact only around 3% of the US total.

Just under 10% of sales are international – the bulk of that (7%) from Australia. This includes the major 1,300 bed Ravenhall Prison scheme, a $700 million dollar PPP project which GEO forecasts will bring in "approximately $75 million in annualized revenues under a 25-year management contract."

GEO makes significant charitable and political donations – notably to Trump's campaign. Trump has reversed previous moves by the federal administration away from private prison management. GEO's attempt to sponsor and name Florida Atlantic University's football stadium was defeated by a local campaign.

Finances. It is profitable and stable: the US prison regime shows no sign of shrinking, and president Trump is a supporter of the private prison industry. Revenue in 2017 was $2.263 million, growing from $2.180 in 2016 and $1.843 in 2015. Profit in 2017 was $146 million, a similar level to previous years. That's a healthy 6.5% profit rate.

GEO pays very low corporation tax of just 8-9%. This is because in 2013 the company restructured as a Real Estate Investment Trust (REIT). This is an effective tax loophole which allows it to make big tax savings on the parts of its income which can be classed as involving real estate investment – e.g. where it builds and owns a prison, rather than just managing it.

Bosses. The big boss, chairman and CEO, is George C. Zoley. It has been alleged that he moonlights as the frontman of a dad rock band. There is a board of six including two black men and two women. Anne Foreman, is a former Under Secretary of the US Air Force. Clarence Anthony is a former Florida mayor and busy political networker, executive director of the "National League of Cities".

GEO UK

It currently has just two UK contracts: Dungavel immigration detention centre in Scotland; and prisoner transport for the Ministry of Justice in England and Wales, run by its UK joint venture GEOAmey.

GEO Group previously held other UK detention centre contracts: it ran Campsfield in 2006-11, and Harmondsworth in 2009-14, but lost these contracts to Serco and Mitie respectively. GEO continues to bid for new detention centre contracts in the UK.

Carlson Wagonlit Travel (CWT)

Carlson Wagonlit is a global business travel services company, i.e. a large scale travel agent and booker for companies and government agencies. Besides general business travel, hotel bookings and events management, CWT provides "specialist travel services" to the oil, gas and other energy industries.

Its official head office is in France, but it is 100% owned by privately owned US conglomerate Carlson Companies Inc. It claims to be active in more than

150 countries, including local partnerships as well as fully owned subsidiary companies and joint ventures. According to its website, in 2017 it processed "over $23 billion" in transactions, bringing in revenue of $1.4 billion.

CWT started as a joint venture between the family run Carlson Companies and the French company Wagonlit, part of the Accor group, but it is now fully owned by Carlson which bought out its remaining partners in 2014. As a privately held US company, Carlson does not release detailed financial and other information.

Carlson's other main businesses were the TGI Fridays restaurants and the Carlson hotels group, which included the Radisson hotels brand. However it sold these business in 2014 and 2016 respectively, and the Carlson Companies is currently just CWT. In May 2018 it launched Carlson Private Capital Partners, an investment fund looking to buy new companies, making investments of "$20 to $100 million"

Carlson appears proud of its "ethical" and philanthropic image, which includes funding a charitable trust called the Carlson Family Foundation.

CWT's deportations contract

Carslon was first contracted to run the Home Office's deportation "travel services" in 2004. The contract was renewed again in 2010, and again in 2017. According to a report on "outsourced contracts" by the Independent Chief Inspector of Borders and Immigration[579], CWT's contract involves:

> management of charter flights and ticketing provision for scheduled flights for migrants subject to enforced removal and escorts, where required, and the management of relationships with carriers to maintain and expand available routes. The annual cost of this contract was approximately £30m, roughly half of which, in FY 2014/15, was the cost of scheduled flight tickets.

> Annually, CWT processed approximately 21,000 booking requests from Home Office caseworkers for tickets for enforced removals. Some booking requests were for multiple travellers and/or more than one flight and might involve several transactions. CWT also managed flight rescheduling, cancellations and refunds. The volume of transactions processed varied from 5,000 to 8,000 per month.

ICIBI goes on to note the value of CWT's service to the Home Office through using its worldwide contacts to facilitate deportations:

> Both Home Office and CWT managers noted that CWT's position as a major travel operator had enabled it to negotiate favourable deals with airlines and, over the life of the contract to increase the range of routes available for enforced removals. (Para 5.10).

Titan Airways

Titan is a charter aircraft operator that provides planes to basically anyone who will pay. Clients include British Airways, Royal Mail, tour operators, airlines, corporate events, sports teams and VIPs, and the military.

It has a fleet of at least 12 planes, and employs around 280 staff. The company is steadily growing, and regularly makes a healthy profit: £4.45 million in the 2016/17 financial year, from a revenue of just under £90 million.[580] About three quarters of the company's sales were in the UK, the rest mainly elsewhere in Europe.

Titan is conveniently based inside Stansted Airport, in a building called Enterprise House, which is right next to the Inflite Jet Centre from where private flights including deportation charters are run.

Titan flights have numbers beginning ZT or AWC. The company's planes have a livery with orange, silver and black ribbons, although some are kept white for clients to customise.

Titan is owned by a parent holding company called Hagondale, which is also the actual owner of its aircraft. Titan/Hagondale is wholly owned by one man, Gene Willson.[581] Willson is a pilot who started the business in 1988 with one light aircraft. He later went into partnership with private equity firm 3i to get capital to expand, but bought them out in 2013 to become the sole shareholder.

Thanks to his dividends from Titan, Willson is reportedly "the 41st richest man in Essex", and lives in a £1.6 million farmhouse in Saffron Walden. Assuming he was the highest paid director in 2016/7, he drew a salary of £363,000; on top of which he then paid himself a £2.75 million dividend. This was down from £4 million the year before.[582]

Contracts and business partners

Titan has contracts and partnerships with many other airlines, tour operators, and others. Unlike other aspects of its business, Titan does not publicise its work on deportation charters or mention these anywhere on its website.

British Airways. There is a recent spate of news articles in papers like the Times and Telegraph by "premium travellers" complaining how they booked BA flights only to be downgraded onto Titan charters. Titan offers both longer term leasing and a "Go Now" short notice service for airlines, with aircraft "on standby 24/7". Aside from BA, Titan's website mentions numerous other airlines that use this service.

Royal Mail. One of Titan's biggest and longest standing cargo customers is the Royal Mail, which has been a mainstay of its business for years. Three "Quick Change" aircraft are leased to Royal Mail "nightly Monday to Friday", but at other times can be converted "on very short notice" to cargo or passenger use for other customers.

Jet2.com. Titan has a long term partnership with low cost airline Jet2.com, including a joint venture called Postal Air Services.

Tour operators. Titan leases planes to run seasonal tours, from winter skiing to summer holidays. Customers names on its website include: Club Med, Corsican Places, Crystal Ski, Cunard cruises, Esprit Holidays, The Gambia Experience, Hurtigruten, Inghams, Neilson, Ski Total, Skiworld. One regular partner, Tangney Tours, hires its planes for pilgrimages to Lourdes.

Specialist, VIP and corporate charters. Titan provides planes for sports teams, bands and musicians, VIPs, and corporate events. For example, Titan says on its website that "Premier League and international football clubs" are notable among its "loyal clientele". It also claims "royalty and heads of state" amongst its clients, and "many years of experience in providing air charter solutions for rock and pop bands, orchestras and film production companies".

Government and military. Titan works for the UK and other governments, including the military. Its website states that it has transported "high profile government ministers" and carried out "the evacuation of civilians, humanitarian missions, search and rescue operations, troop movements and the transportation of military supplies and equipment."

Further reading ...

Rather than a long bibliography, we thought it could be more useful to high-light a few particular recommendations. There are many more references in the text and end notes of this book.

On the UK border regime:

Teresa Hayter: *Open Borders* (Pluto Press, 2004)

Provides a good introduction to the history of the UK immigration system and struggles in the 20th century.

Frances Webber: *Borderline Justice* (Pluto Press, 2012)

Written by a barrister at the forefront of legal campaigns, contains a wealth of insight into the legal side of the UK immigration system, but also the political context of the changing law.

Right to Remain: *Toolkit* (2018)

Very useful pocket-sized reference to the UK asylum system.
Also online at: https://righttoremain.org.uk/toolkit/

Borders in general:

Shahram Khosravi: *Illegal Traveller – an Auto-Ethnography of Borders* (Palgrave Macmillan, 2010)

Short, powerful book on the theory and lived experience of border crossing from an Iranian refugee who is now an academic in Sweden.

Harsha Walia: *Undoing Border Imperialism* (AK Press, 2013)

Book making connections between border regimes, colonialism and global capitalism, from the perspective of a Canada-based "No One is Illegal" activist.

Anonymous: "A No Borders Manifesto" (2012)[583]

Short text with an anarchist vision of the struggle against borders, written by people involved in the UK No Borders network.

Online Sources

You can find a lot of useful information about the UK Border Regime and its private contractors available online. Here are just a few important links. For much more on how to investigate companies, make Freedom of Information (FOI) Act requests, etc., see our *Investigating Companies: a DIY Guide*, which you can download from the Corporate Watch website. And feel free to get in touch with us (email contact@corporatewatch.org) with any specific questions, or if you want help on an investigation.

Statistics

Home Office quarterly immigration statistics
https://www.gov.uk/government/collections/
immigration-statistics-quarterly-release

Home Office migration transparency data
https://www.gov.uk/government/collections/migration-transparency-data

Office for National Statistics quarterly immigration statistics
https://www.ons.gov.uk/peoplepopulationandcommunity/
populationandmigration/internationalmigration

Official inspection reports

Independent Chief Inspector of Borders and Immigration (ICIBI): publishes frequent reports on different aspects of the Border Regime
https://www.gov.uk/government/organisations/independent-chief-inspector-of-borders-and-immigration

Her Majesty's Inspector of Prisons: publishes inspections of detention centres
https://www.justiceinspectorates.gov.uk/hmiprisons/

Independent Monitoring Boards: inspections of detention centres and charter flight deportations
https://www.imb.org.uk/

Freedom of Information Act (FOI) requests

WhatDoTheyKnow: this site makes it easy to send FOI requests to government departments, and has a searchable archive of thousands of requests and replies
https://www.whatdotheyknow.com/

Contracts and Company Information

Contracts Finder: UK government contract announcements
https://www.gov.uk/contracts-finder

Tenders Electronic Daily (TED): contract announcements from all European Union countries
https://ted.europa.eu/TED/main/HomePage.do

Companies House: online company accounts and information
https://beta.companieshouse.gov.uk/

Endnotes

1 For a readable run-through of early British immigration history see Robert Winder: *Bloody Foreigners – the story of immigration to Britain* (Abacus, 2013). A helpful historical introduction on modern UK immigration is Panikos Panayi: *An Immigration History of Britain: Multicultural Racism since 1800* (Longman, 2010).

2 Steve Cohen: *Deportation is Freedom – the Orwellian World of Immigration Controls* (Jessica Kingsley, 2005).

3 On the history of the Daily Mail, including its role in anti-migrant campaigns and much more, see Adrian Addison: *Mail Men: the unauthorised story of the Daily Mail – the paper that divided and conquered Britain* (Atlantic, 2017).

4 For much more detail on right-wing agitation and the Aliens Act see: Steve Cohen: *Standing on the Shoulders of Fascism: from Immigration Control to the Strong State* (Trentham Books, 2006); Panikos Panayi, *An Immigration History of Britain;* Bernard Gainer: *The Alien Invasion: the origins of the Aliens Act of 1905* (Heinemann, 1972); Teresa Hayter: *Open Borders* (Pluto Press, 2004) https://leedsnoborders.files.wordpress.com/2014/02/open-borders-the-case-against-immigration-controls-teresa-hayter.pdf;

5 Hayter: *Open Borders*, p38

6 ONS Migration Statistics Quarterly, November 2017 https://www.ons.gov.uk/peoplepopulationandcommunity/populationandmigration/internationalmigration/bulletins/igrationstatisticsquarterlyreport/november2017#further-characteristics-of-long-term-international-migrants

7 Quoted in Hayter: *Open Borders*, p27

8 https://www.telegraph.co.uk/comment/3643823/Enoch-Powells-Rivers-of-Blood-speech.html

9 Quoted in Hayter: *Open Borders*, p54

10 http://www.thewhitereview.org/feature/notes-history-detention-centre/

11 https://www.versobooks.com/blogs/1282-thatcher-the-pm-who-brought-racism-in-from-the-cold

12 Daniel Trilling *Bloody Nasty People: the rise of Britain's far right* (Verso, 2013) https://www.theguardian.com/books/2012/oct/25/bloody-nasty-people-daniel-trilling-review

13 https://en.wikipedia.org/wiki/National_Front_(UK)

14 https://www.rsc.ox.ac.uk/files/files-1/wp27-evolution-immigration-detention-uk-2005.pdf

15 Article 19: "What's the Story? Sangatte: a case study of media coverage of asylum and refugee issues" (2003) https://www.article19.org/data/files/pdfs/publications/refugees-what-s-the-story-case-study-.pdf

16 Stephen Shaw, Prisons and Probation Ombudsman: "Report of the inquiry into the disturbance and fire at Yarl's Wood Removal Centre", October 2004, p123 (hereafter: Shaw 2004) https://s3-eu-west-2.amazonaws.com/ppo-dev-storage-4dvljl6iqfyh/uploads/2015/11/special-yarls-wood-fire-021.pdf

17 The UNHCR publishes monthly and annual reports on global asylum movements and trends. Its "Asylum levels and trends in industrialised countries, 2010" report gives an overall picture of asylum applications in Europe in 2001-10. Asylum applications in all European countries were just under half a million in 2001 and 2002, but then dropped substantially to just over 200,000 by 2006. http://www.unhcr.org/uk/statistics/unhcrstats/4d8c5b109/asylum-levels-trends-industrialized-countries-2010-statistical-overview.html

It is the case that the UK received the highest number of asylum applications of European countries in 2000-2, and this changed subsequently. Rather than government policy, the most obvious explanation is where refugees came from. In 2000-2, the two main asylum nationalities in Europe were Afghanistan and Iraq. These are both former British colonies and current British war zones, with political and cultural links to the UK, and where English is widely spoken. Afghan and Iraqi refugee numbers both fell after 2002 – although they were on the increase again towards the end of the decade as the US and UK occupying forces lost military control of those countries.

18 https://www.theguardian.com/commentisfree/libertycentral/2009/feb/13/civil-liberties-immigration

19 For further explanation and analysis, this article by the Oxford University Migration Observatory is a good starting point:

"The net migration target and the 2017 election" (May 2017) http://www.migration observatory.ox.ac.uk/resources/commentaries/net-migration-target-2017-election/

For latest figures, and details on how the statistics are calculated, see the Office for National Statistics (ONS) "international migration" page: https://www.ons.gov.uk/peoplepopulationandcommunity/populationandmigration/internationalmigration

20 https://www.telegraph.co.uk/news/politics/labour/11293869/Out-of-context-Read-all-34-mentions-of-immigration-in-Labours-leaked-Ukip-strategy.html

21 https://www.theguardian.com/politics/2013/oct/10/immigration-bill-theresa-may-hostile-environment

22 Home Office Annual Report and Accounts 2016-17, p68 https://assets.publishing.service.gov.uk/government/uploads/system/uploads/attachment_data/file/627853/ho_annual_report_and_accounts_2016_2017.pdf

23 https://www.gov.uk/government/publications/contact-details-for-immigration-compliance-and-enforcement-teams/

24 https://assets.publishing.service.gov.uk/government/uploads/system/uploads/attachment_data/file/584221/Criminal-investigationsv1_0_ext.pdf

25 http://www.manpower.org.uk/borderforce/border_force_office_candidate_pack_10_07_2016.pdf

26 Home Office Annual Report and Accounts 2016-17, p112

27 National Audit Office 2017: A Short Guide to the Home Office https://www.nao.org.uk/wp-content/uploads/2017/09/A-Short-Guide-to-the-Home-Office.pdf

28 The Labour Election Manifesto 2017 promised 500 extra border guards: https://labour.org.uk/manifesto/safer-communities/#second But in a February 2018 speech Diane Abbott doubled the number, seemingly by accident: https://www.huffingtonpost.co.uk/entry/diane-abbott-accidentally-doubles-number-of-border-guards-promised-by-labour_uk_5a8d9b2fe4b00a30a251a0c7

29 This is the Home Office website with links to its latest release: https://www.gov.uk/government/collections/immigration-statistics-quarterly-release

At the time of writing, the latest release, which we are using here, was published in August 2018: https://www.gov.uk/government/statistics/immigration-statistics-year-ending-june-2018

30 This is the ONS website with links to its latest release: https://www.ons.gov.uk/peoplepopulationandcommunity/populationandmigration/internationalmigration

At the time of writing, the latest release, which we are using here, was published in July 2018: https://www.ons.gov.uk/peoplepopulationandcommunity/populationandmigration/internationalmigration/bulletins/migrationstatisticsquarterlyreport/july2018revisedfrommaycoveringtheperiodtodecember2017

31 https://www.gov.uk/types-of-british-nationality/british-citizenship

32 https://www.gov.uk/becoming-a-british-citizen

33 For example, Commonwealth citizens can still claim the right of abode: but only if they were born before 1983, and have a parent born in the UK. Other Commonwealth citizens can get a "UK ancestry" work visa if they have a grandparent born in the UK.

34 https://www.gov.uk/government/uploads/system/uploads/attachment_data/file/683360/citizenship-oct-dec-2017-tables.ods

35 The earlier 2002 Nationality, Immigration and Asylum Act first introduced the power to take away citizenship from people born citizens; the 2006 Act weakened the criteria for doing so.

36 Bridget Anderson: *Us and Them?: The Dangerous Politics of Immigration Control* (Oxford University Press, 2013)

37 https://www.gov.uk/government/statistics/migrant-journey-sixth-report

38 https://www.gov.uk/settle-in-the-uk

39 https://www.gov.uk/government/publications/public-funds--2

40 Home Office staff guidance "European Economic Area (EEA) administrative removal", V4.0 (Dec 2017) https://assets.publishing.service.gov.uk/government/uploads/system/uploads/attachment_data/file/668093/GI-EEA-admin-removal-v4.0EXT.pdf

41 Home Office immigration statistics October to December 2017

42 https://www.gov.uk/browse/visas-immigration/work-visas

43 List of shortage occupations: https://www.gov.uk/guidance/immigration-rules/immigration-rules-appendix-k-shortage-occupation-list

44 Right to Remain: *Toolkit*, 2018 https://righttoremain.org.uk/toolkit/

45 https://www.refugeecouncil.org.uk/glossary

46 All the figures in this paragraph come from UNHCR: "Global Trends: forced displacement in 2017" http://www.unhcr.org/globaltrends2017/

47 https://www.theguardian.com/uk/2010/feb/02/border-staff-asylum-seekers-whistleblower

48 Frances Webber: *Borderline Justice* (Pluto Press, 2012), chapters 2 to 4.

49 Asylum seekers are allowed to work only in limited circumstances: if they have waited more than 12 months without a decision, and then only in jobs on the government's "shortage occupation list". https://researchbriefings.parliament.uk/ResearchBriefing/Summary/SN01908

50 https://www.gov.uk/government/publications/immigration-statistics-october-to-december-2017/how-many-people-do-we-grant-asylum-or-protection-to

51 House of Commons Library briefing paper: "Asylum Statistics", January 2018 https://researchbriefings.parliament.uk/ResearchBriefing/Summary/SN01403#fullreport

52 From the "work in progress" table in the "Asylum Transparency Data: May 2018" statistical release: https://www.gov.uk/government/publications/asylum-transparency-data-may-2018 NB: these figures include "not concluded" cases at all stages, from "awaiting first decision" (20,793) through "post decision" (5,776) and "appeal outstanding" (10,011) to "subject to removal action" (32,037).

53 House of Commons Library briefing paper: "Asylum Statistics", January 2018

54 https://publications.parliament.uk/pa/cm201617/cmselect/cmhaff/637/63704.htm

55 See research on this by Franck Düvell: "Paths into Irregularity: The Legal and Political Construction of Irregular Migration" http://booksandjournals.brillonline.com/content/journals/10.1163/157181611x587

856 Also some summarised points in a blogpost: http://blogs.lse.ac.uk/politicsandpolicy/irregular-migration-10-questions-answered/

56 Ian Gordon, Kathleen Scanlon, Tony Travers and Christine Whitehead: "Economic impact on the London and UK economy of an earned regularisation of irregular migrants to the UK", GLA Economics / LSE, p6 http://www.lse.ac.uk/geographyAndEnvironment/research/london/pdf/irregular%20migrants%20full%20report.pdf

57 United Nations Convention relating to the Status of Refugees, adopted 1951 http://www.unhcr.org/3b66c2aa10 For a detailed discussion see Guy Goodwin-Gill, "Article 31 of the 1951 Convention relating to the Status of Refugees: Non-penalization, Detention and Protection", UNHCR 2001 http://www.unhcr.org/3bcfdf164.pdf

58 Webber: *Borderline Justice*, Chapter 1

59 https://www.theguardian.com/uk-news/2016/oct/13/syrians-conviction-for-using-false-passport-in-asylum-claim-quashed

60 See: Liz Fekete: "The emergence of xeno-racism" (IRR, 2001) http://www.irr.org.uk/news/the-emergence-of-xeno-racism/

61 Harsha Walia: *Undoing Border Imperialism* (AK Press, 2013)

62 This idea of an "assemblage" comes from Gilles Deleuze and Felix Guattari - *1000 Plateaus*. For a more accessible introduction and a detailed account of how it can help us think about social systems and institutions, see Manuel de Landa - *A New Philosophy of Society: Assemblage Theory and Social Complexity* (Bloomsbury, 2006).

63 Right to Remain: Toolkit, 2018 https://righttoremain.org.uk/toolkit/

64 There is a recent overview of the reporting system in an inspection report from the Independent Chief Inspector of Borders and Immigration (ICIBI): "Inspection Report on the Reporting and Offender Management Systems", published November 2017. Facts and figures in this section are taken from this report unless otherwise noted. https://www.gov.uk/government/publications/inspection-report-on-the-reporting-and-offender-management-system

65 Home Office, Immigration Statistics October to December 2016 https://www.gov.uk/government/uploads/system/uploads/attachment_data/file/593038/detention-q4-2016-tables.ods

66 ICIBI report p14: "'"if ROM staff observed that the individual may have driven to the Reporting Centre, they might ask to see the individual's driving licence so that Immigration Enforcement Interventions and Sanctions Directorate (ISD) could liaise with the Driver and Vehicle Licensing Agency (DVLA) to establish whether the licence should be revoked in line with the Immigration Act 2014. Similarly, where an individual reported they were unable to report due to medical treatment, this information would be provided to ISD to liaise with the relevant NHS Trust regarding charging for the treatment."

67 House of Commons Home Affairs Committee (HAC); "Asylum Accommodation", January 2017 https://publications.parliament.uk/pa/cm201617/cmselect/cmhaff/637/63706.htm#_idTextAnchor016

68 National Audit Office (NAO) report: "COMPASS contracts for the provision of accommodation for asylum seekers", January 2014 https://www.nao.org.uk/wp-content/uploads/2014/01/10287-001-accommodation-for-asylum-seekers-Book.pdf

69 Serco written evidence to the Home Affairs Committee, February 2016 http://data.parliament.uk/writtenevidence/committeeevidence.svc/evidencedocument/home-affairs-committee/asylum-accommodation/written/29809.html

70 G4S evidence to the Home Affairs Committee, February 2016 http://data.parliament.uk/writtenevidence/committeeevidence.svc/evidencedocument/home-affairs-committee/asylum-accommodation/written/29580.html

71 UKVI: Asylum Accommodation Support Transformation Briefing Note, November 2017 https://www.local.gov.uk/sites/default/files/documents/Home%20Office_AAST%20Briefing%20Note%20November%202017_FINAL.pdf

72 See the Home Affairs Committee report, and written evidence from G4S and Serco

73 G4S 2017 Full Results presentation transcript 8 March 2018 http://www.g4s.co.id/-/media/g4s/corporate/files/investor-relations/2018/g4s-2017-full-year-results-presentation-transcript-8-march-2018.ashx?la=en

74 https://www.theguardian.com/business/2016/jan/26/g4s-jomast-bosses-admit-number-asylum-seeker-red-doors-too-high-select-committee

An academic analysis of the media's coverage of the "Red Door" scandal: Bates, D. "The "red door" controversy — Middlesbrough's asylum seekers and the discursive politics of racism", Journal of Community and Applied Social Psychology, 2017. https://eprint.ncl.ac.uk/file_store/production/238147/905EE472-B7DD-4018-8136-C783476FD93B.pdf

75 https://www.symaag.org.uk/2017/12/01/daisy-and-the-4-billion-asylum-housing-contracts/

76 https://www.symaag.org.uk/2018/06/05/rodents-bedbugs-mould-uk-asylum-housing-is-a-hostile-environment/

77 Migrant Voice: "Asylum housing in Birmingham", January 2017 https://www.scribd.com/document/338008732/Asylum-Housing-in-Birmingham-Final

78 Asylum Support Appeals Project factsheet: "Section 4 support", https://www.asaproject.org/uploads/Factsheet-2-section-4-support.pdf

79 An academic study of dispersal policy and its implementation: Darling, Jonathan (2016) 'Asylum in austere times : instability, privatization and experimentation within the UK asylum dispersal system.', Journal of refugee studies. http://dro.dur.ac.uk/24997/

80 Hayter: Open Borders, p134

81 https://www.theguardian.com/uk/2008/jun/13/immigration.immigrationpolicy

82 https://en.wikipedia.org/wiki/Glasgow_Girls_(activists)

83 https://peacenews.info/node/3525/unity-glasgow-asylum-seekers

84 https://unitycentreglasgow.org/

85 https://unitycentreglasgow.org/resist-sercos-mass-evictions/

86 This is part of the Home Office's quarterly "Immigration Enforcement transparency data" release, which can be accessed here: https://www.gov.uk/government/collections/migration-transparency-data

87 NB: the deportations figure comes from Home Office data released the quarter after the arrests figure. Thus it only records people deported in the 3-6 months after they were arrested. Some more people may be deported later, after being held for a longer period in detention.

88 ICIBI report on Illegal Working operations, December 2015. Hereafter, we will refer to this as "ICIBI Illegal Working" report. http://icinspector.independent.gov.uk/wp-content/uploads/2015/12/ICIBI-Report-on-illegal-working-17.12.2015.pdf

89 https://www.gov.uk/government/publica tions/contact-details-for-immigration-compliance-and-enforcement-teams/

90 https://www.theguardian.com/uk-news/2018/jun/14/immigration-officers-compe te-on-arrest-numbers-to-win-cake-union

91 The quotes here come from a presentation given at the COMPAS "Does Immigration Enforcement Matter?" conference held in London on 27 October 2017.

92 For example, raids targeting rough sleepers have been focused on East Europeans. Residential raids are likely to hit all nation-alities deemed "removable". A Freedom Of Information request to which the Home Office replied in 2013 (after appeal) also confirms that "restaurants and takeaways" are primary targets. In 2011 there were 2,591 visits to these businesses, leading to 1,939 arrests; in 2012 there were 2,514 visits, with 2,320 arrests. Comparing these figures with the ICIBI Illegal Working re-port, in both years 47% of all raids were to "restaurants and takeaways". Home Office reply to FOI request submitted by Nadeem Badsha, January 2013. https://www.whatdotheyknow.com/request/immigra tion_raids#incoming-351316

93 ICIBI: Inspection report of Border Force and Immigration Enforcement intelligence functions, July 2016. (Hereafter: ICIBI intelligence report 2016). https://www.gov.uk/government/publications/inspection-report-of-border-force-and-immigration-enforcement-intelligence-functions-july-2016

94 Compiled from quarterly Immigration Enforcement transparency data : https://www.gov.uk/government/collections/migration-transparency-data

95 http://antiraids.net/2014/06/03/home-office-immigration-raids-spiked-operation-centurion-ukba/

96 http://www.migrantsrights.org.uk/news/2014/keith-vaz-speaks-out-racial-profiling-used-home-office-operation-centurion

97 The Intelligence Management System (IMS) is the main information recording system for Immigration Enforcement, also used by Border Force. See ICIBI: Inspection report on the intelligence management system, October 2014 http://icinspector.independent.gov.uk/wp-content/uploads/2014/10/An-inspection-of-the-Intelligence-Management-System-FINAL-WEB.pdf IE intelligence officers also have access to various other internal or cross-agency computer systems and are supposed to use these to cross-check intelligence on targets. These include the following: CID; CRS (Case Reference System – a HO database containing details of all visa applications); Experian – commercial database holding credit reference information and personal information held by financial institutions; Warnings Index – a HO System used to ascertain whether individuals are of interest to the Home Office; Home Office National Operations Database; Police National Computer. See ICIBI intelligence report 2016.

98 Again, as part of the quarterly "Immigration Enforcement transparency data" release, which can be accessed here: https://www.gov.uk/government/collections/migration-transparency-data

99 ICIBI intelligence report 2016

100 The Operation Centurion files have not been published themselves because they contain personal information naming businesses and sometimes individuals. Here we quote from the files and anonymise where necessary.

101 http://www.righttoremain.org.uk/blog/byron-burgers-legality-morality-humanity/

102 https://www.theguardian.com/uk-news/2016/jul/31/bugging-byron-activists-release-cockroaches-and-locusts-at-burger-chain

103 https://iwgbclb.wordpress.com/2016/08/12/deliveroo-drivers-on-strike/

104 https://m.facebook.com/story.php?story_fbid=950425175055710&id=467565226675043

105 http://www.islingtongazette.co.uk/news/crime-court/http_www_islingtongazette_co_uk_news_crime_court_three_illegal_immigrants_arrested_at_deliveroo_base_in_islington_1_4563123_1_4563123

106 https://www.indymedia.org.uk/en/2008/11/412669.html

107 http://www.irr.org.uk/news/soas-occupied-after-cleaners-detained-and-forcibly-removed/

108 https://www.gov.uk/government/uploads/system/uploads/attachment_data/file/537725/Illegal_working_operations_v1.pdf

109 ICIBI Illegal Working report para 4.13

110 Anti Raids Network analysis of Operation Skybreaker: https://network23.org/antiraids/2014/09/25/operation-skybreaker/

111 ICIBI Illegal Working report para 4.16

112 https://network23.org/antiraids/2014/09/25/operation-skybreaker/

113 Anti Raids Network write: "During our outreach, we have found that a lot of people have been signing consent forms. However, when we've told people that there is no obligation to sign, many said that they were unaware that it was voluntary, while others said 'you can't do anything to stop them – they do whatever they want'. In practice of course, it is very hard to refuse – regardless of whether this is your legal right."https://network23.org/antiraids/2014/09/25/operation-skybreaker/

114 This legal argument was made in more detail in Corporate Watch's 2016 report "Snitches, Stings and Leaks". Migrants' Rights Network then commissioned Dr. Katie Bales, a lecturer in law at Bristol University, to give a professional opinion on the legal obligations of employers, which backs up our conclusions. We should also note that much of the relevant immigration law has never been tested in court – in part because those targeted in raids often disappear into detention or may indeed be deported. See Katie Bales: "Employment and immigration enforcement: The legal limits of what can be required from employers", Migrants' Rights Network, September 2016. https://migrantsrights.org.uk/wp-content/uploads/2017/12/Katie-Bales-on-HO-raids-in-businesses.pdf

115 The 2016 Immigration Act added "has reasonable cause to believe", which came into force on 12 July 2016. Prior to that, under the 2006 Act, the prosecution had to prove that the employer knew that the employee was working illegally. See the new issue of the government "Employer's Guide to Right to Work Checks":

https://www.gov.uk/government/uploads/system/uploads/attachment_data/file/536953/An_Employer_s_guide_to_right_to_work_checks_-_July_16.pdf

116 More precisely, the procedure is this: Immigration Enforcement (e.g. an ICE team) issues a "referral notice" to the employer stating that they have found illegal workers and that the case will now be handed to the "Civil Penalty Compliance Team" (CPCT); the employer has a chance to object; if the employer does not object or the objection is unsuccessful, they are issued with a second "Notice of Liability" that demands a payment; the employer can also appeal to a civil court to dispute the penalty. See "Code of Practice on Preventing Illegal Working". See page 10 of that document for details of what it means to correctly carry out right to work checks. https://www.gov.uk/government/uploads/system/uploads/attachment_data/file/311668/Code_of_practice_on_preventing_illegal_working.pdf

117 More technically: having a statutory excuse is one of three grounds of objection or appeal to the civil penalty. The others are that the employer is not in fact liable (e.g. they weren't really the illegal worker's employer), or that the penalty is too high. See "Code of Practice on Preventing Illegal Working" https://www.gov.uk/government/uploads/system/uploads/attachment_data/file/311668/Code_of_practice_on_preventing_illegal_working.pdf

NB: there is a Home Office "statutory excuse checksheet" which states clearly what evidence Immigration Officers should look for when judging whether employers made the checks correctly. Basically this amounts to two things: a clear copy of the relevant pages of the worker's passport or other acceptable ID document; and a record of the date when it was checked (for example, by dating the ID document copies). https://www.gov.uk/government/uploads/system/uploads/attachment_data/file/313369/Statutory_Excuse_Checksheet.pdf

118 For example, the Independent Chief Inspector specifically discusses a case where the CPCT penalty team: "considered that the identity documents provided by many of those arrested were fraudulent, but determined that this was not 'readily apparent' so cancelled all but one civil penalty." (ICIBI Illegal Working report, figure 18)

As the Inspector puts it, "employers are either negligent in respect of their obligations to check their employees' 'right to work' or complicit in hiding such work from the authorities." (ICIBI Illegal Working report, forward)

119 Full details are in the Home Office: "Code of practice on preventing illegal working: code of practice for employers" (May 2014) https://www.gov.uk/government/uploads/system/uploads/attachment_data/file/311668/Code_of_practice_on_preventing_illegal_working.pdf

120 http://www.yourlocalguardian.co.uk/news/13646444.Five_arrested_as_Home_Office_immigration_officers_swoop_across_Wandsworth/

121 Government FAQ for employers on illegal working and civil penalties, Answer 44: "If the employer is contracting out specific jobs or services for individuals (contractors and sub-contractors), there is no need for a right to work check when they are not being employed by the employer." https://www.gov.uk/government/uploads/system/uploads/attachment_data/file/426972/frequently_asked_Qs_illegal_working_civil__penalty_May_final.pdf

122 ICIBI Illegal Working report, para 5.18

123 Although this power is framed in terms of licensing law, it doesn't only apply to joint operations with licensing officers. ICE can also enter licensed premises all on their own, "to investigate illegal working following receipt of intelligence on premises they have reason to believe are being used for a licensable activity".

Home Office: "Guidance to licensing authorities to prevent illegal working in licensed premises in England and Wales", 6 April 2017 https://www.gov.uk/government/news/new-powers-to-tackle-illegal-working-in-licensed-premises

Home Office summary statement on the new power from its website: https://www.gov.uk/government/news/new-powers-to-tackle-illegal-working-in-licensed-premises

The actual law is here (see Part 4 on "rights of entry"): http://www.legislation.gov.uk/ukpga/2016/19/schedule/4/enacted

124 ICIBI, "An inspection of the use of the power to enter business premises without a search warrant", March 2014 http://icinspector.independent.gov.uk/wp-content/uploads/2014/03/AD-letters-report-Final-Version-for-Web.pdf

125 ICIBI Illegal Working report, para 5.22

126 ICIBI Illegal Working report, para 5.27 Another legal justification for questioning someone could be that their immigration status is perceived as dependent on that of someone initially under suspicion, e,g., a spouse or other family member.

127 ICIBI Illegal Working report, para 5.28

128 http://antiraids.net/2013/02/04/ukba-raid-disrupted-by-anti-raids-network/

129 https://www.youtube.com/watch?v=pQ0_TFBVots

130 http://antiraids.net/2014/06/03/home-office-immigration-raids-spiked-operation-centurion-ukba/

131 http://antiraids.net/?s=peckham

132 https://theoccupiedtimes.org/?p=14019

133 http://antiraids.net/2015/07/26/why-we-support-the-shadwell-raid-resisters-a-response-to-the-daily-mail/

134 http://antiraids.net/?s=deptford

135 http://antiraids.net/about/

136 http://antiraids.net/2016/07/31/brick-lane-raid-seen-off-it-just-takes-a-few-neighbours/

137 In 2017, we know of at least two people arrested for "obstructing immigration officers" - again, the cases collapsed before or in court. Earlier, the "East Street Three" were people singled out from the resistance on 21 June 2015 and charged with "violent disorder". Two were acquitted by a jury, charges against the third were later dropped. In 2016, ICE teamed up with a Metropolitan Police "gangs unit" for a "sting operation" where a fake raid was staged off Deptford High Street. Two people were arrested for alleged criminal damage - but again, both were acquitted. Of course, there may well be other people we don't know of who have suffered repression for resisting raids. https://trialoftheeaststreet3.wordpress.com/
http://antiraids.net/2016/07/31/cops-immigration-officers-organise-sting-operation-in-deptford-with-bait-immigration-van/

138 https://detainedvoices.com/2018/02/24/i-feel-like-i-have-already-been-removed-from-society/

139 http://www.detentionforum.org.uk/changes/indefinite-detention/

140 https://www.gov.uk/immigration-removal-centre/overview

141 https://assets.publishing.service.gov.uk/government/uploads/system/uploads/attachment_data/file/654123/revised-draft-airports-nps-web-version.pdf

142 Home Office Immigration Statistics, year ending June 2018 (published 23 August) https://www.gov.uk/government/publications/immigration-statistics-year-ending-june-2018/how-many-people-are-detained-or-returned

143 https://www.gov.uk/government/publications/immigration-statistics-october-to-december-2017/how-many-people-are-detained-or-returned#detention

144 Home Office: Immigration Enforcement Data, February 2018 https://www.gov.uk/government/publications/immigration-enforcement-data-february-2018

145 https://www.gov.uk/government/uploads/system/uploads/attachment_data/file/681703/detention-oct-dec-2017-tables.ods see table dt_05

146 https://www.gov.uk/government/publications/immigration-statistics-october-to-december-2017/how-many-people-are-detained-or-returned#detention

147 https://www.gov.uk/government/uploads/system/uploads/attachment_data/file/681703/detention-oct-dec-2017-tables.ods see sheet dt_09

148 https://www.gov.uk/government/publications/immigration-statistics-october-to-december-2017/how-many-people-are-detained-or-returned#detention

149 https://www.gov.uk/government/uploads/system/uploads/attachment_data/file/681703/detention-oct-dec-2017-tables.ods see sheet dt_06

150 Felix Bazalgette: "Notes on the history of a detention centre" (The White Review, September 2017) http://www.thewhitereview.org/feature/notes-history-detention-centre/

151 https://www.rsc.ox.ac.uk/files/files-1/wp27-evolution-immigration-detention-uk-2005.pdf

152 For more on the history of the UK detention system see: http://www.thewhitereview.org/feature/notes-history-detention-centre/ https://www.rsc.ox.ac.uk/files/files-1/wp27-evolution-immigration-detention-uk-2005.pdf

153 1,545 people were detained under Immigration Act powers. Of these, 1,280 (83%) had sought asylum. Control of Immigration - Statistics United Kingdom, 2001, Home Office Statistical Bulletin 11/02. Cited in Yarl's Wood investigation report, footnote p122 https://s3-eu-west-2.amazonaws.com/ppo-dev-storage-4dvljl6iqfyh/uploads/2015/11/special-yarls-wood-fire-021.pdf

154 Home Office immigration statistics quarterly release: detention https://www.gov.uk/government/collections/immigration-statistics-quarterly-release

155 Under the Nationality, Immigration and Asylum Act 2000

156 https://detentionaction.org.uk/verne-closes-shaw-looms

157 http://unlocked.org.uk/blog/unlocking-the-future-of-detention-in-scotland/

158 http://unlocked.org.uk/blog/visiting-dungavel-for-another-year/

159 Stephen Shaw: "Review into the Welfare in Detention of Vulnerable Persons - A report to the Home Office", 2016 (Hereafter: Shaw Review 2016) https://assets.publishing.service.gov.uk/government/uploads/system/uploads/attachment_data/file/490782/52532_Shaw_Review_Accessible.pdf

160 Stephen Shaw: "Assessment of government progress in implementing the report on the welfare in detention of vulnerable persons - A follow-up report to the Home Office", July 2018 (Hereafter: Shaw follow-up report 2018) https://assets.publishing.service.gov.uk/government/uploads/system/uploads/attachment_data/file/728376/Shaw_report_2018_Final_web_accessible.pdf

161 https://www.parliament.uk/documents/commons-committees/home-affairs/Correspondence-17-19/Brook-House-Independent-Investigation.pdf

162 https://www.theguardian.com/uk-news/2018/may/22/former-immigration-detainees-public-inquiry-abuse-claims-brook-house-gatwick

163 https://www.parliament.uk/business/committees/committees-a-z/commons-select/home-affairs-committee/inquiries/parliament-2017/immigration-detention-inquiry-17-19/

164 https://www.asylumaid.org.uk/parliamentary-question-reveals-extent-sexual-assaults-yarls-wood/

165 https://www.bbc.co.uk/programmes/b094mhsn

166 http://www.irr.org.uk/news/2017-the-deadliest-year-in-immigration-detention/

167 http://www.irr.org.uk/news/deaths-in-immigration-detention-1989-2017/

168 http://www.medicaljustice.org.uk/

169 https://www.detentionforum.org.uk/resources/detention-facts/other-reports/

170 https://detainedvoices.com/

171 http://www.barnardos.org.uk/cedars_report_2015.pdf

172 https://www.barnardos.org.uk/news/Barnardos-statement-on-Cedars-accommodation/press_releases.htm?ref=117378

173 http://www.righttoremain.org.uk/blog/g4s-to-provide-child-and-family-welfare-services-at-new-detention-unit/

174 https://corporatewatch.org/true-scale-of-captive-migrant-labour-revealed/

175 https://www.dailyrecord.co.uk/news/scottish-news/dungavel-detention-centre-slave-labour-11851052

176 https://data.gov.uk/data/contracts-finder-archive/search/?buying_org=Commercial%20%26%20Property%20Directorate

177 http://ted.europa.eu/TED/notice/udl?uri=TED:NOTICE:404486-2016:TEXT:EN:HTML

178 https://www.civilserviceworld.com/articles/news/home-office-shelves-plans-new-contract-award-gatwick-immigration-removal-centres

179 https://www.gov.uk/government/news/future-management-of-the-gatwick-immigration-removal-centres

180 Corporate Watch, July 2018, "Detention Centre Profits: 20% and up for the migration prison bosses" https://corporatewatch.org/detention-centre-profits-20-and-up-for-the-migration-prison-bosses/

181 Corporate Watch, July 2015, "Home Office self-audit system for detention centres revealed" https://corporatewatch.org/home-office-self-audit-system-for-detention-centres-revealed/

182 Serco Annual Report 2017 https://www.serco.com/media/2384/serco-annual-report-and-accounts-2017.pdf

183 See account of the Campsfield Nine case by Teresa Hayter in *Open Borders*, pages 128-33.

184 Shaw: Yarl's' Wood report, p4

185 Shaw: Yarl's Wood report, Conclusions 377-380

186 http://www.irr.org.uk/news/campaigners-celebrate-acquittal-of-harmondsworth-4/

187 http://london.noborders.org.uk/node/145

188 Robert Whalley: "Report of the Investigation into the disturbances at Harmondsworth and Campsfield House Immigration Removal Centres", House of Commons, July 2007 https://www.indymedia.org.uk/media/2007/07//376961.pdf

189 Shaw follow-up report 2018, section 2.17

190 http://lesbianimmigrationsupportgroup.blogspot.com/2012/10/women-in-yarls-wood-detention-centre.html

191 https://detainedvoices.com/

192 https://closecampsfield.wordpress.com/tag/expansion/

193 On current official thinking around detention time limits it is worth noting the remarks by Stephen Shaw in his 2018 follow-up report (page viii). He notes: "Support for a time limit has coalesced around a period of 28 days, but I have yet to see a coherent account of how this figure has been arrived at. It is not so long ago that Parliament was presented with a proposal for a 60 day limit, and it is clear that there must be exceptions (it would surely be unacceptable for someone who disrupted a fight on the 27th day of their detention to be released the next day). Indeed, the proposals considered in 2016 during the passage of that year's Immigration Bill specifically excluded those subject to deportation (in other words, the very foreign national offenders (FNOs) who make up the vast majority of those held in detention the longest)."

194 https://labour.org.uk/press/labour-vows-end-mays-hostile-environment-overhaul-uks-detention-system/

195 https://detainedvoices.com/

196 https://detainedvoices.com/2018/02/26/hello-from-yarls-wood/

197 IMB: Heathrow IRCs report 2017 https://s3-eu-west-2.amazonaws.com/imb-prod-storage-1ocod6bqky0vo/uploads/2018/04/Heathrow-IRC-2017-AR.pdf

198 Redacted Colnbrook management contract 2003, archived on Contracts Finder Archive site https://data.gov.uk/data/contracts-finder-archive/contract/699458/

199 Home Office FOI response to Michael Zhang, 7 January 2015, Annex B https://www.whatdotheyknow.com/request/240025/response/602918/attach/4/Annex%20B%20CR%2033555.pdf

200 IMB: Heathrow IRCs report 2017

201 IMB: Heathrow IRCs report 2017

202 https://data.gov.uk/data/contracts-finder-archive/contract/699458/

203 IMB: Heathrow IRCs report 2017

204 IMB: Brook House report 2016 https://www.imb.org.uk/brook-house-irc-annual-report-published-today/

205 https://www.contractsfinder.service.gov.uk/Notice/0a595539-b76e-4296-8987-6ac7233bc2d7

206 Redacted Brook House management contract 2008, archived on Contracts Finder Archive site https://data.gov.uk/data/contracts-finder-archive/contract/599720/

207 https://www.contractsfinder.service.gov.uk/Notice/9f4d386f-621b-426c-b13d-6483e40d3a25

208 IMB: Brook House report 2016

209 IMB: Tinsley House report 2016 https://s3-eu-west-2.amazonaws.com/imb-prod-storage-1ocod6bqky0vo/uploads/2017/06/TINSLEY-HOUSE-2016-1.pdf

210 https://gdwg.org.uk/immigration-detention/gatwick-detention-centres/

211 IMB: Tinsley House report 2016

212 https://www.contractsfinder.service.gov.uk/Notice/d181a58c-104f-41f4-b7b3-f510a8831078

213 IMB: Tinsley House report 2016

214 IMB: Tinsley House report 2016

215 IMB: Campsfield House report 2016 https://s3-eu-west-2.amazonaws.com/imb-prod-storage-1ocod6bqky0vo/uploads/2017/04/Campsfield-House-2016.pdf

216 Redacted Colnbrook management contract 2010, archived on Contracts Finder Archive site https://data.gov.uk/data/contracts-finder-archive/contract/699443/

217 Home Office FOI response to Michael Zhang, 7 January 2015, Annex B

218 IMB: Campsfield House report 2016

219 Redacted Dungavel management contract 20011, archived on Contracts Finder Archive site https://data.gov.uk/data/contracts-finder-archive/contract/699454/

220 https://www.parliament.uk/business/publications/written-questions-answers-statements/written-question/Commons/2016-10-24/49894/

221 Dungavel contract award notice 2011 https://www.contractsfinder.service.gov.uk/Notice/a415f5d7-6b35-4bb1-9e2a-9142249e19d8

222 IMB: Morton Hall report 2016 https://s3-eu-west-2.amazonaws.com/imb-prod-storage-1ocod6bqky0vo/uploads/2017/04/Morton-Hall-2016.pdf

223 Shaw Review 2016

224 Shaw Review 2016, p33

225 IMB: Yarl's Wood report 2016 https://s3-eu-west-2.amazonaws.com/imb-prod-storage-1ocod6bqky0vo/uploads/2017/06/Yarls-Wood-2016.pdf

226 Redacted Yarl's Wood management contract 2006, published on Contracts Finder Archive site https://data.gov.uk/data/contracts-finder-archive/contract/599744/

227 Home Office FOI response to Michael Zhang, 7 January 2015, Annex B

228 IMB: Yarl's Wood report 2016

229 https://www.gov.uk/government/publications/immigration-statistics-october-to-december-2017/how-many-people-are-detained-or-returned All figures used below, unless otherwise noted, come from the tables attached to this Home Office report. The Home Office published quarterly Immigration statistics releases, which includes the basic figures on detention and deportation numbers and nationalities. You can find the latest figures here: https://www.gov.uk/government/collections/immigration-statistics-quarterly-release

230 Corporate Watch: Collective Expulsion – the case against Britain's mass deportation charter flights, 2013 https://corporatewatch.org/publications/2013/collective-expulsion

231 This was the figure published in the Home Office's May 2018 quarterly statistical release. It may be revised higher in later releases, as there is a lag in collecting the "voluntary returns" data while the Home Office waits for confirmation people have left.

232 These figures are not directly comparable, because there has been a change in the Home Office's headline figure. Numbers reported in the older category of "enforced removals" are slightly lower than in the newer category of "enforced returns". This means that the drop in forced deportation numbers

is in fact a bit bigger than these figures represent.

233 https://www.theguardian.com/world/2012/jul/02/iraq-parliament-deported-nationals-europe

234 https://corporatewatch.org/iraqi-deporta tions-the-airlines-helping-the-home-office-deport-refugees-to-war-zones-2/

235 Source: Freedom of Information Requests to the Home Office, published by no-deportations.org.uk

236 Home Office FOI response to Alex Scott, 2 July 2018 https://www.whatdotheyknow.com/request/489809/response/1182364/attach/3/FOI%2048932%20Scott.pdf

237 Home Office FOI response to Thomas Avery, 10 October 2016 https://www.whatdotheyknow.com/request/enforced_removals_and_deportatio#incoming-879337

238 Home Office written question answered by James Brokenshire on 28th July 2015 (Hansard) https://www.theyworkforyou.com/wrans/?id=2015-07-14.6908.h&s=charter+flight#g6908.r0

239 Source: Freedom of Information response published by no-deportations.org.uk. The Home Office says it spent a total £8,895,027 on deporting 1,664 people on charter flights in 2017.

240 On the Sri Lanka case see: Phil Miller: "Did Liam Fox plan deportations to hide Tamil genocide?" https://stopdeportations.wordpress.com/2012/07/05/did-liam-fox-plan-deportations-to-hide-tamil-genocide/

241 See Corporate Watch: Collective Expulsion, p19

242 See ICIBI: "An Inspection of Removals", December 2015. http://icinspector.independent.gov.uk/wp-content/uploads/2015/12/ICIBI-report-on-Removals-17.12.2015.pdf

243 https://corporatewatch.org/home-office-told-to-publish-confidential-reports-on-migrant-detention-sites/

244 https://corporatewatch.org/home-office-self-audit-system-for-detention-centres-revealed/

245 https://corporatewatch.org/g4s-and-carlson-wagonlit-profiteers-scrabble-for-more-home-office-contracts/

246 "Provision of travel services for immigration purposes" Home Office contract award notice, 30 May 2017

247 See: ICIBI "Inspection of Outsourced Contracts" published March 2016; and article on Carlson Wagonlit Travel in Corporate Watch: "The Rules of Engagement" (2011),. http://icinspector.independent.gov.uk/wp-content/uploads/2016/03/ICIBI-report-on-Outsourced-Contracts-and-Cedars-Final.pdf

https://corporatewatch.org/product/magazine-49-the-rules-of-engagement/

248 E.g. a recent report by Sahara Reporters on 2 August 2018 reported a deportation to Nigeria on Titan Flight ZT9131 http://saharareporters.com/2018/08/02/deported-36-nigerians-illegally-residing-uk

249 The guidelines are contained in a Home Office document called "Judicial Reviews and Injunctions". The latest edition at time of writing is version 15.0, May 2018: https://assets.publishing.service.gov.uk/government/uploads/system/uploads/attachment_data/file/709719/chapter-60-judicial-reviews_v15.0.pdf

250 The latest edition at time of writing is version 15.0, May 2018: https://assets.publishing.service.gov.uk/government/uploads/system/uploads/attachment_data/file/709719/chapter-60-judicial-reviews_v15.0.pdf

251 http://www.irr.org.uk/news/excessive-use-of-restraint-during-charter-deportation-flight/

252 IMB charter flight monitoring team: Annual Report 2017 https://s3-eu-west-2.amazonaws.com/imb-prod-storage-1ocod6bqky0vo/uploads/2018/06/IMB-Charter-Flights-2017-annual-report.pdf

253 IMB charter flight monitoring team: Annual Report 2017

254 https://twitter.com/uribemonic/status/1001848402806755328

255 https://www.theguardian.com/uk-news/2018/feb/21/home-office-contractors-cuffed-detained-migrants-inside-coach-on-fire

256 http://www.inflitejetcentre.co.uk/welcome.htm

257 HMIP report on a Third Country charter flight, May 2018 https://www.justiceinspectorates.gov.uk/hmiprisons/wp-content/uploads/sites/4/2018/05/January-2018-TCU-escort-

https://www.contractsfinder.service.gov.uk/Notice/36f67d6d-2b26-4ecb-88c6-41291aa8af37

web-2018.pdf; IMB charter flight monitoring team Annual Report 2017

258 A few useful articles and eyewitness accounts on deportation flights: James Bridle - "Planespotting" http://booktwo. org/notebook/planespotting/; Unity Centre Glasgow on May 24 2016 flight to Nigeria and Ghana http://unitycentreglasgow.org/ mass-deportation-charter-flight-to-nigeria-and-ghana-set-for-may-24th/;

"Ghosted Away: UK's secret removal flights examined" by Lotte Lewis Smith https:// www.opendemocracy.net/uk/shinealight/ lotte-ls/ghosted-away-uk-s-secret-removal-flights-examined;

"Rough handling and restraint: UK forced removals still a nasty business" by Lotte Lewis Smith https://www.opendemo cracy.net/uk/shinealight/lotte-ls/rough-handling-and-restraint-UK-forced-removals-still-nasty-business

259 https://detainedvoices.com/2015/10/09/ before-i-was-helpless-but-then-i-was-powerful/

260 https://freedomnews.org.uk/sweden-activist-prevents-deportation-of-a-man-to-afghanistan/

261 https://detentionaction.org.uk/news /iraq-charter-flight-cancelled

262 https://www.theguardian.com/world/ 2012/jul/02/iraq-parliament-deported-nationals-europe

263 Report of 2009 Tinsley House blockade from Indymedia, March 2009: https://www.indy media.org.uk/en/2009/03/424608.html

Reports of 2009 Heathrow blockade from Indymedia and The Guardian, May 2009: https://www.indymedia.org.uk/ en/2009/05/430420.html https://www.theguardian.com/uk/2009/ may/12/colnbrook-detention-centre-protest

Report of 2011 Heathrow blockade from Indymedia, June 2011: https://www.indymedia.org.uk/ en/2011/06/481148.html

Report of November 2011 Heathrow blockade from Indymedia: https://www.indymedia.org.uk/ en/2011/12/490205.html

Report of February 2012 Heathrow blockade from London No Borders: http://london.noborders.org.uk/news/ migration-prison-blockade-delays-charter-numerous-detainees-did-not-fly

Report of September 2012 Heathrow blockade from London No Borders: http://london.noborders.org.uk/news/direct-action-gets-goods-blockade-helps-stop-35-people-being-deported

264 https://enddeportations.wordpress.com/

265 Home Office FOI response to Ms Strickland, 28 February 2018 https://www. whatdotheyknow.com/request/cancelled_charter_flight_bound_f#incoming-1119877

266 https://calaismigrantsolidarity.wordpress. com/deaths-at-the-calais-border/

267 https://calaismigrantsolidarity.wordpress. com/videos-and-articles-2/this-border-kills-our-dossier-of-violence/

268 https://www.freightlink.co.uk/knowledge/ articles/port-dover-freight-volumes-reach-record-levels

269 https://www.getlinkgroup.com/ uploadedFiles/assets-uk/the-channel-tunnel/EY-Channel-Tunnel-UK.pdf

270 https://www.eurotunnelgroup.com/uk/ the-channel-tunnel/founding-documents/

271 Sangatte Protocol between Government of UK and French Republic: http://treaties. fco.gov.uk/docs/fullnames/pdf/1993/ TS0070%20%281993%29%20CM-2366%201991%2025%20NOV,%20 SANGATTE%3B%20PROTOCOL%20 BETWEEN%20GOV%200F%20UK,%20 NI%20&%20FRENCH%20REPUBLIC%20 CONCERNING%20FRONTIER%20 CONTROLS%20&%20POLICING,%20CO-OPERATION.pdf

272 The media campaign, particularly as it turned against the Sangatte camp, is surveyed and analysed in a report by Article 19: "What's the story? Sangatte: a case study of media coverage of asylum and refugee issues" (2004) https://www.article19.org/data/files/ pdfs/publications/refugees-what-s-the-story-case-study-.pdf

273 http://www.lacimade.org/la-loi-des-jungles/

274 https://calaismigrantsolidarity.wordpress. com/2009/09/22/jungle-destroyed-despite-resistance/

275 https://calaismigrantsolidarity.wordpress. com/?s=victor+hugo

276 Home Office contract award notice "Border Force South East and European Coach Services", August 2016 https:// www.contractsfinder.service.gov.uk/ Notice/0c1e111e-49d4-4123-95f4-7bc45e442ba0

277 All of this has been documented on the Calais Migrant Solidarity website, and in local press: https://calaismigrantsolidarity.wordpress.com/2014/09/22/6401/ https://calaismigrantsolidarity.wordpress.com/2015/11/20/segragation-in-the-swimming-pool/

http://www.lavoixdunord.fr/region/migrants-de-calais-des-mesures-prises-pour-eviter-leur-ia33b48581n3167998

278 https://calaismigrantsolidarity.wordpress.com/2014/05/14/communique-salut-o-toit/

279 https://calaismigrantsolidarity.wordpress.com/2013/10/25/natacha-bouchart-the-mayoress-of-calais-posted-an-e-mail-adress-on-facebook-to-denunciate-the-migrant-squatters/

280 https://luttennord.wordpress.com/2014/02/22/sauvons-calais-les-miliciens-sont-dans-la-rue/

281 http://www.lavoixdunord.fr/region/pour-sauver-le-port-de-calais-des-employes-reclament-que-ia31b0n3197859

282 https://calaismigrantsolidarity.wordpress.com/2013/10/21/4420/

283 See our detailed Eurotunnel company profile: https://calaisresearch.noblogs.org/eurotunnel/

284 https://www.insidermedia.com/insider/national/110221-mities-12m-security-contract-renewed

285 www.waronwant.org/media/uk-and-france-paid-24m-euros-calais-migrants-isds-case; news.vice.com/article/eurotunnel-wants-france-and-britain-to-pay-105-million-to-cope-with-migrant-crisis-in-calais.

286 http://www.eurotunnelgroup.com/uploadedFiles/assets-uk/Shareholders-Investors/Publication/Registration-Doc/2015-Registration-Document-GET-SE.pdf

287 http://www.independent.co.uk/news/uk/home-news/britain-pledges-pound15m-to-tighten-border-controls-1734049.html

288 http://ec.europa.eu/dgs/home-affairs/financing/fundings/migration-asylum-borders/asylum-migration-integration-fund/index_en.htm

289 http://uk.reuters.com/article/uk-europe-migrants-funding-idUKKCN0QF16620150810

290 https://www.gov.uk/government/uploads/system/uploads/attachment_data/file/359914/BFpartnerBulletinSep14.pdf

291 http://www.bbc.com/news/uk-33992952

292 https://www.gov.uk/government/publications/joint-ukfrench-ministerial-declaration-on-calais

293 http://ec.europa.eu/dgs/home-affairs/what-is-new/news/news/2015/20150831_1_en.htm

294 http://www.france24.com/en/20160303-hollande-cameron-calais-migrants-drone-deal-franco-british-summit

295 https://www.flightglobal.com/news/articles/analysis-anglo-french-fcas-feasibility-study-kicks-405711/

296 https://fullfact.org/immigration/36-million-isnt-just-close-calais-jungle/

297 http://www.bbc.com/news/uk-37411314_http://www.eamuscork.com/spip.php?article64 http://ted.europa.eu/udl?uri=TED:NOTICE:39786-2017:TEXT:EN:HTML

298 Company website: http://www.wagtailuk.com/ Contract award notice: https://www.contractsfinder.service.gov.uk/Notice/ef402d0f-aa43-404d-b5c6-6cf9f8c46c16

299 http://www.lavoixdunord.fr/region/camp-pour-migrants-a-calais-une-bonne-opportunite-pour-ia33b48581n3222429

http://cettesemaine.info/breves/spip.php?article1411&lang=fr

300 Calais Research: Vinci company profile https://calaisresearch.noblogs.org/vinci/

301 https://www.jacksons-security.co.uk/News/transport-case-studies/improving-perimeter-safety-and-security-at-the-eurotunnel-terminal-in-coquelles-calais-6566.aspx

302 http://www.themigrantsfiles.com/

303 https://calaisresearch.noblogs.org/contractors/#sdfootnote73anc

304 See Calais Migrant Solidarity blog for numerous accounts, and particularly this video from August 2015: https://calaismigrantsolidarity.wordpress.com/2015/08/02/a-night-of-migrants-collective-strength-and-severe-police-repression/

305 Calais Migrant Solidarity: "Lies in the media about No Borders: a CMS response", March 2016 https://calaismigrantsolidarity.wordpress.com/2016/03/04/lies-in-the-media-about-no-borders-a-cms-response/

"Non, le mouvement No Border n'est pas responsable de l'augmentation de la tension dans le Calaisis" – Text of support for "No Borders" against state allegations, signed by more than 20 associations working in Calais, November 2015: https://calaismigrantsolidarity.wordpress.com/2015/11/21/texte-de-soutien-des-associationstext-of-support-from-associations/

Calais Migrant Solidarity: "What is 'No Border'?", August 2015 https://calaismigrantsolidarity.wordpress.com/page/39/

306 https://www.telegraph.co.uk/news/uknews/immigration/9291483/Theresa-May-interview-Were-going-to-give-illegal-migrants-a-really-hostile-reception.html

307 This wording is from the more formal language of the introduction to the 2014 Immigration Act http://www.legislation.gov.uk/ukpga/2014/22/introduction/enacted

There is a handy summary of the Act here: https://www.jcwi.org.uk/sites/jcwi/files/Immigration%20Act%202014%20Summary%20Provisions.pdf

308 Technically, the rules are called the "National Health Service (Charges to Overseas Visitors) (Amendment) Regulations 2017". The Department of Health publishes guidance on how to implement these; the latest guidance eat time of writing was published in May 2018 https://www.gov.uk/government/publications/guidance-on-overseas-visitors-hospital-charging-regulations#history

309 The government's plans were set out clearly in a February 2017 report by the Department of Health called "Making a fair contribution" https://assets.publishing.service.gov.uk/government/uploads/system/uploads/attachment_data/file/590027/Cons_Response_cost_recovery.pdf

310 https://www.gov.uk/government/news/health-charge-for-temporary-migrants-will-increase-to-400-a-year

311 Department of Health: "Making a fair contribution", February 2017 https://assets.publishing.service.gov.uk/government/uploads/system/uploads/attachment_data/file/590027/Cons_Response_cost_recovery.pdf

312 On GP charges, it says (on page 12): "*While we believe that primary care has an important role in establishing chargeable status and charging overseas visitors and migrants we will take a phased approach to implementing this over a longer time scale.*" This will involve working "with stakeholders including the Royal College of GPs, the British Medical Association (BMA)'s General Practitioners' Committee (GPC) and the General Dental Council to consider how best to extend the charging of overseas visitors and migrants into primary care." In particular: "*We will work with the BMA GPC to consider how we extend charging to primary medical services so that overseas visitors and migrants not exempt in the Charging Regulations will have to pay for these services, (excluding GP/nurse consultations).*" The negative responses on A&E and ambulance charges mean these proposals will be further delayed. But they are still on the table. The report concludes, in a section called "areas for further development": "*Therefore, in the case of A&E care and ambulance services, we are still considering the points raised by respondents and exploring the feasibility of implementing the proposals. We will therefore respond on those points later in the year.*"

313 https://www.publications.parliament.uk/pa/cm201617/cmselect/cmpubacc/771/771.pdf see page 6, recommendation 3

314 http://www.peterboroughtoday.co.uk/news/health/health-regulator-to-keep-peterborough-and-stamford-hospitals-open-despite-fall-into-financial-crisis-1-5480914

315 https://fullfact.org/health/health-tourism-whats-cost/

316 http://www.docsnotcops.co.uk/

317 https://www.doctorsoftheworld.org.uk/

318 https://www.medact.org/2018/news/media-appearances/over-150-health-professionals-call-for-scrapping-of-charges-id-checks-for-migrants-in-a-letter-to-the-evening-standard/

319 https://www.theguardian.com/society/2017/feb/06/hospitals-check-patients-entitled-free-nhs-care-law-jeremy-hunt

320 https://www.standard.co.uk/news/health/8900-checks-on-nhs-health-tourists-find-just-50-liable-to-pay-a3850121.html

321 https://www.gov.uk/government/publications/information-requests-from-the-home-office-to-nhs-digital

322 NHS Digital and the PDS do not cover Scotland and Northern Ireland, and nor does the Home Office memorandum. We do not know what other arrangements are in force in those countries.

323 http://webarchive.nationalarchives.gov.uk /20160921135209/ http://systems.digital. nhs.uk/demographics/spineconnect/ spineconnectpds.pdf

324 NB: according to the PDS user guide: "When allocating a new NHS number, the local system should encourage the local system user to select 'male' or 'female' rather than 'not known'. The fourth value of 'not specified' should never be pro-actively set by local systems. Setting gender to anything other than 'male' or 'female' will make the patient difficult to trace."

325 In 2013, the government introduced its controversial "care.data" scheme to combine all patient information from both GPs and hospitals under the control of NHS Digital, then called the Health and Social Care Information Centre (HSIC). This scheme was officially shelved after a review of "data security and consent" by the National Data Guardian for Health and Care, Fiona Caldicott. (http://www.parliament.uk/ business/publications/written-questions-answers-statements/written-statement/ Commons/2016-07-06/HCWS62) However, although the "care.data" programme is officially no more, centralised data gathering from GP surgeries is already well under way and continues apace. For much more on care.data and other NHS data confidentiality issues see the campaigning website medconfidential.org.

326 Patients can request that their entries are flagged as "sensitive", which means that only NHS number, name, gender and date of birth will be visible to ordinary NHS staff accessing the database. However this is only granted in exceptional circumstances, e.g. for victims of domestic violence. In any case, the full range of data will still be available to NHS digital Back Office, and so can be passed to the Home Office.

327 https://www.theguardian.com/ society/2018/may/09/government-to-stop-forcing-nhs-to-share-patients-data-with-home-office

328 https://www.theguardian.com/society/ 2018/jan/31/nhs-chiefs-stop-patient-data-immigration-officials

329 This MoU was released in response to a Freedom of Information request by Jen Persson. The earliest version released was signed in June 2015, after a year of exchanging numerous drafts. It was updated with a "version 2.1" in October 2016. https:// www.whatdotheyknow.com/request/377285/ response/941438/attach/5/20161016%20 DfE%20HO%20MoU%20redacted.pdf

330 Section 15.1.2

331 A school can also collect the information on another nearby date if there are "unusual circumstances".

332 DfE and Home Office memorandum of understanding 16 October 2016, redacted in response to FOI request by Jen Persson, 22 February 2017 https://www.whatdothey know.com/request/pupil_data_off_ register_back_off

333 Including in a 31 October 2016 debate in the House of Lords. Lord Nash stated: "Where the police or Home Office have clear evidence of illegal activity or fear of harm to children, limited data, including a pupil's name, address and some school details, may be requested. To be absolutely clear, this does not include data on nationality, country of birth or language proficiency." https://hansard.parlia ment.uk/lords/2016-10-31/debates/6D06F 8D5-7709-43DF-87ED-33CBBC7324FF/ Education%28PupilInformation%29 %28England%29%28Miscellaneous Amendments%29Regulations2016

334 https://schoolsweek.co.uk/dfe-had-agreement-to-share-pupil-nationality-data-with-home-office/

335 See the Schools ABC website for accounts from teachers, and details on the right to refuse: https://www.schoolsabc.net/

336 DfE: "Schools Census 2016/17 guide" https:// www.gov.uk/government/uploads/system/ uploads/attachment_data/file/580078/ School_census_2016_to_2017_guide_v1_5. pdf pages 66 and 67 Schools "must not request to see for any child, for example, a passport or birth certificate to verify the information declared by the parent / guardian or pupil for the purposes of the census."

337 http://schoolsweek.co.uk/nationality-data-was-compromise-on-theresa-mays-school-immigration-check-plan/

338 https://schoolsweek.co.uk/pupils-who-were-not-white-british-told-to-send-in-birthplace-data/

339 https://www.schoolsabc.net/

340 https://schoolsweek.co.uk/campaigners-launch-judicial-review-proceedings-to-stop-collection-of-pupil-nationality-data/

341 https://schoolsweek.co.uk/schools-fail-to-obtain-nationality-data-on-quarter-of-pupils/

342 As well as post-16 education, independent schools are also allowed to be Tier 4 visa sponsors for children under 16. The latest student guidance for Tier 4 applicants is here: https://www.gov.uk/government/uploads/system/uploads/attachment_data/file/591777/T4_Migrant_Guidance_February_2017.pdf The latest guidance for sponsoring institutions is here: https://www.gov.uk/government/publications/sponsor-a-tier-4-student-guidance-for-educators

343 https://www.theguardian.com/education/2013/jan/08/immigration-foreign-students-universities

344 Home Office Tier 4 Sponsor guidance – Document 2: Sponsorship Duties, Version 07/2018, page 7 https://www.gov.uk/government/uploads/system/uploads/attachment_data/file/571831/Tier_4_Sponsor_Guidance_-_Document_2-Sponsorship_Duties.pdf

345 Ibid pages 63-4

346 https://www.jcwi.org.uk/blog/2012/11/14/attendance-monitoring-has-gone-too-far-%E2%80%93-nus-pulls-out-stop-sign

347 See this 2012 report from the UCU union on some universities' practices and their impact: https://www.ucu.org.uk/media/5816/Impact-of-points-based-immigration-UCU-report-May-12/pdf/Impact_of_Points_Based_Immigration_-_UCU_Report.pdf

348 https://www.theguardian.com/uk-news/2018/jul/12/ucl-row-email-immigration-check-fine-draconian-discriminatory?CMP=Share_iOSApp_Other

349 https://en-gb.facebook.com/UnisResist.BorderControls/

350 On threats against striking lecturers see Jen Bagelman and Jon Cinamon: "Border Enforcement: the university – a conversation", May 2018 https://societyandspace.org/2018/05/29/border-enforcement-the-university-a-conversation/

On issues for international academic staff more generally, see USSBriefs: "The Hostile Environmet in British Universities", June 2018 https://medium.com/ussbriefs/the-hostile-environment-in-british-universities-c8d2c04da064

351 The Home Office guide on the rules: https://www.gov.uk/government/collections/landlords-immigration-right-to-rent-checks A guide from Shelter: http://england.shelter.org.uk/housing_advice/private_renting/right_to_rent_immigration_checks And one from the Joint Council for the Welfare of Immigrants (JCWI): https://www.jcwi.org.uk/policy/reports/jcwi-right-rent-guides-tenants-advisors

352 http://www.jcwi.org.uk/news-and-policy/passport-please

353 https://www.theguardian.com/uk-news/2018/jun/02/legal-challenge-rent-rules-discriminate-non-uk-nationals

354 Corporate Watch "The Round Up: rough-sleeper immigration raids and charity collaboration", March 2017 https://corporatewatch.org/the-round-up-rough-sleeper-immigration-raids-and-charity-collaboration-2/

355 See Corporate Watch: "Court Victory against St Mungos and Thames Reach rough sleeper raids – what next?", December 2017 https://corporatewatch.org/court-victory-against-st-mungos-and-thames-reach-rough-sleeper-raids-what-next/

356 For details on this and other points in this section see Corporate Watch "The Round Up"

357 Full court judgement: http://www.bailii.org/ew/cases/EWHC/Admin/2017/3298.html

358 Home Office immigration statistics, year ending June 2018, Returns tables volume 1, table 2q https://www.gov.uk/government/publications/immigration-statistics-year-ending-june-2018/how-many-people-are-detained-or-returned

359 http://icinspector.independent.gov.uk/wp-content/uploads/2016/10/Hostile-environment-driving-licences-and-bank-accounts-January-to-July-2016.pdf

360 http://icinspector.independent.gov.uk/wp-content/uploads/2016/10/Hostile-environment-driving-licences-and-bank-accounts-January-to-July-2016.pdf para 5.81

361 https://www.cifas.org.uk/immigration_act

362 The membership list is here: https://www.cifas.org.uk/cifas_members Cifas says on its website (here https://www.cifas.org.uk/immigration_act) that all of its members have access to the immigration "disqualified persons" database which would include members who are not banks or building societies.

363 See ICIBI: "Inspection report of the hostile environment measures relating to driving licences and bank accounts", October 2016, chapter 6. (Hereafter: ICIBI hostile environment measures report 2016). http://icinspector.independent.gov.uk/wp-content/uploads/2016/10/Hostile-environment-driving-licences-and-bank-accounts-January-to-July-2016.pdf

364 ICIBI hostile environment measures report 2016

365 ICIBI hostile environment measures report 2016, chapter 6

366 ICIBI hostile environment measures report 2016, para 6.23

367 https://www.theguardian.com/uk-news/2018/may/17/home-office-suspends-immigration-checks-on-uk-bank-accounts

368 ICIBI: "Inspection report on hostile environment provisions for tackling sham marriage", December 2016. Para 3.3. http://icinspector.independent.gov.uk/wp-content/uploads/2016/12/Sham_Marriage_report.pdf

369 https://www.bbc.co.uk/news/uk-44074572

370 https://www.libertyhumanrights.org.uk/news/blog/operation-nexus-dangerous-and-discriminatory-it-needs-go

371 The AIRE centre's legal argument can be read on their website: http://www.airecentre.org/data/files/AIRE_centre_v_SSHD_subs_skeletonfinal.pdf

372 https://www.freemovement.org.uk/operation-nexus-judicial-review-appeal-aire-centre-fundraising/

373 Home Office: "Controlling Migration Fund prospectus November 2016"

https://www.gov.uk/government/publications/controlling-migration-fund-prospectus

374 Home Office: "Controlling Migration Fund: bidding through the fund 2017/8" https://assets.publishing.service.gov.uk/government/uploads/system/uploads/attachment_data/file/658247/Controlling_Migration_Fund_-_FAQ.pdf

375 https://www.whatdotheyknow.com/request/176653/response/489096/attach/3/IR28948%20Mehta%20Report.pdf According to this 2014 FOI response to S. Mehta linked above, the database has "186 screens" with many more data entry fields.

376 https://www.theregister.co.uk/2014/07/22/home_office_tossed_away_347m_on_failed_assylum_tech_project/

377 https://www.theregister.co.uk/2018/04/12/uk_government_immigration_database/

378 https://www.theregister.co.uk/2018/05/18/home_office_hands_91m_digital_visa_contract_to_sopra_steria/

379 https://assets.publishing.service.gov.uk/government/uploads/system/uploads/attachment_data/file/695321/An_inspection_of_exit_checks.pdf It claimed to capture 100% of people leaving the UK by air, except through the "Common Travel Area" which includes the Republic of Ireland. It only captured 89% of people coming in to the UK. Border Force is continually trying to increase these figures, and there are new agreements with Ireland to register passenger information.

380 https://euobserver.com/justice/141919

381 For how the ISA system works and how it is used see ICIBI: "An Inspection of Exit Checks" (March 2018) https://assets.publishing.service.gov.uk/government/uploads/system/uploads/attachment_data/file/695321/An_inspection_of_exit_checks.pdf

382 https://www.theregister.co.uk/2016/03/04/eborders_at_least_eight_years_late_and_will_cost_more_than_1bn/

383 https://www.theregister.co.uk/2017/12/08/uk_border_risks_being_exposed_post_brexit_due_to_lack_of_it_planning_warn_mps/

384 On the NRC and NARRATE, valid as of 2015, see ICIBI "An inspection of removals" (2015) https://assets.publishing.service.gov.uk/government/uploads/system/uploads/attachment_data/file/547681/ICIBI-report-on-Removals-_December_2015.pdf

385 Birth certificates and other records are still currently on paper, stored in the GRO building in Southport. Only the index of all these records, with basic ID information, is electronic; this should change in the next few years.

386 The PND was created and is maintained by a company called CGI which will run it until at least 2019 https://www.cgi-group.co.uk/case-study/police-national-database-joins-forces https://www.cgi-group.co.uk/news/home-office-extends-cgis-police-national-database-contract-for-a-further-three-years

387 https://www.gov.uk/government/publications/ho-government-major-projects-portfolio-data-2016

388 https://bigbrotherwatch.org.uk/wp-content/uploads/2018/05/Face-Off-final-digital-1.pdf

389 https://gizmodo.com/facial-recognition-used-by-wales-police-has-90-percent-1825809635

390 https://www.gov.uk/government/publications/home-office-biometrics-strategy

391 https://www.gov.uk/government/news/biometrics-commissioners-response-to-the-home-office-biometrics-strategy

392 https://www.gov.uk/government/uploads/system/uploads/attachment_data/file/509831/6.1770_Modern_Crime_Prevention_Strategy_final_WEB_version.pdf

393 https://ict.police.uk/

394 https://www.digitalmarketplace.service.gov.uk/digital-outcomes-and-specialists/opportunities/5999

395 https://ec.europa.eu/home-affairs/what-we-do/policies/borders-and-visas/schengen-information-system_en

396 https://www.soprasteria.com/en/media/press-release/steria-successfully-launches-the-second-generation-schengen-information-system-for-the-european-commission-(sis-ii)

397 https://euobserver.com/justice/141919

398 John Grayson, "Meet the UK's latest weapon against organised crime and asylum seekers", Open Democracy, 16 March 2015 https://www.opendemocracy.net/shinealight/john-grayson/meet-uk-s-latest-weapon-against-organised-crime-and-asylum-seekers

HM Government: "Contest: the United Kingdom's strategy for countering terrorism", July 2011 https://assets.publishing.service.gov.uk/government/uploads/system/uploads/attachment_data/file/97994/contest-summary.pdf

399 https://www.sia.homeoffice.gov.uk/Pages/individual-licensing-privacy-notice.aspx

400 http://www.experian.com/blogs/news/2017/06/13/data-accuracy-police/

401 https://www.experian.co.uk/blogs/latest-thinking/identity-and-fraud/right-to-work-checks/

402 Big Brother Watch: "A closer look at Experian big data and artificial intelligence in Durham police", April 2018 https://bigbrotherwatch.org.uk/2018/04/a-closer-look-at-experian-big-data-and-artificial-intelligence-in-durham-police/

403 https://www.gov.uk/government/uploads/system/uploads/attachment_data/file/585928/MOU_v3.pdf pages 4-7

404 http://www.legislation.gov.uk/ukpga/2017/30/section/35/enacted

405 http://www.legislation.gov.uk/ukpga/2017/30/schedule/4/enacted

406 http://www.legislation.gov.uk/ukpga/2018/12/schedule/2/enacted

407 https://www.digitalmarketplace.service.gov.uk/

408 https://www.theregister.co.uk/2016/06/03/home_office_mega_database/

409 http://www.computerweekly.com/feature/Hadoop-starts-to-trumpet-way-through-UK-public-sector ; http://searchdatamanagement.techtarget.com/feature/Inside-the-Hortonworks-open-enterprise-Hadoop-distribution

410 http://www.computerweekly.com/blog/Data-Matters/Is-Hadoop-fit-for-government-IT-purpose

411 https://hortonworks.com/

412 http://diginomica.com/2015/09/11/using-hadoop-inside-jaguar-land-rover-zurich-insurance-and-the-home-office/

413 E.g. this advert for Home Office Biometrics app development, May 2018: https://www.digitalmarketplace.service.gov.uk/digital-outcomes-and-specialists/opportunities/6827

414 https://en.wikipedia.org/wiki/Agile_software_development

415 https://www.theregister.co.uk/2016/10/27/home_office_extends_fujitsu_contract/

416 https://www.thenation.com/article/tech-workers-fighting-back-collusion-ice-department-defense/

417 https://techworkerscoalition.org/

418 https://www.gov.uk/government/uploads/system/uploads/attachment_data/file/589815/Ipsos_MORI_Cost_Recovery.pdf

419 http://blog.mungos.org/helping-people-sleeping-rough-from-europe-and-beyond/

420 For further explanation and analysis, this article by the Oxford University Migration Observatory is a good starting point: "The net migration target and the 2017 election" (May 2017) http://www.migrationobservatory.ox.ac.uk/resources/commentaries/net-migration-target-2017-election/

For latest figures, and details on how the statistics are calculated, see the Office for National Statistics (ONS) "international migration" page: https://www.ons.gov.uk/peoplepopulationandcommunity/populationandmigration/internationalmigration

421 https://www.ons.gov.uk/peoplepopulationandcommunity/populationandmigration/internationalmigration/bulletins/migrationstatisticsquarterlyreport/november2017#further-characteristics-of-long-term-international-migrants

422 https://www.ons.gov.uk/peoplepopulationandcommunity/populationandmigration/internationalmigration/bulletins/migrationstatisticsquarterlyreport/july2018revisedfrommaycoveringtheperiodtodecember2017

423 https://www.theguardian.com/uk-news/2018/feb/22/net-migration-of-eu-nationals-to-britain-falls-by-75000

424 ICIBI Illegal Working report, para 4.7

425 https://www.theguardian.com/politics/2013/oct/10/immigration-bill-theresa-may-hostile-environment

426 ICIBI hostile environment measures report 2016

427 Both quoted in Shaw: Yarl's Wood report 2004, p127-8

428 https://www.gov.uk/government/uploads/system/uploads/attachment_data/file/681246/returns1-oct-dec-2017-tables.ods

429 Presentation at the COMPAS "Does Immigration Enforcement Matter?" conference held on 27 October 2017

430 Ipsos MORI: "Shifting Ground" (2015) https://www.ipsos.com/ipsos-mori/en-uk/shifting-ground-attitudes-towards-immigration-and-brexit

431 Ipsos MORI: "Perceptions and reality: shifting public attitudes towards immigration" (2013) https://www.ipsos.com/sites/default/files/publication/1970-01/sri-perceptions-and-reality-immigration-report-2013.pdf

432 Ipsos MORI: Issues Index December 2017 https://www.ipsos.com/ipsos-mori/en-uk/issues-index-december-2017-more-britons-see-brexit-and-nhs-important-issues-month

433 Lord Ashcroft: "Small Island: public opinion and the politics of immigration" (2013) https://lordashcroftpolls.com/wp-content/uploads/2013/08/LORD-ASHCROFT-Public-opinion-and-the-politics-of-immigration2.pdf

434 Scott Blinder, Migration Observatory: "UK public opinion towards migration: determinants of attitudes" (2011) http://www.migrationobservatory.ox.ac.uk/resources/briefings/uk-public-opinion-toward-migration-determinants-of-attitudes

435 Here Blinder refers to Card, David, Christian Dustmann, and Ian Preston. "Immigration, Wages, and Compositional Amenities." NBER Working Paper No. w15521, The National Bureau of Economic Research, Cambridge MA, 2009. http://papers.ssrn.com/sol3/papers.cfm?abstract_id=1505844.

436 One theoretical discussion we find generally helpful is Manuel Castells: Communication and Power (2009). Stefan Walgrave and Peter Van Aelst in "The Contingency of the Mass Media's Political Agenda Setting Power: Toward a Preliminary Theory" (2006) give a survey of many empirical studies up to that point. Note that a lot of this literature is focused on US and other powers' foreign policy, and above all on war. Much of the empirical literature works with paradigms of "agenda setting" and "framing". Robert Entman is among the leading theorists here, see e.g. Robert Entman: "Framing Bias: Media in the Distribution of Power". http://www.communicationcache.com/uploads/1/0/8/8/10887248/framing_bias_media_in_the_distribution_of_power.pdf

437 Scott Blinder, Migration Observatory: "UK public opinion towards migration: determinants of attitudes" (2011) http://www.migrationobservatory.ox.ac.uk/resources/briefings/uk-public-opinion-toward-migration-determinants-of-attitudes/

438 Ipsos MORI: "Perceptions and reality: shifting public attitudes towards immigration" (2013) https://www.ipsos.com/sites/default/files/publication/1970-01/sri-perceptions-and-reality-immigration-report-2013.pdf

439 https://medium.com/oxford-university/where-do-people-get-their-news-8e850a0dea03

440 Stefaan Walgrave and Peter Van Aelst: "The Contingency of the Mass Media's Political Agenda Setting Power: Toward a Preliminary Theory" (Journal of Communication, 2006) http://citeseerx.ist.psu.edu/viewdoc/download?doi=10.1.1.612.5724&rep=rep1&type=pdf

441 Article 19: "What's the Story? Sangatte: a case study of media coverage of asylum and refugee issues" (2003) https://www.article19.org/data/files/pdfs/publications/refugees-what-s-the-story-case-study-.pdf

Greg Phil, Emma Briant and Pauline Donald: *Bad News for Refugees* (Pluto Press, 2013) http://www.jstor.org/stable/j.ctt183p4bm

UNHCR: "Press coverage of the refugee and migrant crisis in the EU" (UNHCR, 2015) http://www.unhcr.org/56bb369c9.pdf

David Allen: "A decade of immigration in the British press" (Migration Observatory, 2016) http://www.migrationobservatory.ox.ac.uk/resources/reports/decade-immigration-british-press/

442 A basic introduction to framing theory: https://masscommtheory.com/theory-overviews/framing-theory/

443 Roy Greenslade: "Seeking Scapegoats: the coverage of asylum in the UK press" (IPPR, 2005) https://www.ippr.org/files/images/media/files/publication/2011/05/wp5_scapegoats_1359.pdf

444 Nick Medic: "Making a meal of a myth" (2011) http://www.mediawise.org.uk/wp-content/uploads/2011/03/Making-a-meal-of-a-myth.pdf

445 Press Gazette http://www.pressgazette.co.uk/national-newspaper-print-abcs-daily-star-overtakes-daily-telegraph-for-first-time-in-over-a-year/

446 http://www.huffingtonpost.co.uk/entry/question-time-ukip-nigel-farage_uk_58d95295e4b03787d35ae186

447 Media Reform Coalition: "Who owns the media?" (2015) http://www.media reform.org.uk/who-owns-the-uk-media

448 Adrian Addison: *Mail Men: the unauthorised story of the Daily Mail* (Atlantic, 2017)

449 http://www.independent.co.uk/news/media/murdoch-admits-editorial-control-760297.html

450 https://www.lrb.co.uk/v39/n11/andrew-ohagan/whos-the-real-cunt

451 https://www.theguardian.com/media/2018/jun/13/paul-dacre-warns-against-softening-daily-mail-brexit-stance

452 https://www.huffingtonpost.com/2014/06/18/rupert-murdoch-immigration-reform_n_5509876.html

453 https://edition.cnn.com/2015/07/12/politics/rupert-murdoch-trump-tweets/index.html

454 https://www.theguardian.com/media/2005/apr/19/citynews.politics

455 Edward S. Herman and Noam Chomsky: *Manufacturing Consent: the political economy of the mass media* https://archive.org/stream/pdfy-NekqfnoWlEuYgdZl/Manufacturing%20Consent%20%5BThe%20Political%20Economy%20Of%20The%20Mass%20Media%5D_djvu.txt

456 Kirsty Milne: "Manufacturing Dissent" (Demos, 2005) https://www.demos.co.uk/files/manufacturingdissent.pdf

457 https://www.nytimes.com/2017/05/02/world/europe/london-tabloids-brexit.html

458 https://www.theguardian.com/media/2016/jun/24/mail-sun-uk-brexit-newspapers

459 https://drive.google.com/file/d/0B4IqRxA4qQpjakI1UEd5WEFIRGc/view

460 Roy Greenslade: "Seeking Scapegoats: the coverage of asylum in the UK press" (IPPR 2005)

461 Edward Bernays: *Propaganda* https://archive.org/details/EdwardL.BernaysPropaganda

462 Jacques Ellul: *Propaganda* https://archive.org/details/Propaganda_201512

463 Lynton Crosby youtube campaign master class: https://www.youtube.com/watch?time_continue=2&v=H_YareK6WKk

464 https://www.conservativehome.com/thetorydiary/2015/06/the-computers-that-crashed-and-the-campaign-that-didnt-the-story-of-the-tory-stealth-operation-that-outwitted-labour.html

465 http://eprints.lse.ac.uk/72066/1/Anstead_Data-driven%20campaigning_2017.pdf

466 https://www.politico.eu/article/theresa-may-campaign-war-room-conservative-stephen-gilbert-lynton-crosby/

467 https://www.politico.eu/article/theresa-may-campaign-war-room-conservative-stephen-gilbert-lynton-crosby/

468 https://www.theguardian.com/uk-news/cambridge-analytica

469 https://www.theguardian.com/politics/2016/jan/20/lynton-crosby-and-dead-cat-won-election-conservatives-labour-intellectually-lazy

470 https://www.researchgate.net/publication/230269354_Having_One's_Cake_and_Eating_It_Too_Cameron's_Conservatives_and_Immigration

471 https://www.youtube.com/watch?v=2Zefc_LwTVo

472 https://www.theguardian.com/politics/2015/mar/29/diane-abbott-labour-immigration-controls-mugs-shameful

473 Tim Finch and David Goodhart, editors: "Immigration under Labour" (Prospect and IPPR, 2010) https://www.ippr.org/files/images/media/files/publication/2011/05/Immigration%20under%20Labour%20Nov2010_1812.pdf

474 Marcus Roberts: "Revolt on the left: Labour's UKIP problem and how it can be overcome" (Fabian Society, 2014) https://www.fabians.org.uk/wp-content/uploads/2014/10/RevoltOnTheLeft-Final4.pdf

475 https://en.wikipedia.org/wiki/Blue_Labour

476 https://www.ipsos.com/ipsos-mori/en-uk/immigration-now-top-issue-voters-eu-referendum

477 https://i.telegraph.co.uk/multimedia/archive/03138/CampaigningAgainst_3138005a.pdf

478 https://labour.org.uk/manifesto/safer-communities/#second

479 https://www.theguardian.com/politics/2000/jan/10/jackstraw.labour1

480 http://news.bbc.co.uk/2/hi/uk_news/politics/3872675.stm

481 Webber: Borderline Justice, p165

482 Hannah Jones, Yasmin Gunaratnam, Gargi Bhattacharyya, William Davies, Sukhwant Dhaliwal, Kirsten Forkert, Emma Jackson and Roiyah Saltus: *Go Home: the politics of immigration controversies* (Manchester University Press, 2017) http://www.manchesteruniversitypress.co.uk/9781526113221/

483 http://www.irr.org.uk/news/pr-and-the-selling-of-border-controls/

484 Lisa Thomas: *The UK media-state nexus in the context of post-9/11 terrorism policy* (PhD thesis, University of Bedfordshire, 2014)http://uobrep.openrepository.com/uobrep/handle/10547/565808

485 Tony Blair: *A Journey* (Scumbags-r-us, 2010) https://en.wikipedia.org/wiki/A_Journey

486 Peter Oborne and Simon Walters: *Alastair Campbell* (Aurum, 2004), https://www.theguardian.com/politics/2004/may/24/uk.pressandpublishing

487 Aeron Davis: *The Mediation of Power* (Routledge, 2007) https://www.amazon.com/Mediation-Power-Critical-Introduction-Communication/dp/0415404916

488 Peter Van Aelst and Stefan Walgrave: "Information and Arena – the dual function of the news media for political elites" in Van Aelst and Walgrave (Eds.), *How Political Actors Use the Media* (Palgrave, 2017) https://www.researchgate.net/publication/320204091_Information_and_Arena_The_Dual_Function_of_the_News_Media_for_Political_Elites

489 http://www.bbc.com/news/uk-politics-36031743

490 https://hackinginquiry.org/mediareleases/whittingdale-should-never-have-interfered-with-press-regulation/

491 https://www.theguardian.com/the-scott-trust/2015/jul/26/the-scott-trust-board

492 Edward S. Herman and Noam Chomsky: *Manufacturing Consent: the political economy of the mass media*

493 Tamasin Cave and Andy Rowell: *A Quiet Word: Lobbying, Crony Capitalism and Broken Politics in Britain* (Bodley Head, 2014) http://www.spinwatch.org/index.php/issues/lobbying/item/5638-your-guide-to-corporate-lobbying

494 http://www.bbc.com/news/uk-politics-36977840

495 https://www.electoralcommission.org.uk/find-information-by-subject/political-parties-campaigning-and-donations/donations-and-loans-to-political-parties

496 https://www.iod.com/Portals/0/PDFs/Campaigns%20and%20Reports/Europe%20and%20trade/Immigration-Report-2016.pdf

497 http://www.cbi.org.uk/news/cbi-submission-to-the-migration-advisory-committee/

498 http://www.cbi.org.uk/cbi-prod/assets/File/pdf/cbi-business-priorities-for-a-new-migration-system-dec%20-016.pdf

499 http://www.londonfirst.co.uk/wp-content/uploads/2017/07/London-First-immigration-proposal_300617.pdf

500 Shahram Khosravi: *Illegal Traveller* (Palgrave Macmillan, 2010) https://www.palgrave.com/gp/book/9780230230798

501 Calais Research: Eurotunnel company profile https://calaisresearch.noblogs.org/eurotunnel/

502 Calais Research: the port of Calais https://calaisresearch.noblogs.org/port-of-calais/

503 Calais Research: freight industry https://calaisresearch.noblogs.org/freight-industry/

504 Barnardo's "Cedars: recommendations for a new government" http://www.barnardos.org.uk/cedars_report_2015.pdf

505 Mark Akkerman: "Border Wars" (TransNational Institute and Stop Wapenhandel, 2016) https://reliefweb.int/sites/reliefweb.int/files/resources/border-wars-report-web.pdf

506 https://badboysofbrexit.com/the-money-men/

507 Aristotle Kallis "When fascism became mainstream" http://www.pacedifesa.org/public/documents/Kallis%20-%20When%20Fascism%20Became%20Mainstream.pdf

508 Paul Stocker: "Infection of the far right? How extremism went mainstream in UK politics" (New European, 2017) http://www.theneweuropean.co.uk/top-stories/infection-of-the-far-right-1-5236047

509 Steve Cohen: *Standing on the Shoulders of Fascism: from Immigration Control to the Strong State* (Trentham Books, 2006)

510 https://en.wikipedia.org/wiki/National_Front_(UK)

511 http://news.bbc.co.uk/2/hi/uk_news/politics/1949863.stm

512 https://www.newstatesman.com/politics/politics/2012/09/blighting-burnley

513 Nigel Copsey and David Renton: British Fascism, the Labour Movement and the State (Palgrave Macmillan, 2005) https://www.palgrave.com/us/book/9781403939166

514 https://www.theguardian.com/politics/2009/jan/30/brown-british-jobs-workers

515 https://uk.news.yahoo.com/british-jobs-british-workers-far-111223812.html

516 https://wikileaks.org/wiki/British_National_Party_membership_and_contacts_list%2C_2007-2008

517 https://www.telegraph.co.uk/news/politics/ukip/10735155/Nigel-Farage-I-am-proud-to-have-taken-a-third-of-the-BNPs-support.html

518 Anders Widfeldt and Heinz Brandenburg: "The populist beauty and the fascist beast? Comparing the support bases of UKIP and the BNP" http://www.lancaster.ac.uk/fass/events/epop2013/docs/Widfeldt-Brandenburg%20-%20EPOP2013%20-%20draft.pdf

519 https://www.lrb.co.uk/v38/n15/john-lanchester/brexit-blues

520 https://forums.digitalspy.com/discussion/2214981/mays-policies-and-the-bnp-2005-manifesto

521 http://www.dailymail.co.uk/news/article-2427617/Gordon-Brown-considered-putting-troops-streets-banks-crashed-reveals-Damian-McBride.html

522 Powerbase: Migration Watch UK http://powerbase.info/index.php/Migration_Watch_UK

523 https://www.theguardian.com/commentisfree/2007/mar/16/watchingdavidcoleman1

524 Powerbase: Cross Party Group on Balanced Migration http://powerbase.info/index.php/Cross_Party_Group_on_Balanced_Migration

525 Home Office: ministerial gifts, hospitality, travel and meetings transparency release: https://www.gov.uk/government/collections/home-office-ministers-hospitality-data

526 https://www.independent.co.uk/arts-entertainment/tv/news/kate-hopkins-lbc-radio-manchester-attack-final-solution-daily-mail-muslims-racism-a7756776.html

527 https://www.newstatesman.com/politics/politics/2012/09/blighting-burnley

528 https://en.wikipedia.org/wiki/Question_Time_British_National_Party_controversy

529 https://www.huffingtonpost.co.uk/entry/question-time-ukip-nigel-farage_uk_58d95295e4b03787d35ae186

530 http://powerbase.info/index.php/Migration_Watch_UK#cite_note-9

531 https://www.mirror.co.uk/news/uk-news/sir-andrew-green---an-apology-523654

532 http://powerbase.info/index.php/Migration_Watch_UK#cite_note-9

533 https://www.theguardian.com/media/2011/feb/23/churnalism-pr-media-trust

534 https://www.bbc.co.uk/search?q=%22migration+watch%22

535 http://www.politics.co.uk/blogs/2016/06/13/buried-in-a-migration-watch-report-the-truth-about-immigrati

536 http://iasc-culture.org/THR/channels/Infernal_Machine/2017/02/politics-is-downstream-from-culture-part-1-right-turn-to-narrative/

537 Richard Cockett: *Thinking the Unthinkable* (HarperCollins, 1994) https://www.independent.co.uk/voices/book-review-unthinkable-thoughts-make-history-thinking-the-unthinkable-richard-cockett-harpercollins-1419873.html

538 https://www.politico.com/magazine/story/2018/02/25/overton-window-explained-definition-meaning-217010

539 http://www.mackinac.org/overtonwindow#Explanation

540 https://www.economist.com/blogs/freeexchange/2008/07/summer_book_club_capitalism_an

541 Generalised Anxiety Disorder affects around 6% of the UK population. With post traumatic stress disorders (PTSD), phobias, obsessive compulsive disorder (OCD) and "panic disorder", these conditions affect at least one in ten adults at any time. These figures, of course, only refer to people who have been medically diagnosed. https://www.gov.uk/government/uploads/system/uploads/attachment_data/file/556596/apms-2014-full-rpt.pdf

542 Stuart Ewen: *Captains of Consciousness – advertising and the social roots of the consumer culture* https://www.crashdebug.fr/media/Docs/ewen.captainsconsciousness.pdf

543 https://www.youtube.com/watch?v=H_YareK6WKk

544 https://www.youtube.com/watch?v=d1UGic5-Z0o

545 https://www.nytimes.com/2017/05/02/world/europe/london-tabloids-brexit.html

546 See Frances Webber: *Borderline Justice* for many more earlier examples.

547 Frederick Douglass: West India Emancipation speech, 1857 http://www.blackpast.org/1857-frederick-douglass-if-there-no-struggle-there-no-progress

548 Webber: Borderline Justice, page 11. This book is a detailed account of many of these contests, involving both victories and defeats, from the experience of a key protagonist over several decades.

549 As Voltairine de Cleyre put it: "one common struggle against those who have appropriated the earth, the money and the machines." Voltairine de Cleyre: "Direct Action" http://www.spunk.org/texts/writers/decleyre/sp001334.htmlhttps://salirdelghetto.files.wordpress.com/2014/09/voltairine_de_cleyre_sharon_presley_crispin_sarbookzz-org.pdf

550 Contracts Finder: https://www.contractsfinder.service.gov.uk/Search

TED: https://ted.europa.eu/TED/main/HomePage.do

551 Sources: Contracts Finder Archive list of detention centre contracts issued pre-October 2012: https://data.gov.uk/data/contracts-finder-archive/search/?buying_org=Commercial%20%26%20Property%20Directorate

Home Office FOI response to Michael Zhang, 7 January 2015, Annex B https://www.whatdotheyknow.com/request/240025/response/602918/attach/4/Annex%20B%20CR%2033555.pdf

Brook House contract award notice, published March 2009: https://www.contractsfinder.service.gov.uk/Notice/9f4d386f-621b-426c-b13d-6483e40d3a25

Tinsley House contract award notice, published May 2009: https://www.contractsfinder.service.gov.uk/Notice/d181a58c-104f-41f4-b7b3-f510a8831078

Dungavel contract award notice, published September 2011 https://www.contractsfinder.service.gov.uk/Notice/a415f5d7-6b35-4bb1-9e2a-9142249e19d8

552 National Audit Office: Yarl's Wood IRC, July 2016 https://www.nao.org.uk/wp-content/uploads/2016/07/Yarls-Wood-Immigration-Removal-Centre.pdf

553 Contract notice published June 2018: https://www.contractsfinder.service.gov.uk/Notice/8e94f338-6049-48f7-8b82-9dea24af8857

554 Contract notice published July 2017: https://ted.europa.eu/TED/notice/udl?uri=TED:NOTICE:261853-2017:TEXT:EN:HTML

555 Independent Monitoring Board: Annual Report of IMB Charter Flight monitoring team 2017, Published June 2018 https://s3-eu-west-2.amazonaws.com/imb-prod-storage-1ocod6bqky0vo/uploads/2018/06/IMB-Charter-Flights-2017-annual-report.pdf

556 https://www.opendemocracy.net/shinealight/phil-miller/security-industry-provides-medics-for-uk-deportation-flights

557 Tender announcement published July 2017: https://www.contractsfinder.service.gov.uk/Notice/00c48c77-6e89-4b77-9fac-65104453c74e

558 Contracts Finder Archive list of UKBA COMPASS contracts https://data.gov.uk/data/contracts-finder-archive/search/?buying_org=UK%20Border%20Agency

559 G4S evidence to the Home Affairs Committee, February 2016 http://data. parliament.uk/writtenevidence/committe eevidence.svc/evidencedocument/home-affairs-committee/asylum-accommo dation/written/29580.html

560 Serco written evidence to the Home Affairs Committee, February 2016 http://data.parliament.uk/writtenevidence/ committeeevidence.svc/evidencedocument/ home-affairs-committee/asylum-accommodation/written/29809.html

561 Contract award notice published February 2017: https://ted.europa.eu/TED/notice/ udl?uri=TED:NOTICE:39786-2017:TEXT: EN:HTML

562 Contract award notice published March 2015: https://www.contractsfinder. service.gov.uk/Notice/ef402d0f-aa43-404d-b5c6-6cf9f8c46c16

563 Contract award notice published February 2017: https://www.contractsfinder.service. gov.uk/Notice/35b3fffe-090a-4cd2-be99-2040fd632e3e

564 Tender announcement published March 2018: https://www.contractsfinder. service.gov.uk/Notice/66b2ec5a-f948-4849-9fb2-7825b0eb9ccb

565 Contract award notice published March 2017 https://www.contractsfinder.service. gov.uk/Notice/c96e6fef-efe5-4b50-bff7-ec545defb9bb

566 Contract award notice published January 2018: https://www.contractsfinder. service.gov.uk/Notice/a05423ad-ed56-47e3-9b59-e1cf3b215a55

567 Contract award notice published May 2018: https://www.contractsfinder.service.gov. uk/Notice/5caa2d89-98d8-4bc3-8bc6-c4284762130c

568 Contract award notice published May 2018: https://www.contractsfinder.service.gov. uk/Notice/13c2219a-7033-441b-9efc-0cb5fb73d8b9

569 Contract award notice and redacted contract documents published August 2018: https://www.contractsfinder.service.gov. uk/Notice/5e36782a-b120-4781-aae6-e907315836a2

570 Contract award notice published August 2017: https://www.contractsfinder.service. gov.uk/Notice/6cd9615a-13c7-4b60-924c-309d6a18d3ae

571 Contract award notice published August 2017: https://www.contractsfinder.service.

gov.uk/Notice/c50896cd-557d-41ba-8249-b16f419480c0

572 Tender notice published June 2018: https://www.contractsfinder.service.gov. uk/Notice/7c01639f-2c15-4746-8ec8-b3c9472b35f1

573 Contract award notice published April 2018 https://www.contractsfinder.service.gov. uk/Notice/05a79a16-9f1b-4f0c-8627-f1b184fe7e6d

574 https://www.theregister.co.uk/2018/05/18/ home_office_hands_91m_digital_visa_ contract_to_sopra_steria/

575 This is a brief summary of Corporate Watch: "G4S: Company Profile 2018" (June 2018). See that for references and more information. https://corporatewatch.org/g4s-company-profile-2018/

576 This is a brief summary of Corporate Watch: "Mitie: Company Profile 2018" (June 2018). See that for references and more information. https://corporatewatch.org/mitie-company-profile-2018/

577 This is a brief summary of Corporate Watch: "Serco: Company Profile 2018" (June 2018). See that for references and more information. https://corporatewatch.org/serco-company-profile-2018/

578 This is a brief summary of Corporate Watch: "GEO: Company Profile 2018" (June 2018). See that for references and much more detail. https://corporatewatch.org/geo-company-profile-2018/

579 ICIBI: "Inspection of Outsourced Contracts" March 2016, para 5.10 http://icinspector. independent.gov.uk/wp-content/uploads/ 2016/03/ICIBI-report-on-Outsourced-Contracts-and-Cedars-Final.pdf

580 See Titan's latest accounts and other filings on the Companies House website: https://beta.companieshouse.gov.uk/ company/02212225/filing-history

581 He was the only shareholder in the parent company Hagondale as of the most recently published Confirmation Statement, December 2017.

582 See latest accounts of Hagondale on the Companies House website: https://beta.companieshouse.gov.uk/ company/02670425/filing-history

583 Available online here: https://illwilleditions.no blogs.org/files/2015/10/a-no-borders-mani festo-READ.pdf or here: https://theanarchist library.org/library/a-no-borders-manifesto

dariush @ corporatewatch.org

No Borders